The Creevey Papers

The Creevey Papers

Edited by

JOHN GORE

B. T. Batsford Ltd
LONDON

FIRST PUBLISHED 1902

Made and printed in Great Britain
by William Clowes and Sons, Limited, London and Beccles
for the publishers B. T. Batsford Limited
4 Fitzhardinge Street, Portman Square, London W.1

Contents

Acknowledgment

The Publishers wish to thank the following for permission to reproduce the illustrations included in this book:

J. Blackett-Ord, Esq., for page 120 (both); Brooks's for page 184; the Mansell Collection for page 121 (top); the National Portrait Gallery for pages 105 (bottom), 185 (top), 200 (bottom) and 201 (both); the Countess of Portarlington for page 105 (top); the *Radio Times* Hulton Picture Library for page 185 (bottom); Lord Sefton for page 200 (top); the Trustees of the Victoria and Albert Museum for page 104.

List of Illustrations

THOMAS CREEVEY

A Brief Biography

ON FEBRUARY 5, 1838, in his lodgings at 17 Jermyn Street, died Thomas Creevey. A month short of seventy, he was well known in political circles and in Whig society. He was forgotten in no time, as are all but the giants and the freaks in life's circus. At the beginning of this century he was a vague name, recurrent only in Hansard, and the dust of half a century was still being piously and regularly wiped off his 'literary remains,' a vast pile of notes and correspondence, neatly arranged and wrapped up in the attics of Whitfield Hall, Northumberland. The history of these papers must be set down briefly. They consisted largely of letters Creevey had written to his wife and his stepdaughter, Elizabeth Ord, at various times, of correspondence between himself and his political and other contemporaries, of short memoranda and reminiscences he had prepared for 'a history of his own times' which he intended to write in his final retirement and had indeed begun to plan when he died suddenly. Miss Elizabeth had fair copied a great deal of them, for Creevey's handwriting was shocking. From Elizabeth Ord the papers passed to her sister Anne, the wife of Lt.-Col. Hamilton and ultimately to Mr. John Blackett Ord of Whitfield Hall, Hexham, who has kindly authorised the use of a few brief linking passages, of which he still holds the copyright.

One very wet Sunday about 1900 a tour of the house led to those attics and provoked an inquiry concerning the contents. The result was *The Creevey Papers*, edited by Sir Herbert Maxwell; two volumes of sparkling political and social gossip which took Edwardian London by storm. Happier than Greville in the hour of his 'come-back,' Creevey was not cursed for a key-hole spy. He was the lion of the season in 1904. But no one could throw much light on his career. In the memoirs of his own day there was little to glean. Brougham, his crony, barely mentioned him, Greville gave him three or four paragraphs. His name (without much substance) occurred occasionally elsewhere. The few survivors from his age, who had as children known him well, were themselves too old to recall him clearly. For another generation after 1904 the schoolboy's 'three lines' easily comprised the known details of his career. It was not until 1934, when the chance was offered me to re-examine the still enormous, unused mass of papers at Whitfield, that any attempt was made to investigate his origins and to penetrate the mysteries of his career. Researches made before and continued since the publication of *Creevey's Life and Times* now enable me to set forth a more or less complete account of his life.

He was born on March 5, 1768, at Liverpool in a house in School Lane, near the Blue Coat School. His mother was Phoebe Prescott who was married in 1764 to William Creevey, a locally well-known mariner, a merchant captain of slave-carrying vessels trading out of Liverpool to the African Coast; and a daughter was born to them before or during 1766. Mrs. Creevey was twenty-four at the time of her marriage. The Captain was often from home on his lawful or unlawful occasions, and twice indeed suffered imprisonment at the hands of the French. There is strong but not conclusive evidence that during one such absence in 1767 a liaison between Mrs. Creevey and young Lord Molyneux of Croxteth resulted in the birth of Thomas Creevey in March, 1768. These evidences are set forth in an Appendix in this volume. The Captain died soon after Creevey's birth, his will being proved in November, 1769. Mrs. Creevey subsequently married again, dying in 1812 as Mrs. Lowe at the age of seventy-four. There is evidence of a lack of sympathy in the relations of mother and son after Creevey's school days ended. Like her husband, she was largely illiterate and of very humble origin.

The boy from the first was brought up above his station. At twelve or thirteen he was sent to Newcome's at Hackney, a private-public school, for generations patronised by aristocratic Whig families. Creevey was turned off at seventeen with a smattering of general education, but better grounded in mathematics and political history, and with a taste for sound reading. He made at the school one friend, Charles Callis Western (afterwards Lord Western), who proved of the utmost help in the early stages of his career. He went on to Queens' College, Cambridge, in the Newcome tradition, and in 1784 graduated as Seventh Wrangler. The question of his future began to be debated by his family advisers, an uncle, John Eaton, and Dr. James Currie, a liberal-minded specialist in fevers and Robert Burns's first editor and biographer. There were at one time serious thoughts of sending him into the Church, but ultimately Currie's intellectual circle at Liverpool, which gave Creevey an access of liberal education, decided his professional career.

Round Currie in Liverpool gathered many of the rising lights of the Bar, among them Romilly and Scarlett, and Michael Angelo Taylor, who became a famous host of the Whig party and one of Creevey's closest friends; and Sir John Moore and his sailor brother, Graham. Creevey soon made Currie's friends his own and impressed them with his ability. No doubt the example of Romilly influenced the choice of the Bar as his profession. He was admitted a student of the Inner Temple in 1789 and of Gray's Inn in 1791. In 1792 he took his M.A. degree and was called to the Bar two years later. He decided to practise on the Chancery side. If there is little in his papers to show that he fully realised the dangers and political significance of those times, he undoubtedly made headway in his profession, absorbed the new theories of the Revolution, and began to practise a natural talent for public speaking by supporting his political friends on the hustings. Western put conveyancing business in his way and turned his thoughts towards politics. He introduced him to his neighbour in Essex, Lord Petre, who also sent him business and was soon persuaded to put this adroit young lawyer forward for the borough of Thetford, of which the patronage alternated between Petre and the Duke of Norfolk.

It was at Western's house that Creevey met a charming widow, several years older than himself, Eleanor Ord, daughter of Charles Brandling of Gosforth, a man of property and patronage. She had married and buried William Ord, another landowner in Northumberland and sometime M.P. for Newcastle, and on his death was left with a comfortable life interest and a family of two sons and three daughters, of whom the elder son was just coming of age and into his considerable inheritance. Mrs. Ord was on intimate terms with her distant cousin, Charles Grey (Lord Grey of the Reform Bill), and was a friend of the Prince of Wales, of Sheridan and later of Mrs. Fitzherbert. Creevey was not blind to the social and political advantages of her position. In 1802 he was able to announce a double event to the admiring circle at Liverpool: in the year of his marriage he could write M.P. after his name. He was thirty-four years of age. The Creeveys set up house at Park Place, St. James's, and cut quite a substantial figure in Whig circles. The stepdaughters took to him at once. He was their 'dear, dear Beau-père.' Mrs. Creevey was known as 'Nummy,' Creevey became 'Diddy' or 'Mr. Nummy.'

He threw in his lot with Fox whom he admired 'next idolatry,' and with his lieutenant, Grey, which signified the old Pavilion Gang; and for the next few years he worked assiduously for his party, taking with good humour a number of hard knocks. His allotted part was obstruction; he harassed the Government, a gadfly in the flanks of Addington and later of the dying Pitt; an ungrateful task from which Grey shrank. In 1804 he made his first important speech (war in Ceylon). Fox remarked to Lord King that it was 'very good indeed, real good stuff, not a word of nonsense.' A letter which Fox wrote to him, also in 1804, soliciting his influence with his brother-in-law Brandling, M.P. for Newcastle, testifies to the value of Mrs. Creevey's connections in launching him in politics; and socially, in Whig Society, her position was no less valuable to him. He began to fill the pages of Hansard—in the course of his political career he made more than one hundred and fifty speeches—and to be reckoned by friend and foe a redoubtable fighter.

While his women-folk followed fashion to Brighton, Creevey, spurning any but political society, stuck to his two professions. A short and brilliant chapter began in 1806. Pitt dead, Grenville was called in and the King compelled to admit the Foxites to the 'Ministry of All the Talents.' Creevey's bruises were salved with the balm of office. He was appointed Secretary to the Board of Control with a salary of £1,200 a year. It was the high tide of his political career, but sadly brief. In 1807 the Ministry crashed on the rocks of Catholic Relief and the Whigs streamed out into the wilderness, there to wander in disunity for twenty-three years of Creevey's prime.

Swallowing his chagrin, he moved to a smaller house, and fought on. Brougham was out of the House in 1812 and easily persuaded Creevey to join him in contesting his native Liverpool (which Creevey had consistently taken under his wing in Parliament) against Gascoigne and Canning. Backed by the new Lord Sefton[1] (who knew all about him) and the Roscoe interests, he and Brougham were beaten out of the field, and Creevey fell back on Thetford. Unfortunately, unguarded words he had used during the campaign laid him open to a charge of libel. He was convicted and fined, Brougham defending him. He was bitterly chagrined and for a time lost interest in politics. His wife's health was now breaking up, and in 1814 he left England and established his family in Brussels, where he remained for five years. If exile interrupted his parliamentary career, it enabled him to write a page of vivid history. To it we owe his famous picture of the Duke after Waterloo and his piquant conversation with the Duke of Kent on the subject of patriotic marriage. Mrs. Creevey died in 1818, leaving Creevey for some time inconsolable and almost destitute. He refused his step-daughters' entreaty that he should make his home with them, being unwilling to trench on what remained to them of their mother's income. He returned to England in July, 1819, with the unmarried stepdaughters, and the second phase of his career began. He was fifty-two, and all was to build up again save the store of his experience. Norfolk disposed of Thetford elsewhere, and the party man became the house-party man. Paradoxically it is from the dozen trivial years of his poverty spent among the flesh-pots that his present fame is derived. For now began the series of letters to Bessy Ord but for which his name to-day would signify nothing. The phrase needs a qualification. Creevey regained his interest in politics; indeed, he was in again as member for Appleby by 1820 and was soon turning out hard-hitting pamphlets which delighted Brougham and the rest.

His most constant hosts were all men of wealth. Sefton (well nick-named 'The Pet') grew more and more to depend on him. He played his part to suit his company. He would talk racing with the 'legs,' would gossip for hours with the old Dowagers, Newcastle and Salisbury, carried hymn-books for Lady Duncannon, and convulsed Lady Augusta Milbank with his broad stories. And as his assurance grew in society, so did his political authority. He took on the character of Elder Statesman. Grey in his retirement relied on him for news of political trends and of Brougham's pranks;

[1] 2nd Earl and son of Creevey's reputed father.

Brougham never ceased to canvass his opinion. Whitbread to the end of his life had set store by him and so quite genuinely did others of the small band of sincere Radical social-reformers, such as Henry Grey Bennet. An even more convincing proof that he was widely regarded as a man of some account is gained by a study of his relations with the Duke of Wellington. The women were always on his side. For three or four he felt a respect and devotion which placed them beyond the range of his barbs. He was shrewd enough to distinguish between a great lady and an important one. He kept his head and (unlike Tierney) his heart. He never gambled; he rarely borrowed.

In 1826 a family bereavement crushed Sefton, and Creevey from that day forward became essential to him. There is some evidence that now both families acknowledged among themselves the fact of Creevey's parentage. Henceforth his assurance becomes complete, and he frequently refers to the Molyneux as 'his own, his *real*, family.'[2] When in 1830 the new King, William IV, summoned Lord Grey, the faithful received their rewards, and after the lions had been appeased, crumbs were found for the mice. Creevey ('Old Grey Pantaloons' to the lampooners), whose sandy hair had turned to pepper and salt in the service of Reform, received a sinecure bestowed with charming grace by Grey. He was sixty-two, but still robust; and the Treasurership of the Ordnance carried £1,000 a year salary.

He was brought back into Parliament whilst the battle of Reform was fought out. In 1834 the Whig Ministry was upset largely by Brougham's intrigues, and the Coercion Bill gave Grey his chance to retire, after securing a last favour for Creevey. The Treasurership was properly axed, but the wood of privilege was still extensive. Creevey's fever of righteous indignation was assuaged with a Commissionership of Greenwich Hospital, £600 a year, and a charming house. But the label 'placeman' in Creevey's case needs qualification also. It was in dignified form, carrying the sub-title of 'Elder Statesman.' His political shrewdness and his good sense were ever more acknowledged and used by his friends, and no one can read the letters written to him at the end of his life by Lord and Lady Grey without acknowledging that his character and worth as political

[2] For the light on the riddle of Creevey's parentage, see Appendix I.

adviser, and as philosopher and friend, were held in high estimation in the final phase.

His sister's death in 1835 assured him an income from all sources of £1,000 a year. He chose this juncture to take to himself a mistress from the 'nocturnal pavement' (as Greville relates), a certain Emma Murray. He lived long enough to glance into the new world which began with the accession of Victoria, and to recognise its significance. On February 2, 1838, he stayed over-long at Greenwich gossiping with Sir Thomas Hardy's daughters.[3] He returned seriously ill, and at 6 o'clock in the morning of the 5th he died in his London lodgings.

The news was soon over the town, and Sefton and Brougham (Greville relates) instructed Vizard, the solicitor, instantly to negotiate with Mrs. Murray, who was left residuary legatee, for the purchase of diaries believed to exist and to contain 'revelations.' Whether any such papers were bought and burned will be briefly considered at the end of this book. He was buried in the Hospital grounds, Francis Molyneux representing his father as a chief mourner.

Estimates of Creevey by such different people as Melbourne, Greville, Broughton, and Lady Holland indicate that politically and socially he was indeed a man of some account. Circumstances alone prevented his rising higher in political life, for which he was well qualified by shrewdness, resource, courage, ability, and useful debating gifts. This question of his status will also be considered at the end of the book in greater detail. It is easy enough to understand his social success. In a robust age he possessed good health, inexhaustible spirits, and a constant flow of broad humour. Intensely alive and interested in the human drama, past and present, he was never bored, never boring in his own circles. He was adroit, self-sufficient, and of marked independence of mind. He recommended himself with remarkable tact and discrimination to women of every age, rank and type. His charm and sympathy in the company of young people of both sexes were acknowledged by the evidence of persons alive in 1904 who had known him well in their childhood, notably by Augusta (Ponsonby), Countess of Kerry, by Lady Georgina Grey, and by the Grenfell grandchildren of Lord Sefton.

[3] *Nelson's Hardy and His Wife* by John Gore, p. 198, note.

If he adopted the aristocratic attitude of his hosts, he was neither snob nor toady.

His letters rank high in their *genre*, and the reason is not far to seek. His natural gifts above referred to had as full play in his letters as in his conversation. He was besides a natural, untaught painter in words. He had almost the 'Austen touch' with his quick strokes. You can see Wellington walking up and down the room in Brussels on June 19, 1815; you can still *hear* Lady Sefton drawling and Lady Augusta Milbank's deep-throated roar of laughter. His nicknames are précis of character and indestructible labels. The letters place him on the fringe of history (a service they did for others also) and in a guise more trivial than his work and character warrant.

JOHN GORE

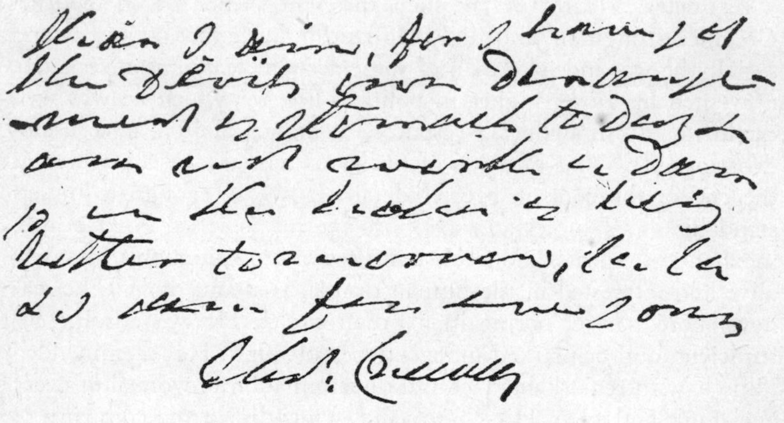

Facsimile of Creevey's handwriting

SOME NICKNAMES USED BY CREEVEY

Barney . . .	12th Duke of Norfolk; also *Twitch*, *Scroop*.
Beau, The . .	Duke of Wellington.
Billy, Our . .	William IV.
Bogey . . .	Lord Grenville.
Bruffam . . .	Henry Brougham; also *Wickedshifts*, *Beelzebub*, and finally *Guy Vaux*.
Ciss	Lady Cecilia Underwood, daughter of 2nd Earl of Arran. 2nd wife of H.R.H. Duke of Sussex, created Duchess of Inverness in 1840.
Clunch . . .	Lord Althorp.
Cocky . . .	Hon. H. G. Bennet.
Cole, Old or Mrs. .	G. Tierney.
Cole, Young . .	James Abercromby, Speaker 1835–9.
Comical Bob . .	Lord Robert Spencer, son of 3rd Duke of Marlborough.
Dear Eddard . .	Hon. R. Edward Petre.
Doctor, The . .	Henry Addington (Lord Sidmouth).
Fergy . . .	General Sir R. Ferguson of Raith.
Frog, The . .	King William I of Holland.
Frog, Young . .	The Prince of Orange.
Jack the Painter .	Thomas Spring Rice.
Jaffa	General Sir Robert Wilson.
Jenky . . .	Lord Liverpool.
Jockey . . .	11th Duke of Norfolk.
King Jog . . .	J. G. Lambton (afterwards Lord Durham); also *The Monarch*. *'One can jog along on £40,000 a year.'*
King Tom . .	Coke of Norfolk (afterwards Lord Leicester).
Madagascar . .	Lady Holland.
Mull	Lord Molyneux, son of Lord Sefton.
Niffy Naffy . .	Lord Darlington (afterwards Duke of Cleveland).
Og	Lord Kensington.
P., Mrs. . . .	Princess of Wales (Queen Caroline).
Prinney . . .	The Regent. (This nickname originated with the Misses Ord, who saw much of the Prince in childhood.)

P, Young	Princess Charlotte.
Pet, The	Lord Sefton.
Pie and Thimble	Lord John Russell; also *Widow's Mite.*
Pop, The	Lady Darlington; also *Poplolly, Haradan.*
Punch	Charles Greville.
Roscius	Lord Henry Petty (Lord Lansdowne).
Sally	Sarah, Lady Jersey.
Sally, Old or Dow	Emily Mary, Lady Salisbury.
Scroop	12th Duke of Norfolk.
Sherry	R. B. Sheridan.
Slice	H.R.H. Duke of Gloucester.
Snip	Lord Goderich.
Squire, Stiffrump	C. Western; also *The Turkey.*
Suss	H.R.H. Duke of Sussex.
Taffy	W. J. Hughes, Lord Dinorben.
Twitch	12th Duke of Norfolk.
Vesuvius	Hon. Douglas Kinnaird.
Vic or Viccy	Queen Victoria.
Wickedshifts	H. Brougham.
Widow's Mite	Lord John Russell.

THE CREEVEY PAPERS

chapter one

1793–1805

THE EARLIEST LETTER preserved in the huge mass of Creevey's correspondence is a very brief one; but it strikes the note which carried dismay and indignation into every court in Europe, and was the prelude to twenty years of widespread war.

Hon. Charles Grey, M.P. [afterwards 2nd Earl Grey], to Mrs. Ord.

24th Jan. 1793

DEAR MRS. ORD,

I have only a moment before the post goes out.... An account is come that the King of France was executed on Monday morning. Everything in Paris bore the appearance of another tumult and massacre. Bad as I am thought, I cannot express the horror I feel at this atrocity.

Yours affectionately,

C. GREY.

'War is certain, and—God grant we may not all lament the consequences of it!'

There are few letters during the remaining years of the eighteenth century referring to anything except private affairs. Dr. J. Currie of Liverpool wrote pretty regularly to Creevey, who was reading for the Bar at this time.

Dr. Currie to Creevey

Liverpool, 30th Dec., 1795

...I once thought you a modest fellow—now I laugh at the very idea of it. Upon my soul, Creevey, it was all a damned hum. What with your election songs and your rompings—what with your carousings with the men and your bamboozlings with the women, you are a most complete hand indeed. Widow, wife, or maid, it is all one to you....If you go on in this way, and keep out of Doctors Commons, the Lord knows what you may rise to....

20th Jan., 1801

...I envy you the company you keep. When you tell me of meeting Erskine, Parr and Mackintosh familiarly, I sigh at my allotment in this corner of the Island. It is impossible not to rust here, even if one had talents of a better kind. In London, and perhaps there only, practice and exercise keep men polished and bright.... So you are become an intimate friend of Lady Oxford. My dear Creevey—these women—these beautiful women—are the devil's most powerful temptation—but I will not moralize, on paper at least....

Liverpool, 11th Feb., 1802[1]

...I have at length received your long expected letter, and can truly say that I never received one from you that gave me so much pleasure. I could very easily suppose that you would find it difficult to write, and while uncertainty hung over you, readily excused your not writing at all. It never occurred to me that you had any suspicion of my reserve. I very seriously and solemnly assure you I conducted myself with perfect prudence....I could not indeed help hearing the report in question. It was very general before you last came to us from the north, for people here take a great interest in you, and knowing our friendship talk much of you to me....I have been lately attending your Mother or rather calling on her as I passed, in consequence of the state of the eye, which you saw, and which continues. *She* mentioned the subject to me, and afterwards what you said to her about it; which I desired her not to repeat to any other; which she assured me she would not....Every part of your letter gave me true pleasure. This young squire[2] rises upon me much. Upon my soul he has done the thing most handsomely. But let everything be signed and sealed. Generosity is a vigorous plant, but shortlived. Self interest is a little shrub, that gradually increases, and that becomes at length the monarch of the forest....

And your success at Morpeth too! upon my soul it is quite the thing. On this one may look a step further. Orde may, will very likely, bring in

[1] Exceptionally, I have here inserted one letter printed in my *Creevey's Life and Times*—Currie to Creevey 11 Feb. 1802. This letter, referring to his engagement to Mrs. Ord, affords picturesque evidence of Creevey's early environment. It shows that an admiring circle of family and friends at Liverpool regarded him as something of a 'card' and possibly a trump card and watched his progress with admiration not untinged with cynicism. J. G.

[2] William Ord, Mrs. Ord's elder son.

two members. Be this as it may, your way is clear. Creevey will come in before long, etc., etc. I am truly happy you are taking root. I know you well and love you very much, and have thought of you at times not without some anxiety.

In your progress upwards, the first steps are the most difficult to a man like you—to a man of pride and sensibility. Give you a firm footing, enable you to stand secure, and your rise, your consideration, will be speedily secured. The connection you are about to form is in every way desirable. I am a fool if it is not preferable to your marrying a Liverpool or a London Miss with £30,000.... I never had an opportunity of thanking you for your skill in showing off Mackintosh[3] in such a stile. He is a wonderful Lion; not what you would call a Scotchman—but an indolent, thoughtless, innocent sort of man that will be continually in scrapes, and that will not get forward with all his extraordinary talents, unless somebody take him up and push him on....

Say a word or two of politics when you write—kind regards to our friend Scarlett[4] to whom I shall write soon. Adieu my Creevey. Thou art a damned knowing one after all....

In 1802 Creevey was returned to Parliament as member for Thetford, a pocket borough in the gift of the Duke of Norfolk and Lord Petre. He was an enthusiastic Whig of the advanced type which was about to reject that time-worn title, and adopt the more expressive one of Radical. Indeed, the animosity of this section against the old Whigs, under the lead of Lord Grenville, was almost as intense as it was against the Tories under Pitt.

Sir Francis Burdett, M.P., to Creevey

Piccadilly, August 18th, 1802

My dear Creevey,

I have scarcely time to turn round, but will not defer sending a line in answer to your very kind letter—as I am entirely of your opinion in every point. I look upon your advice as excellent, and intend consequently to follow it. You know by this time the Petition[5] is taken out of my hands, in a manner most flattering and honourable. The conduct of the Sheriffs I believe quite unprecedented, but whether they will be punished, protected or rewarded exceeds my sagacity to foretell, perhaps both the latter.

[3] Sir James Mackintosh (1765–1832), barrister and philosopher.
[4] Lord Chief Baron of the Exchequer (1834); created Lord Abinger (1835).
[5] The Middlesex Election fought out for 4 years.

I regard the issue of this contest exactly in the same light as you do—a subject of great triumph and not of mortification. My friend is compleatly satisfied. I have done my duty and the Public acknowledge it—surely this is sufficient to satisfy the ambition of an honest man.

I, however, cannot help envying you your happiness and comfort, and wish most heartily I was of the party. You cannot think how friendly Ord was nor how much I feel obliged to him—we used his house, but I hope not injured it.

Sherry is quite grown loving again; he came here yesterday with all sorts of [*illegible*] from the Prince, Mrs. Fitzherbert, &c., &c.; it is a year and half, I believe before this Election, since we almost spoke. Mrs. Sheridan came one day on the Hustings, and was much delighted and entertained at being hailed by the multitude as Mrs. Burdett....

Yours sincerely,

F. BURDETT.

Creevey to Currie

Great Cumberland Place, 8th Nov., 1802

... The Grenvilles are in great spirits; the *Morning Post*, and *Morning Chronicle* too, are strongly suspected of being in their pay, and to-day it is said Tom Grenville is to be started as Speaker against Abbott. Great are the speculations about Pitt; it is asserted that he is fonder of his relations [the Grenvilles] than the Doctor,[6] but I hear of no authority for this opinion. I, for one, if they try their strength in the choice of a Speaker, tho' I detest Abbott, will vote for him or anybody else supported by Addington, in opposition to a Grenville or a Pittite. I am affraid of this damned Addington being bullied out of his pacific disposition. He will be most cursedly run at, and he has neither talents to command open coadjutors, nor sufficient skill in intriguing to acquire private ones. Still I think we cannot surely be pushed again into the field of battle.

Now for France—all the world has been there, and various is the information imported from thence. Whishaw was my first historian, and I think the worst. He was at Paris only a fortnight, but he travelled through France. I apprehend, either from a scanty supply of the language of proper introductions, he has been merely a stage coach traveller. He has seen soldiers in every part of his tour, and superintending every department of the Government... and has returned quite scared out of his wits at the dreadful power and villainy of the French Govern-

[6] Henry Addington, created Viscount Sidmouth in 1805. He was nicknamed 'the Doctor' because his father was a physician.

ment.... Romilly[7] is my next relator, and much more amusing. His private friends were the Liancourts, de la Rochefoucaults, &c., and he dined at different times with Talleyrand, Berthier, and all the other Ministers at their houses. Ministers, however, and statesmen are alike in all countries; they alone are precluded from telling you anything about the country in whose service they are, and emigrants are too insecure to indulge any freedom in conversation. Romilly's account, therefore, as one might suppose, makes his society of Paris the most gloomy possible. He says at Talleyrand's table, where you have such magnificence as was never seen before in France, the Master of the House, who as an exile in England without a guinea was the pleasantest of Men, in France and in the midst of his prosperity sits the most melancholy picture apparently of sorrow and despair. Romilly sat next to Fox at Talleyrand's dinner, and had all his conversation to himself; but not a word of public affairs—all *vertu* and French *belles lettres*. Romilly would not grace the court of Buonaparte, but left Paris with as much detestation of him and his Government as Whishaw, and with much more reason.

But the great lion of all upon the subject of Paris is Mackintosh. He has really seen most entertaining things and people. He, too, dined with Ministers and has held a long consultation with the Consul[8] upon the Norman and English laws; but his means of living with the active people of France has far exceeded that of any other English. I think his most valuable acquaintance must have been Madame de Souza. She is a Frenchwoman, was a widow, and is now the wife of the Portuguese ambassador. She is the friend and companion and confidante of Madame Buonaparte, and satisfied all Mackintosh's enquiries respecting her friend and her husband the Consul. Her history to Mackintosh (confirmed by Madame Cabarrus, late Madame Tallien) of Madame Buonaparte and her husband is this.—Madame Buonaparte is a woman nearly fifty, of singular good temper, and without a tittle of intrigue. She is a Creole, and has large West India possessions. On these last accounts it was that she was married by the Viscount Beauharnois—a lively nobleman about the old Court; and both in his life and since his death his wife remained a great favorite in Paris.

Immediately previous to the directorial power being established in 1795, the Sections all rose upon the Convention or Assembly, whatever it was, in consequence of an odious vote or decree they had made. At this period, no general would incur the risque of an unsuccessful attack

[7] Samuel Romilly, K.C., entered Parliament in 1806, appointed Solicitor-General. An ardent Reformer, he committed suicide in 1818.

[8] Bonaparte.

upon the Sections; Buonaparte alone, who was known only from having served at the siege of Toulon, being then in Paris, said if any General would lend him a coat, he would fight the Sections. He put his coat on; he peppered the Sections with grape shot; the establishment of the Directory was the consequence to them, and to him in return they gave the command of the army of Italy. He became, therefore, the fashion, and was asked to meet good company, and he was asked to Tallien's to put him next the widow Beauharnois, that he might vex Hoche, who was then after her and her fortune. Madame Tallien did so, and the new lovers were married in ten days. She never was Barras' mistress; Madame Cabarrus told Mackintosh that was calumny, for that she herself was his mistress at that very time.[9] Madame de Souza says no one but Madame Buonaparte could live with the Consul; he is subject to fits of passion, bordering upon derangement, and upon the appearance of one of these distempered freaks of his, he is left by all about him to his fate and to the effects of time. It is a service of great danger, even in his milder moments, to propose anything to him, and it is from his wife's forbearance in both ways that she can possibly contrive to have the respect she meets with from him.

Every wreck of the different parties in France for the last ten years that is now to be found in Paris, Mackintosh met and lived familiarly with—La Fayette, [*illegible*], Jean Bon Saint-André, Barthelemy, Camille Jourdan, Abbé Morelaix, Fouché, Boissy Danglas, &c., &c. Tallien.[10]

Mackintosh dined at Barthelemy's the banker—the brother of the ex-director—with a pleasant party. The ex-director was there, and next to him sat Fouché—now a senator—but who formerly, as Minister of Police, actually *deported* the ex-director to Cayenne. There was likewise a person there who told M. he had seen Fouché ride full gallop to preside at some celebrated massacre, with a pair of *human ears* stuck one on each side of his hat.[11] The conversation of this notable assembly was as charming as the performers themselves; it turned principally upon the blessings of peace and humanity.

[9] The beautiful Madame de Tallien, previously Comtesse de Fontenay, was as fickle as she was frail, for she was also the mistress of the rich banker Ouvrard. Tallien obtained a divorce in 1802, and she married the Prince de Chimay.

[10] Jean Lambert Tallien, one of the chief organisers and bloodiest agents of the Terror, leader in the overthrow of Robespierre.

[11] Joseph Fouché had as yet but accomplished half his cycle of cynical tergiversation, which brought him to office under Louis XVIII after the fall of Napoleon. He died in 1820, a naturalised Austrian subject, having amassed enormous wealth.

All the others whom I have mentioned above have no connection with Fouché or Tallien, and are reasonable men, perfectly unrestrained in their conversation, quite anti-Buonapartian, and as much devoted to England. To such men Fox has given great surprise by his conversation, as he has given offence to his friends here. He talks publicly of Liberty being *asleep* in France, but *dead* in England. He will be attacked in the House of Commons certainly, and I think will find it difficult to justify himself. He has been damned imprudent.

At the time of Creevey's entrance to the House of Commons, Pitt was in seclusion. He had retired from office in March, 1801, putting up the former Speaker, Mr. Addington, as Prime Minister and Leader of the House of Commons. George III heartily approved of this arrangement, although on the face of it were all the signs of instability. Taking Pitt and Addington aside at the Palace one day —'If we three keep together,' said he, 'all will go well.' But as the months went on, Pitt chafed at his own inactivity and fretted at the incapacity of his nominee. Pitt's friends were importunate for his return; he himself was burning to take the reins again, but was too proud, perhaps too loyal to Addington, to adopt overt action to effect it. Moreover, Addington, who had been an excellent Speaker, had no suspicion of the poor figure he cut as head of the Government. It never occurred to him to take any of the numerous hints offered by Canning and other Tories, until the necessity for some change was forced upon him by the imminence of disaster from the disaffection of his followers. He offered to resign the Treasury in favour of a peer, Pitt and he to share the administration of affairs as Secretary of State. This proposal Pitt brushed contemptuously, almost derisively, aside; matters went on as before, except that the former friendship of Pitt and Addington was at an end. When Parliament met on November 24, Pitt did not appear in the House.

Creevey to Currie

25th Nov., 1802

I went yesterday to the opening of our campaign, with some apprehension, I confess, as I knew Fox was to be there, lest his sentiments upon the subject of France and England should diminish my esteem for him. His conduct, however, and his speech were, in my mind, in every respect *perfect*; and if he will let them be the models for his future imitation, he will keep in the Doctor and preserve the peace. God continue Fox's prudence and Pitt's gout! The infamous malignity and misrepresentation of that scoundrel Windham did injury only to himself: never creature less deserved it than poor Fox. You cannot imagine the pleasure I feel in having this noble animal still to look up to as my champion. Nothing can be so whimsical as the state of the House of Commons. The Ministers, feeble beyond all powers of caricaturing, are unsupported—at least by the acclamations—of that great mass of persons who always support all Ministers, but who are ashamed *publicly* to applaud them. They are insulted by the indigent, mercenary Canning, who wants again to be in place, and they are openly pelted by the sanguinary faction of Windham and the Grenvillites as dastardly poltroons, for not rushing instantly into war. Under these circumstances their only ally is the old Opposition.... If they are so supported, I see distinctly that Fox will at least have arrived at this situation that, tho' unable to be Minister himself, he may in fact prevent one from being turned out.... God send Pitt and Dundas anywhere but to the House of Commons, and much might, I think, be done by a judicious *dandling* of the Doctor.

Lord Henry Petty and I dined together yesterday. He is as good as ever. We both took our seats behind old Charley.

The treaty of Amiens had been concluded in March, 1802, but Bonaparte's restless ambition, and especially his desire to re-establish the colonial power of France, menaced the maritime ascendancy of Great Britain, and Addington watched uneasily the war-clouds gathering again upon the horizon.

In February, 1803, M. Talleyrand demanded from Lord Whitworth, British Ambassador in Paris, an assurance of the speedy evacuation of Malta by King George's Government, in compliance with the tenth article of the Treaty of Amiens. Negotiations dragged on till, on 13th March, Whitworth had a stormy interview with Bonaparte, who charged the British Government with being determined to drag him into war. Finally, on 12th May the rupture was complete; Lord Whitworth requested his passport, and the two countries were at war.

Creevey to Currie

11th March, 1803

...No one knows the precise point on which the damn'd Corsican and the Doctor have knocked their heads together, but I must think, till I know more, that Addington has been precipitate. The injury done is incalculable. I defy any man to have confidence in public credit in future, till a perfectly new order of things takes place.... As long as the neighbouring Monster lives, he will bully and defy us; and being once discovered, as it now is, that even Addington will bluster as well as him in return, I see no prospect of prosperity in this country, that is—the prosperity of *peace*—as long as Buonaparte lives.... Was it not lucky that I sold out at 74¼? They are to-day about 64.

7th April, 1803

...I have barely time to say that of all the Men I have ever seen, your countryman General Moore is the greatest prodigy. I thank my good fortune to have seen so much of him—such a combination of acknowledged fame, of devotion from all who have served under him—of the most touching simplicity and yet most accomplished manners—of the most capital understanding, captivating conversation, and sentiments of honour as exalted as his practice.... Think of such a beast as Pitt treating, almost with contempt, certainly with injury, such a man as Moore....

Currie to Creevey

Liverpool, May 1st, 1803

I was infinitely obliged by your last report, and beg of you to give me another, as matters draw fast to a crisis. I will expect to have a few lines at latest by the post of Wednesday.

I fear this Billy[12] will come in after all.

I have to tell you one or two things about your friends here.

First, I have been attending your aunt, Mrs. Eaton, who was very ill, but is recovered. I was to have written to you about the time she got better, but neglected it. But in answer to her earnest enquiries, I delivered your love (God forgive me) and your congratulations on her recovery. I said everything kind and civil for you to Eaton too, so that you are not to pretend that you did not hear of her illness. But you are now to write a few lines either to him or her as soon as convenient, saying what you see fit on so affecting an occasion—now do not forget this. I cannot think how the old lady came to trust herself in my hands, for I had just been in at the death of two of her neighbours, and I consider my being called to her as a symptom of great attachment to you, and probably in its consequences no way unfavourable to you. For I must tell you that she and I are wondrous great, and we talk you over by the

[12] Mr. Pitt.

half-hour together. She and he seem very much devoted to you.... They are quite pleased, too, with Mrs. Creevey.

Give my love to Moore[13] when you see him. Scarlett has been here with his brother; a very worthy fellow. He says you are coming on. What sort of a thing is this presentation? I see you are a nominee in the Boston election. I hope it is for Maddock, whom I know a little and like a great deal.

We are all cursed flatt here about the spun out negotiations. Nothing doing. Everything stagnated. We shall have war, because it is just the most absurd thing in creation.

Creevey to Currie

11th May

...I supped last night with Fox at Mrs. Bouverie's.... There were there Grey, Whitbread, Lord Lauderdale, Fitzpatrick, Lord Robert Spencer, Lord John Townshend and your humble servant.... You would be perfectly astonished at the vigour of body, the energy of mind, the innocent playfulness and happiness of Fox. The contrast between him and his old associates is the most marvellous thing I ever saw—they having all the air of shattered debauchees, of passing gaming, drinking, sleepless nights, whereas the old leader of the gang might really pass for the pattern and the effect of domestic good order.... A telegraphic dispatch announces that Lord Whitworth has left Paris.[14]

Saturday, 14th May

... A messenger has arrived to-day who left Paris at 9 o'clock Thursday night, and Lord Whitworth was to leave it in the night, or rather morning, at two; so I presume he will be in England on Monday. Think only what a day Monday or Tuesday will be in the House of Commons! and think likewise what a damn'd eternal fool the Doctor must turn out to be. Upon my soul! it is too shocking to think of the wretched destiny of mankind in being placed in the hands of such pitiful, squirting politicians as this accursed Apothecary and his family and friends! ...

On 16th May the King sent a message to the House of Commons calling upon it to support him in resisting the aggressive policy of France and the ambitious schemes of the First Consul. Pitt might no longer hold aloof.

[13] Captain (afterwards Admiral Sir Graham) Moore, brother of John Moore.
[14] News was telegraphed by semaphore signals.

Creevey to Currie

20th

...This damned fellow Pitt has taken his seat and is here, and, what is worse, it is certain that he and his fellows are to support the war. They are to say the time for criticism is suspended; that the question is not now whether Ministers have been too tardy or too rash, but the French are to be fought. Upon my soul! the prospect has turned me perfectly sick....

21st

...It is really infinitely droll to see these old rogues so defeated by the Court and Doctor. I really think Pitt is done: his face is no longer red, but yellow; his looks are dejected; his countenance I think much changed and fallen, and every now and then he gives a hollow cough. Upon my soul, hating him as I do, I am almost moved to pity to see his fallen greatness. I saw this once splendid fellow drive yesterday to the House of Lords in his forlorn, shattered equipage, and I stood near him behind the throne till two o'clock this morning. I saw no expression but melancholy on the fellow's face—princes of the blood passing him without speaking to him, and, as I could fancy, an universal sentiment in those around him that *he was done*....

An offer of mediation between Britain and France having been received from the Emperor Alexander of Russia, a debate arose in the House of Commons.

24th May, 1803

...Lord Hawkesbury[15] then began and made a very elaborate speech of two hours, containing little inflammatory matter, and being a fair and reasonable representation of his case and justification of the war. Erskine followed in the most confused, unintelligible, inefficient performance that ever came from the mouth of man. Then came the great fiend himself—Pitt—who, in the elevation of his tone of mind and composition, in the infinite energy of his style, the miraculous perspicuity and fluency of his periods, outdid (as it was thought) all former performances of his. Never, to be sure, was there such an exhibition; its effect was dreadful. He spoke nearly two hours—all for war, and for war without end. He would say nothing for Ministers, but he exhorted or rather *commanded* them to lose no time in establishing measures of

[15] Afterwards Earl of Liverpool and Prime Minister.

finance suited to our situation.... Wilberforce made an inimitable speech for peace and on grounds the most calculated for popular approbation.... It is said the House of Commons never behaved so ill as in their reception of this speech. They tried over and over again to cough him down, but without effect...

The speech referred to above was universally acknowledged as one of the finest ever delivered by Pitt; but it is not included among his published speeches, owing to the accidental exclusion of reporters from the gallery. Fox replied on the second night of the debate in a speech of equal merit; but there is a gap in Creevey's letters covering the whole of the rest of the session, and we know not, though we may imagine, the effect of his leader's eloquence upon his mind.

Creevey to Currie

22nd Aug., 1803

...I saw a great deal of Sheridan. We dined together several times, got a little bosky, and he took great pains to convince me he was sincere and confidential with me.... A plan of his relates to Ireland, and it is the substitution of a Council for the present Viceroy, the head of the Council to be the Prince of Wales, his assistants to be Lord Moira, Lord Hutchinson and Sheridan himself. The Prince is quite heated upon the subject; nothing else is discussed by them. Lord Hutchinson is as deep in the design as any of them, but God knows it is about as probable as the embassy of old Charley to Russia. I believe Sherry is very much in the confidence of the Ministers. They have convinced him of the difficulty of pressing the King for any attentions to the Prince of Wales; he is quite set against him, and holds entirely to the Duke of York, who, on the other hand, is most odious to the Ministry.... Have you begun your visits to Knowsley yet? ...If you see Mrs. Hornby, cultivate her. She is an excellent creature; her husband, the rector, is the most tiresome, prosy son of a —— I ever met with, but is worthy....

Sir John Moore to Creevey

Sandgate, 15th Sept., 1803

...The newspapers have disposed of me and my troops at Lisbon and Cherbourgh, but we believe that we have not moved from this place. I begun to despair of seeing you here, and am quite happy to find that, at last, I am to have that pleasure. If the Miss Ords do not think they can trust to the Camp for beaux, or if they have any in attendance whose curiosity to see soldiers they may chuse to indulge, assure them that whoever accompanies them shall be cordially received by everybody here....

Capt. Graham Moore, R.N., to Creevey

Plymouth, August 7th, 1803

...I never had to do with a new ship's company before made up of Falstaff's men—'decayed tapsters,' &c., so I do not bear that very well and I get no seamen but those who enter here at Plymouth, which are very few indeed. The Admiralty will not let me have any who enter for the ship at any of the other ports, which cuts up my hopes of a tolerable ship's company....I hear sometimes from my brother Jack. He says they have had a review of his whole Corps before the Duke of York.... My mother was more delighted with the scene than any boy or girl of fifteen. N.B.—she is near 70....She is an excellent mother of a soldier. I am not afraid of showing her to Mrs. Creevey, altho' she is of a very different cast from what she has generally lived with. If Mrs. Creevey does not like her, I shall never feel how the devil she came to like me.

Jack says his Corps are not at all what he would have them, yet that they will beat any of the French whom he leads them up to. I am convinced the French can make no progress in England, and do not believe now that they will attempt it; but how is all this to end? However that may be, as I am in for it, I wish to God I was tolerably ready, and scouring the seas. What the devil can Fox mean by his palaver about a military command for the Prince of Wales? That may come well enough from Mrs. Barham perhaps.

Indefatigable, *Cawsand Bay, Sept. 16th, 1803*

...It has pleased the Worthies aloft to keep us in expectation of sailing at an hour's notice since Sunday last. This is very proper, I am sure, and rather inconvenient too. I hate to be a-going a-going. It is disagreeable to Jack, because I have sent all his wives and his loves on shore, and altho' I have made him an apology, he must think the Captain is no great things. The blackguards will know me by-and-by. They seem a tolerable set, and I am already inclined to love them. If they fight, I shall worship them....There is another very fine frigate here, as ready as we are—the *Fisgard*, commanded by a delightful little fellow, Lord Mark Kerr. He is an honour to Lords as they go....If there is to be a war with Spain, it would be well to let us know of it before we sail, as money—altho' nothing to a philosopher—is something to me. I am growing old, and none of the women will have me now if I cannot keep them in style, and you know there is no carrying on the war ashore in the peace, when it comes, without animals of that description.... The most cheerful fellow on politics is my brother Jack; you'll hear no croaking from him. He says it's all nonsense....

Creevey to Currie

London, Dec. 21, 1803

...My impression of Addington and his colleagues during this short part of the Session, has been pretty much what it has heretofore been. They are, upon my soul, the feeblest—lowest almost—of Men, still more so of Ministers. When there is anything like a general attack upon them, they look as if they felt it all; they blush and look at one another in despair; they make no fight; or, if they offer to defend themselves, no one listens but to laugh at them....

The impression of Pitt was what his enemies most triumphantly delight in; but what they never could have been sanguine enough to expect, his speech was the production of the dirtiest of mankind, and so it was received. His intimates—his nearest neighbours—Canning and Co., sat mute, astounded and evidently thinking themselves disgraced by the shuffling tacticks of their military leader. His lingering after Addington, tho' at open war with him in print—his caution of touching either Fox or Windham, those proscribed victims of fortune—his senseless vapouring and most untrue and envious criticism upon volunteers, and, above all, his officious and disgusting sentiment as to the recovery of his Majesty's electoral dominion,[16] accommodated all his hearers with sufficient reasons for condemnation, and, for once in his life, I have no doubt their prodigy of art and elocution had in his favorite theatre not a single admirer. Canning and Sturges, talking to me afterwards about the excellence of Fox's speech, said what a pity it was Pitt had not taken the same manly part. I asked why he had not done so, and they shrugged up their shoulders and said a man who had been minister eighteen years was a *bad opposition man*.

Old Charley was *himself*, and of course was exquisitely delightful. Unfettered by any hopes or fears—by any systems or connection—he turned his huge understanding loose amongst these skirmishers, and it soon settled, with its usual and beautiful perspicuity, all the points that came within the decision of reasoning, judgment, experience and knowledge of mankind. In addition to the correctness of his views and delineations, he was all fire and simplicity and sweet temper; and the

[16] The kingdom of Hanover.

effect of these united perfections upon the House was as visible in his favor as their disappointment and disgust had been before at the unworthy performance of Colonel Pitt.

It is almost too advanced a state of my letter to take in the Windhams and Co. We all know that he and the Grenvilles have been the merciless bloodhounds of past times, and no friend of Fox can ever forget or forgive the bitter malignity with which Windham pursued and hunted down the great and amiable creature. But as a party, and with such a foil to it as the present administration, they are entitled to greater weight than they have.

One constantly hears lamentation from grave persons over the deterioration of the House of Commons from some past ideal; but just as people are accustomed now to look back upon the time when Pitt and Fox were protagonists as the true parliamentary golden age, so it was in that day. In concluding this long letter, Creevey, who had just one year of parliamentary experience, moralises upon the lowered tone of the debates.

Windham, Lord Grenville and Elliott have great parliamentary talents, and Tom Grenville is most respectable in the same way, and of a high and unsullied character. They are of the old school as compared with the Ministry; they are full of courage, of acquirements, of elevated manners; there is nothing low in the fellows, there is no cringing to power or popularity. In Fox's absence they are the only representatives of past and better days in Parliament.

Pitt's intolerance of Addington now passed into an active phase, and the unfortunate Prime Minister found himself under a crossfire directed by the two most powerful men in the House—Pitt and Fox. The following notes dispel any doubt which may still exist as to the formal and explicit understanding between these ancient antagonists for the object which both had at heart, though for very different reasons, namely the overthrow of Addington:—

Charles Fox to Creevey

Arlington St., Saturday [*1804*]

DEAR SIR,

I enclose you a part of a letter from Grey. If you can speak to Brandling[17] upon the subject you may tell him that in all the divisions

[17] Mr. Brandling, M.P. for Newcastle-on-Tyne, was Mrs. Creevey's brother.

we shall have this next week, either Mr. Pitt will be with us or we with him.

Yours,

C. J. Fox.

Enclosure in above

My dear Fox,

I forgot yesterday to answer your question about Brandling. He is not at present in this county [Northumberland], and I don't know whether he is in London or in Yorkshire. Creevey, his brother-in-law, will be able to suggest the best mode of applying to him; but I should think, notwithstanding his hatred of the Doctor, that he would not vote against him without Pitt.

The unnatural alliance between Pitt and Fox was manifested in its least commendable aspect upon the occasion of Pitt's motion for an inquiry into the administration of the First Lord of the Admiralty, Earl St. Vincent, who had not only contributed to securing for his country the mastery of the ocean, but, by means of the Commission of Inquiry which he established as First Lord, had exposed and put an end to many abuses in the service. Pitt's motion, of course, was hostile to the gallant admiral, through whose discredit he sought to bring Addington's Government into disgrace; and Fox supported the motion in a speech the insincerity of which was not inferior to that of Pitt, and staggered even such a good party man as Creevey.

Creevey to Currie

22nd March, 1804

...With respect to the debate...nothing could be...so unlike a *case* against Lord St. Vincent: I really doubted the fidelity of my ears all the time I listened to him (Fox), he was so very unlike himself. His first reply was a great and striking display of his powers, but the charge against the Admiralty derived little support or elucidation from it. I confess I felt a wish that Fox would not have taken the part he did, because I cannot reconcile it to my notions either of private friendship or parliamentary justice to put a man upon his trial, because I am sure he is innocent. There were, however, most powerful arguments urged by Fox that in a great measure reconciled me to the vote I gave, and indeed had they been much less and much weaker, I should most readily have gone with him. A Leader of a Party has a most difficult part imposed upon him on such an occasion. It is impossible he can be alone influenced by the abstract question of merit or demerit of the motion but of course must calculate *in every way* upon the effects of his vote. As a private of a party there is nothing so fatal to publick principle, or one's own private respect and consequence, as acting for oneself upon great questions. I am more passionately attached every day to Party. I am certain that without it nothing can be done, and I am more certain from every day's experience that the leader of the party to which I belong is as superior in talents, in enlightened views, in publick and private virtues, to all other party leaders as one human being can be to another. He must therefore give many, many votes that I may think are wrong, before I vote against him or not with him.

I scarcely know an earthly blessing I would purchase at the expense of those sensations I feel towards the incomparable Charley!

2nd April

... The fact is I believe, as I have always done, that the Regal function will never more be exercised by him (George III), and the Dr. has most impudently assumed these functions in doing what he has done.

And now again for speculation. I can swear to what Sheridan will try for, if the thing does not too suddenly come to a crisis. His insuperable vanity has suggested to him the brilliancy of being first with the Prince and governing his councils. He will, if he sees it practicable, try, and is now trying, to alienate the Prince from Fox, and to reconcile him to the wretched Addington. The effect of such a diabolical project is doubtless to be dreaded with a person so unsteady as the Prince; but then again there are things that comfort me. If the Prince has a point on which he is uniform, it is a proud and just attachment to the old Nobility of the country, articles which fortunately find no place in the composition of the present ministers. His notion, too, of Sheridan, I believe, has not much to do with his qualities for a statesman. Devonshire House, too, is his constant haunt, where every one is against Sheridan; and where the Prince, at his own request, met Grey three weeks ago and offered him any pledge as a security for his calling Fox to his councils whenever he had the power. Master Sherry does not know this, and of course it must not be known; but I know it and am certain of the fact. Sheridan displays evident distrust of his own projects, and is basely playing an under game as Fox's friend, in the event of defeat to him and his Dr. I never saw conduct more distinctly base than his.

1st May

... The enemy of mankind is Pitt. I detest from the bottom of my heart him and all his satellites. I am sure, too, that, independent of his dispositions, his mind is of a mean and little structure, much below the requisite for times like these—active, intriguing and most powerful, but all in detail, quite incapable of accompanying the elevated views of Fox.

Addington stuck stiffly to his post, but the forces allied against him in the Commons proved irresistible in the end; in May, 1804, he resigned, and Pitt entered upon his last administration. Addington, smothering his resentment of the rough handling he had received, joined Pitt's Cabinet as President of the Council in January, 1805, accepting at the same time the peerage which he had previously declined. Pitt would have given Fox a share in the administration hardly inferior to his own, but the King would not hear of it, and thus was lost for ever the noble project of uniting the chief political parties for the defence of the Empire.

Creevey to Currie

2nd May, 1804

... It is felt by the Pittites that the Prince and a Regency must be resorted to, and as the Prince evinced on every occasion the strongest decision in favor of Fox, the Pittites are preparing for a reciprocity of good offices. God send we may have a Regency, and then the cards are in our hands. I wish you had seen the party of which I formed one in the park just now. Lord Buckingham, his son Temple, Ld. Derby, Charles Grey, Ld. Fitzwilliam, Canning, Ld. Morpeth and Ld. Stafford. ... The *four* physicians were at Buckingham House this morning: I feel certain he (the King) is devilish bad....

3rd May

Under our present circumstances no news is good news, because it shows there are great difficulties in making the peace between the King and Pitt.... The King has communicated to him that he will see him to-morrow or Saturday, *which communication Pitt immediately forwarded to Fox*. There is, I hope, much value in these facts; they show, I hope, that the Monarch *is done*, and can no longer make Ministers; they show too, I hope, that Pitt thinks so. Why this delay at such a time if the King is well? Why this civility from Pitt to Fox? if the former did not suspect no good was to come of his interviews with his

Master. We are all in better spirits—by 'all,' I mean the admirers of Fox and haters of Pitt....

8th May

...I was too late for last night's post, and besides I was struck dumb and lifeless by the elevation of that wretch Pitt to his former fatal eminence—sick to death, too, with something like a sensation of Fox's disgrace and defeat, and of the termination of all our hopes. But I am better to-day; the Grenvilles and Windhamites have to a man stuck fast to Fox and refuse to treat with Pitt. The Prince, too, loads Fox with caresses, and swears his father's exception to Fox alone is meant as the last and greatest of personal injuries to himself, because the King knows full well that Fox is the first favorite of the Prince.

Park Place, June 2nd, 1804

...Well—I think, considering we have certainly been out-jockeyed by the villain Pitt, we are doing famously. Pitt, I think, is in a damnable dilemma; his character has received a cursed blow from the appearance of puzzle in his late conduct, from the wretched farce of [*illegible*] turning out Addington, and keeping those who were worse than him; and from his having produced no military plans yet, after all his anathemas against the late Ministers for their delay. The country, I now firmly believe, was tired of Pitt and even of the Court, and conceived some new men and councils, and above all an union of all great men, was a necessary experiment for the situation. Pitt has disappointed this wish and expectation, and has shown no necessity that has compelled him so to do. He has all the air of having acted a rapacious, selfish, shabby part; he is surrounded by shabby partizans; in comparison with his own relations, the Grenvilles, he is degraded; he has no novelty to recommend him; his Master[18] is on the wane, and to a certain extent is evidently hostile to him. In addition to all this, the daily and nightly attendance of Dr. Simmonds and four physicians at Buckingham House must inevitably increase the Prince's power, and diminish that of Pitt. I saw these five Drs. and Dundass, the surgeon from Richmond, come out of Buckingham House with Pitt half an hour ago. Simmonds and one of the physicians always return at five in the evening—the former for the night—the latter for some hours. I have watched and know their motions well. This must end surely at no distant period—a Regency—and then I hope the game's our own! In the mean time, these dinners and this activity of the Prince are certainly doing good, and our friends are much more numerous than I expected. We are a great body—the

[18] George III.

Prince at the head of us. Fox, Grey, &c., are all in great spirits. . . . Your humble servant partakes in the passing festivities of these Opposition grandees. I dine to-morrow at Lord Fitzwilliam's, this day week at *Carlton House*; Monday I dine at Lord Derby's. I really believe I have played my cards, so far, excellently with these people.

Sir John Moore to Creevey

Sandgate, 27th Aug., 1804

. . . We understand that Government have positive information that we are to be invaded, and I am told that Pitt believes it. The experience of the last twelve months has taught me to place little confidence in the information or belief of Ministers, and as the undertaking seems to me so arduous, and offering so little prospect of success, I cannot persuade myself that Bonoparte will be mad enough to attempt it. He will continue to threaten, by which means alone he can do us harm. The invasion would, I am confident, end in our glory and in his disgrace.

The newspapers continue to mention secret expeditions, and have sometimes named me as one of the Generals to be employed. I put these upon a par with the invasion. We have at present no disposeable force, and, if we had, I see no object worthy upon which to risk it. Thus, without belief in invasion or foreign expeditions, my situation here becomes daily more irksome, and I am almost reduced to wish for peace. I am tired of the confinement, without the occupation, of war.

Lord Henry Petty to Creevey

Bath, Nov. 23rd, 1804

. . . [We are] within a few doors here of Ld. Thurlow's house, which has been recently honor'd with a Royal visit, when, as you may suppose, the whole scene of ministerial intrigue and family negociation was laid open: some *legal business* of importance was also transacted, for one lawyer came down with the P., and another was sent for while he remained. . . . Most probably it relates to some arrangement for the Princess. I am really glad to find he has conducted himself with so much firmness, and at the same time with some decorum. I give *him* the more credit for it, as I suspect the councils of Carlton House are not composed of the most highminded or immaculate statesmen.[19]

19 'At that period we had a kind of Cabinet, with whom I used to consult. They were the Dukes of York, Portland, Devonshire and Northumberland, Lord Guilford (that was Lord North), Lords Stormont, Moira and Fitzwilliam and Charles Fox.'—*Statement by George IV to F. W. Croker* [The Croker Papers, i. 289].

chapter two

1805

THE FOLLOWING HOLOGRAPH note, without date, probably belongs to the year 1805, and is interesting as being written by the future William IV on behalf of the future George IV:—

H.R.H. the Duke of Clarence to Creevey
[holograph]

St. James's, Friday night

DEAR SIR,

The Prince desires you will meet at dinner here on Saturday the Eighteenth instant at six o'Clock Lord [*illegible*] and Sheridan. I hope I need not add how happy your presence will make me. I remain

Yours sincerely,

WILLIAM.

Foreign politics during these years absorbed all the energies of Ministers, and diverted Pitt from those schemes of reform which undoubtedly lay near his heart. But the spirit of reform was awake, though it was crushed out of the plans of the Cabinet by stress of circumstance. The Opposition enjoyed more freedom and less responsibility. Creevey attached himself to that section of it which was foremost in hunting out abuses and proposing drastic measures of redress. At this time Henry Dundas, Viscount Melville, was First Lord of the Admiralty. The 10th Report of the Commission appointed 'to inquire into frauds and abuses in the Royal Navy' contained grave charges against Melville, who was accused in the House of Commons of malversation in his office of Treasurer of the Navy, committed in years subsequent to 1782. The division on 8th April showed 216 votes in each lobby, when the Speaker gave his casting vote in favour of Whitbread's motion. Melville at once resigned, and his name was erased from the list of Privy Councillors. He was impeached before the House of Lords and acquitted, but not till 12th June, 1806, six months after Pitt's death. 'I have ever thought,' wrote Lord Fitzharris, 'that an aiding cause in Pitt's death, certainly one that tended to shorten his existence, was the result of the proceedings against his old friend and colleague Lord Melville.'

Creevey to Currie

13th March, 1805

...I am trying to learn my lesson as a future under-secretary or Secretary of the Treasury.... We had a famous debate on Sheridan's motion; never anything was so hollow as the argument on our side. Sherry's speech and reply were both excellent. In that part of his reply when he fired upon Pitt for his treachery to the Catholics, Pitt's eyes started with defiance from their sockets, and seemed to tell him if he advanced an atom further he would have his life. Sherry left him a little alone and tickled him about of the greatness of his mind and the good temper of Melville; and then he turned upon him again with redoubled fury.... Never has it fallen to my lot to hear such words before in publick or in private used by man to man.

April 13, 1805

...We have had indeed most famous sport with this same Leviathan, Lord Melville. His tumbling so soon was as unexpected by all of us as it was by himself or you. It was clear from the first that he was ruined sooner or later, but no one anticipated his defeat upon the first Attack, and supported as he was by the Addingtons as well as Pitts, and with the nostrum held out, too, of further enquiry by a secret Committee. The history of that celebrated night presents a wide field of attack upon Pitt under all the infinite difficulties of his situation; a clamour for reform in the expenditure of the publick money is at last found to be the touchstone of the House of Commons and of the publick....Grey is to give notice immediately when we meet to bring in a bill appointing Commissioners to examine into abuses in the Army, in the Barracks—the Ordnance—the Commissariat Departments. This plan, if it is worth anything...must place Pitt in the cursedest dilemma possible. Can he refuse enquiry when it is so loudly called for; or, if he grants it, what must become of the Duke of York and the Greenwoods and Hammersleys and Delaneys, &c., &c., &c., whose tricks with money in these departments would whitewash those of Trotter by comparison....I have no hesitation in saying that Pitt must be more than man to stand it....

London, May 11, 1805

Our campaign for the last six weeks has been a marvellous one.... The country has surprised me as much as the votes of the 8th and 10th, and these meetings and resolutions have brought us safe into port, as far, at least, as relates to Melville. Pitt, too, is greatly, if not irrepairably damaged by Melville's defeat and by certain irregularities of his own. Whitbread's select committee has done great additional injury to Melville, and has got sufficient matter established for a *resolution* against Pitt.... It is a damned thing, too, for the friends and admirers of this once great man, to see him sent for by Whitbread, and to hear him examined for anything like money irregularities. He is, I am certain, infinitely injured in the estimation of the House of Commons; and then think of his situation in other respects—his right hand, Melville, lopped off—a superannuated Methodist at the head of the Admiralty, in order to catch the votes of Wilberforce and Co. now and then—all the fleets of France and Spain in motion—the finances at their utmost stretch—not an official person but Huskisson and Rose to do anything at their respective offices—publick business multiplied by opposition beyond all former example—and himself more averse to business daily—disunited with Addington—having quite lost his own character and with a King perfectly mad and involving his ministry in the damnedest scrapes upon the subject of expense.... I know Pitt's friends think he can't go on, and they all wish him not to try it. You may guess how the matter is when I tell you that Abercromby, the member for Edinburgh, and Hope, the member of your county, have struck and fled, declaring they won't support Pitt any longer, whom they both pronounce to be a damned rascal. My authority is James Abercromby,[1] and I will answer for the truth of these facts.

...Bennet[2] has been here, and is now returned to Bath. He is most desirous to know you, and I promised I would write to you and mention him by way of introduction. He is most amiable, occasionally most *boring*, but at all times most upright and honorable. Make him introduce you to Lord and Lady Tankerville. The former is very fond of me; he is a haughty, honorable man—has lived at one time in the heart of political leaders—was the friend of Lansdowne—has been in office several times, and is now a misanthrope, but very communicative and entertaining when he likes his man. His only remaining passion is for clever men, of which description he considers himself as one, tho' cer-

[1] Hon. James Abercromby; Speaker 1835–9; created Lord Dunfermline 1839; died 1858.

[2] Hon. H. G. Bennet, M.P., 2nd son of 4th Earl of Tankerville.

tainly unjustly. Lady Tankerville has perhaps as much merit as any woman in England.[3] She is, too, very clever, and has great wit; but she, like her Lord, is depress'd and unhappy. They compose together the most striking libel upon the blessing of Fortune; they are rich much beyond their desires or expenditure, they have the most elevated rank of their country, I know of nothing to disturb their happiness, and they are apparently the most miserable people I ever saw.

Thorndon [Lord Petre's], 28th July, 1805

...You must know that I came out of the battle [of the session] very sick of it and of my leaders. It appears to me we had Pitt upon his very last legs, and might have destroyed him upon the spot; instead of which, every opportunity for so doing was either lost or converted to a contrary purpose. Could the most inveterate enemy of Pitt have wished for anything better than to find him lending £40,000, appropriated by law to particular publick purposes, to two bankrupt members of parliament who voted always with him?[4] and could the most pertinacious derider of Fox's political folly have dared to conceive that Fox on such an occasion should acquit Pitt of all corruption, and should add likewise this sentiment to his opinion, that to have so detected him in corruption would have made him (Fox) the most miserable of men? ... In short, between ourselves, my dear Doctor, I believe that Fox has no principle about publick money, and that he would give it away, if he had the power, in any way or for any job quite as disgusting as the worst of Pitt's. It is a painful conclusion this to come to, and dreadfully diminishes one's parliamentary amusement. You can have no conception how feverish I became about Fox's conduct during this damned Athol business.[5] I talked *at* him in private, and no doubt vexed him infernally; but this you'll say is but poor work, to be making myself enemies in the persons whose jobs I oppose, and to quarrel with my own friends for not opposing the jobs too. I must have some discussion with my conscience and

[3] She was Emma, daughter and co-heiress of Sir James Colebrooke, Bart.

[4] Boyd, Benfield and Co., to whom Pitt advanced the sum named out of money voted for Navy services. They were Government agents, and shortly afterwards went bankrupt.

[5] The 3rd Duke of Athol having inherited the sovereignty of the Isle of Man through his wife, daughter and heiress of his uncle, the 2nd Duke, sold the same in 1765 to the Government for £70,000 and a pension of £2,000 for their joint lives, but reserving their land rents. The 4th Duke, after two failures, succeeded in getting a bill through Parliament in 1805, settling one-fourth of the customs of the island upon him and the heirs general of James Stanley, 7th Earl of Derby. The bill was vigorously opposed, and Creevey denounced it as a job. The fourth of the customs was subsequently commuted for £409,000.

my temper before the next campaign, to see whether I can't go on a little more smoothly, and without prejudice to my interest.... I see a great deal of Windham. He has dined with me, but my opinion of him is not at all improved by my acquaintance with him. He is, at the same time, *decidedly* the most agreeable and witty in conversation of all these great men....

The following notes are without date, but the allusion to Tom Sheridan's bride shows that they belong to the summer of 1805.

R. B. Sheridan, M.P., to Creevey

Richmond Hill,
Monday—the third day of Peace and Tranquillity

My dear Creevey,

You must make my excuse to the Lord Mayor. Pray vouch that you should have brought me, but my cold is really so bad that I should infallibly lay myself up if I attempted to go. Here are pure air, quiet and innocence, and everything that suits me.

Pray let me caution you not to expose yourself to the *air* after Dinner, as I find malicious people disposed to attribute to wine what was clearly the mere effect of the atmosphere. My last hour to your Ladies, as I am certainly going to die; till when, however,

Yours truly,
R. B. S.

Thursday evening

My dear Creevey,

If you don't leave town to-morrow, come and eat your mutton with me in George St. and meet Adam and McMahon, and more than all, my Son and Daughter.

Mrs. Creevey will excuse you at my request, and you will be a Piece of a Lion to have seen so early Mrs. T. S.,[6] whom I think lovely and engaging and interesting beyond measure, and, as far as I can judge, with a most superior understanding.

Yours ever,
R. B. S.

[6] Sheridan's only son [by his first marriage. J. G.], Tom [1775–1817], married Caroline Henrietta Callander in 1805. She was a celebrated beauty, wrote three novels which had some popularity, and was the mother of four sons and three beautiful daughters—Mrs. Blackwood, afterwards Lady Dufferin, and lastly, Countess of Gifford; The Hon. Mrs. Norton, afterwards Lady Stirling-Maxwell of Keir; and the youngest, the Duchess of Somerset, Queen of Beauty at the Eglinton Tournament.

Grosvenor Place, Saturday morning

My dear Mrs. Creevey,

I left Hester about two hours ago; she violently expects you. Remember we have a bed for you, a fishing rod for Creevey on Monday morning. If you will stay over Monday, Hester and Richmond Hill will make you quite well, and there are, not cockney, but classical Lions for Creevey to see....

It is difficult in these later days to realise the degree in which Royal personages were allowed, and even expected, to interfere with politics and the work of Parliament under the Hanoverian dynasty. It is notorious that, George III having evinced his determination to have a Tory Cabinet, the Heir Apparent chose his friends and counsellors from the Whig Opposition, trafficking in seats in Parliament as keenly as any boroughmonger of them all. Among others whom he sought to enlist in his Parliamentary party was the gentle and erudite Samuel Romilly, whose name must ever be associated with the unwearying efforts he made to reform and mitigate the atrociously sanguinary penal code of England. Measured by the extent of the immediate success of these efforts, Romilly's influence upon the statute-book may be reckoned trifling, seeing that all he was able to effect against Lord Ellenborough and the House of Lords was the repeal, in 1812, of the law which prescribed the death penalty upon any soldier or mariner who should presume to beg, without permission from his commanding officer or a magistrate. Nevertheless the fruits of his life-work ripened after his untimely death by his own hand in 1818, and although he cannot be reckoned among the noisiest nor among the most profusely munificent philanthropists, the influence of Samuel Romilly was indeed one of the most powerful and beneficent ever exerted in the cause of humanity.

Samuel Romilly to Creevey

Little Ealing, Sept. 23rd, 1805

Dear Creevey,

I have just received your letter....It has indeed very much surprised me, and I am afraid my answer to it will occasion as much surprise in you. I cannot express to you how much flattered I am by the honor which the Prince of Wales does me. No event in the whole course of my life has been so gratifying to me....I have formed no resolution to keep out of Parliament; on the contrary, it has long been my intention and is still my wish, to obtain a seat in the House, though not immediately.[7] If I had been a member from the beginning of the present Parliament, my vote would have been uniformly given in a way which I presume would have been agreeable to the Prince of Wales.... Upon all questions I should have voted with Mr. Fox; and yet, with all this, I feel myself obliged to decline the offer which his Royal Highness has the great condescension to make me....

Lord Henry Petty[8] to Creevey

Dublin, Sept. 15th, 1805

DEAR CREEVEY,

I have for some time meditated writing to you, more, I confess, in the hope of procuring an answer, than with that of being able to communicate anything that can interest you from this country, altho' it affords me a great deal of amusement as a traveller.

The town of Dublin is full of fine buildings, fine streets, &c., but so ill placed and imperfectly finished as to give it the appearance of a great piece of patchwork, made up without skill and without attention. The Custom House, is, however, an exception, and in every respect a noble edifice....

Belfast, Oct. 24th, 1805

What great events are passing on the Continent. It is terrible to think that Pitt has so much of the fate of England and of Europe in his hands. I understand there has been some disagreement with Russia in consequence of the D. of Y. being intended for the command of a combined army of Russians and English, against which the Court of Petersburgh demonstrated. How disgracefull to be indebted to a foreign court for teaching us commonsense and our own interest at such a crisis!

At Christmastide, 1805, Pitt received his death-blow. He had staked the existence of his country and the freedom of Europe upon the coalition of Austria, Russia, and England against Bonaparte and the destructive energies of France. But before these formidable allies could come into line, even before the British force had embarked for Germany, Napoleon swept through the Black Forest

[7] He was elected member for Queenborough in 1806, on taking office as Solicitor-General in 'All the Talents.'

[8] Chancellor of the Exchequer in 'All the Talents,' 1806–7, and afterwards 3rd Marquess of Lansdowne.

with 100,000 men. The Austrian commander Mack, posted on the Iller from Ulm to Memmingen, was surprised, taken in rear, and laid down his arms on October 19th, Werneck's corps having done the like the day before to Murat. By the end of the month the Austrian field force of 80,000 was no more. When rumours reached Pitt of the capitulation of Ulm—'Don't believe it,' he exclaimed; 'it is all a fiction.' Next day the terrible news received confirmation; the shock could not be repaired, even by the glorious intelligence which arrived four days later of the destruction of the French and Spanish fleets at Trafalgar. That, indeed, revived shattered hopes for the moment, but it was followed closely by the news of Austerlitz, where the second partner in the coalition had been crushed with a loss of 26,000 men. Not only was the coalition at an end, but its author passed quickly into the shadow of death.

Hon. Charles Grey, M.P. (afterwards 2nd Earl Grey), to Creevey

Howick, Dec. 29th, 1805

. . . Your details, which I had received from no other person, have left no doubt upon my mind. Of the delay of fresh intelligence I think nothing. I remember the same thing happened after the battle of Ulm, when the same inferences were drawn from it, and the opportunity taken to circulate the same reports of the defeat of the French. It seems Robert Ward sent to all the newspapers the paragraphs which you wd. see, asserting the Russian capitulation and Count Palfy's letters to be forgeries; and this, I am assured, without the least authority for doing so, except his own foolish belief. All this, I agree with you, is as much calculated to hurt Pitt, when it is completely exposed, as the disasters themselves, and the folly of doing it is inconceivable. If the defeat of the 2nd[9] was as calamitous as I believe it to have been, it is nonsense to talk any more of Continental confederacies. The game is too desperate even for Pitt himself, desperate as he is; and the King of Prussia certainly would not expose himself alone, which in the first instance he must do, to all the power and vengeance of France. I am more inclined to think that they [Pitt's Cabinet] really do flatter themselves against all evidence into a belief in these renewed battles and consequent change of fortune. There is nothing too absurd for them in a military view. They are naturally confident and sanguine, and this is their last hope.

[9] At Austerlitz.

chapter two (*continued*)

1805

THE FOLLOWING REMINISCENCES were written by Creevey in the reign of William IV, but as they refer chiefly to his doings in 1805, they find their proper sequence in this place. At the time they were written Creevey's feelings towards George IV had undergone a complete revulsion; but in 1805 he was full of enthusiasm for the Heir Apparent, upon whom the hopes of the whole Whig party were fixed,

It was in 1804 when I first began to take a part in the House of Commons, at which time the Prince of Wales was a most warm and active partizan of Mr. Fox and the Opposition. It was then that the Prince began first to notice me, and to stop his horse and talk with me when he met me in the streets; but I recollect only one occasion, in that or the succeeding year, that I dined at Carlton House, and that was with a party of the Opposition, to whom he gave various dinners during that spring. On that occasion Lord Dundas and Calcraft sat at the top and bottom of the table, the Prince in the middle at one side, with the Duke of Clarence next to him; Fox, Sheridan and about 30 opposition members of both Houses making the whole party. We walked about the garden before dinner without our hats.

The only thing that made an impression upon me in favour of the Prince that day (always excepting his excellent manners and appearance of good humour) was his receiving a note during dinner which he flung across the table to Fox and asked if he must not answer it, which Fox assented to; and then, without the slightest fuss, the Prince left his place, went into another room and wrote an answer, which he brought to Fox for his approval, and when the latter said it was quite right, the Prince seemed delighted, which I thought very pretty in him, and a striking proof of Fox's influence over him.

During dinner he was very gracious, funny and agreeable, but after dinner he took to making speeches, and was very prosy as well as highly injudicious. He made a long harangue in favour of the Catholics and took occasion to tell us that his brother William and himself were the only two of his family who were not *Germans*—this too in a company which was, most of them, barely known to him. Likewise I remember his halloaing to Sir Charles Bamfyld at the other end of the table, and asking him if he had seen Mother Windsor[1] lately. I brought Lord Howick[2] and George Walpole home at night in my coach, and so ended that day.

At the beginning of September, 1805, Mrs. Creevey and myself with her daughters, went to Brighton to spend the autumn there, the Prince then living at the Pavilion. I think it was the first, or at furthest the second, day after our arrival, when my two eldest daughters[3] and myself were walking on the Steyne, and the Prince, who was sitting talking to old Lady Clermont, having perceived me, left her and came up to speak to me, when I presented my daughters to him. He was very gracious to us all and hoped he should see me shortly at dinner. In two or three days from this time I received an invitation to dine at the Pavilion.... Mrs. Fitzherbert, whom I had never been in a room with before, sat on one side of the Prince, and the Duke of Clarence on the other.... In the course of the evening the Prince took me up to the card table where Mrs. Fitzherbert was playing, and said—'Mrs. Fitzherbert, I wish you would call upon Mrs. Creevey, and say from me I shall be happy to see her here.' Mrs. Fitzherbert did call accordingly, and altho' she and Mrs. Creevey had never seen each other before, an acquaintance began that soon grew into a very sincere and agreeable friendship, which lasted the remainder of Mrs. Creevey's life....

...Immediately after this first visit from Mrs. Fitzherbert, Mrs. Creevey and her daughters became invited with myself to the Prince's parties at the Pavilion, and till the first week in January—a space of about four months—except a few days when the Prince went to see the King at Weymouth, and a short time that I was in London in November, there was not a day we were not at the Pavilion, I dining there always once or twice a week, Mrs. Creevey frequently dining with me likewise, but in the evening we were always there.

During these four months the Prince behaved with the greatest good humour as well as kindness to us all. He was always merry and full of his jokes, and any one would have said he was really a very happy man. Indeed I have heard him say repeatedly during that time that he never should be so happy when King, as he was then.

I suppose the Courts or houses of Princes are all alike in one thing,

[1] A notorious procuress in King's Place.
[2] Afterwards Earl Grey, the Prime Minister.
[3] His stepdaughters, the Miss Ords.

viz., that in attending them you lose your liberty. After one month was gone by, you fell naturally and of course into the ranks, and had to reserve your observations till you were asked for them. These royal invitations are by no means calculated to reconcile one to a Court. To be sent for half an hour before dinner, or perhaps in the middle of one's own, was a little too humiliating to be very agreeable.

... Lord Hutchinson[4] was a great feature at the Pavilion. He lived in the house, or rather the one adjoining it, and within the grounds.... As a military man he was a great resource at that time, as we were in the midst of expectations about the Austrians and Buonaparte, and the battle which we all knew would so soon take place between them. It was a funny thing to hear the Prince, when the battle *had* taken place, express the same opinion as was given in the London Government newspapers, that it was all over with the French—they were all sent to the devil, and the Lord knows what. Maps were got out to satisfy everybody as to the precise ground where the battle had been fought and the route by which the French had retreated. While these operations were going on in one window of the Pavilion, Lord Hutchinson took me privately to another, when he put into my hand his own private dispatch from Gordon, then Secretary to the Commander-in-Chief, giving him the true account of the battle of Austerlitz, with the complete victory of the French. This news, unaccountable as it may appear, was repeated day after day at the Pavilion for nearly a week; and when the truth began at last to make its appearance in the newspapers, the Prince put them all in his pockets, so that no paper was forthcoming at the Pavilion, instead of half-a-dozen, the usual number.... We used to dine pretty punctually at six, the average number being about sixteen.... Mrs. Fitzherbert always dined there, and mostly one other lady—Lady Downshire very often, sometimes Lady Clare or Lady Berkeley or Mrs. Creevey. Mrs. Fitzherbert was a great card-player, and played every night. The Prince never touched a card, but was occupied in talking to his guests, and very much in listening to and giving directions to the band. At 12 o'clock punctually the band stopped, and sandwiches and wine and water handed about, and shortly after the Prince made a bow and we all dispersed.

I had heard a great deal of the Prince's drinking, but, during the time that I speak of, I never saw him the least drunk but once, and I was myself pretty much the occasion of it. We were dining at the Pavilion,

[4] Brother of the 1st Earl of Donoughmore; a general officer, succeeded Sir Ralph Abercromby in command of the army in Egypt, and was raised to the peerage in 1801.

and poor Fonblanque, a dolorous fop of a lawyer, and a member of Parliament too, was one of the guests. After drinking some wine, I could not resist having some jokes at Fonblanque's expense, which the Prince encouraged greatly. I went on and invented stories about speeches Fonblanque had made in Parliament, which were so pathetic as to have affected his audience to tears, all of which inventions of mine Fonblanque denied to be true with such overpowering gravity that the Prince said he should die of it if I did not stop.... In the evening, at about ten or eleven o'clock, he said he would go to the ball at the Castle, and said I should go with him. So I went in his coach, and he entered the room with his arm through mine, everybody standing and getting upon benches to see him. He was certainly tipsey, and so, of course, was I, but not much, for I well remember his taking me up to Mrs. Creevey and her daughters, and telling them he had never spent a pleasanter day in his life, and that 'Creevey had been very great.' He used to drink a great quantity of wine at dinner, and was very fond of making any newcomer drunk by drinking wine with him very frequently, always recommending his strongest wines, and at last some remarkable strong old brandy which he called Diabolino.

It used to be the Duke of Norfolk's custom to come over every year from Arundel to pay his respects to the Prince and to stay two days at Brighton, both of which he always dined at the Pavilion. In the year 1804, upon this annual visit, the Prince had drunk so much as to be made very seriously ill by it, so that in 1805 (the year I was there) when the Duke came, Mrs. Fitzherbert, who was always the Prince's best friend, was very much afraid of his being again made ill, and she persuaded the Prince to adopt different stratagems to avoid drinking with the Duke. I dined there on both days, and letters were brought in each day after dinner to the Prince, which he affected to consider of great importance, and so went out to answer them, while the Duke of Clarence went on drinking with the Duke of Norfolk. But on the second day this joke was carried too far, and in the evening the Duke of Norfolk showed he was affronted. The Prince took me aside and said—'Stay after everyone is gone to-night. The Jockey's got sulky, and I must give him a broiled bone to get him in good humour again.' So of course I stayed, and about one o'clock the Prince of Wales and Duke of Clarence, the Duke of Norfolk and myself sat down to a supper of broiled bones, the result of which was, having fallen asleep myself, I was awoke by the sound of the Duke of Norfolk's snoring. I found the Prince of Wales and the Duke of Clarence in a very animated discussion as to the particular shape and make of the wig worn by George II.

Among other visitors to the Pavilion came Sheridan, with whom I was then pretty intimate, though perhaps not so much so as afterwards. I was curious to see him and the Prince daily in this way, considering the very great intimacy there had been between them for so many years. Nothing, certainly, could be more creditable to both parties than their conduct. I never saw Sheridan during the period of three weeks (I think it was) take the least more liberty in the Prince's presence than if it had been the first day he had ever seen him. On the other hand, the Prince always showed by his manner that he thought Sheridan a man that any prince might be proud of as a friend. So much of *manners*; but I was witness to a kind of altercation between them in which Sheridan could make no impression on the Prince. The latter had just given Sheridan the office of Auditor of the Duchy of Cornwall, worth about £800 per annum, and Sheridan was most anxious that the Prince should transfer the appointment to his son, Tom Sheridan, who was just then married. What Sheridan's object in this was, cannot be exactly made out; whether it really was affection for Tom, or whether it was to keep the profit of the office out of the reach of his creditors, or whether it was to have a young life in the patent instead of his own. Whichever of these objects he had in view, he pursued it with the greatest vehemence; so much so, that I saw him *cry bitterly* one night in making his supplication to the Prince. The latter, however, was not to be shaken... he resisted the demand upon the sole ground that Sheridan's reputation was such, that it made it not only justifiable, but most honourable to him, the Prince, to make such a selection for the office....

This reminds me of another circumstance relating to the same office when in Sheridan's possession. In the year 1810, Mrs. Creevey, her daughters and myself were spending our summer at Richmond. Sheridan and his wife (who was a relation and particular friend of Mrs. Creevey's) came down to dine and stay all night with us. There being no other person present after dinner, when the ladies had left the room, Sheridan said:—

'A damned odd thing happened to me this morning, and Hester [Mrs. Sheridan] and I have agreed in coming down here to-day that no human being shall ever know of it as long as we live; so that nothing but my firm conviction that Hester is at this moment telling it to Mrs. Creevey could induce me to tell it to you.'

Then he said that the money belonging to this office of his in the Duchy being always paid into Biddulph's or Cox's bank (I think it was) at Charing Cross, it was his habit to look in there. There was one particular clerk who seemed always so fond of him, and so proud of his acquaintance, that he every now and then cajoled him into advancing him £10 or £20 more than his account entitled him to.... That morning he thought his friend looked particularly smiling upon him, so he said:—

'I looked in to see if you could let me have ten pounds.'

'Ten pounds!' replied the clerk; 'to be sure I can, Mr. Sheridan. You've got my letter, sir, have you not?'

'No,' said Sheridan, 'what letter?'

It is literally true that at this time and for many, many years Sheridan never got twopenny-post letters,[5] because there was no money to pay for them, and the postman would not leave them without payment.

'Why, don't you know what has happened, sir?' asked the clerk. 'There is £1,300 paid into your account. There has been a very great fine paid for one of the Duchy estates, and this £1,300 is your percentage as auditor.'

Sheridan was, of course, very much set up with this £1,300, and, on the very next day upon leaving us, he took a house at Barnes Terrace, where he spent all his £1,300. At the end of two or three months at most, the tradespeople would no longer supply him without being paid, so he was obliged to remove. What made this folly the more striking was that Sheridan had occupied five or six different houses in this neighbourhood at different periods of his life, and on each occasion had been driven away literally by non-payment of his bills and consequent want of food for the house. Yet he was as full of his fun during these two months as ever he could be—gave dinners perpetually and was always on the road between Barnes and London, or Barnes and Oatlands (the Duke of York's), in a large job coach upon which he would have his family arms painted....

...As I may not have another opportunity of committing to paper what little I have of perfect recollection of what Sheridan told me in our walks at Brighton respecting his early life, and as he certainly was a very extraordinary man, I may as well insert it here.

He was at school at Harrow, and, as he told me, never had any scholastic fame while he was there, nor did he appear to have formed any friendships there. He said he was a very low-spirited boy, much given to crying when alone, and he attributed this very much to being neglected by his father, to his being left without money, and often not

[5] The charge at this time for letters sent and delivered within the metropolitan district was only *2d.*, payable by the recipient; but country letters were charged from *10d.* to *1s. 6d.* and more, according to distance.

taken home at the regular holidays. From Harrow he went to live in John Street, out of Soho Square, whether with his father or some other instructor, I forget, but he dwelt upon the two years he spent there as those in which he acquired all the reading and learning he had upon any subject.

At the end of this time his father determined to open a kind of academy at Bath—the masters or instructors to be Sheridan the father, his eldest son Charles, and our Sheridan, who was to be *rhetorical usher*. According to his account, however, the whole concern was presently laughed off the stage, and then Sheridan described his happiness as beginning. He danced with all the women at Bath, wrote sonnets and verses in praise of some, satires and lampoons upon others, and in a very short time became the established wit and fashion of the place.

It was at this period of his life he fell in love with Miss Lin(d)ley, whom he afterwards married, but she was carried off by her father at that time to a convent in France, to be kept out of his way. Then it was he became embroiled with Mr. Mathews, who was likewise a lover of Miss Lin(d)ley, as well as her libeller. Sheridan fought two duels with Mr. Mathews upon this subject, both times with swords.

The (second) duel was fought at King's Weston (if I recollect right). According to Sheridan's account, never was anything so desperate. Sheridan's sword broke in a point blank thrust into Mathews's chest; upon this he closed, and they both fell, Mathews uppermost; but, in falling, his sword broke likewise, sticking into the earth and snapping. However, he drew the sharp end out of the ground, and with this he stabbed Sheridan in the face and body, over and over again, till it was thought he must die. Sheridan named both the seconds, but I forget them. He said they were both cut for ever afterwards for not interfering. He said, likewise, there was a regular proceeding before the Mayor of Bristol, on the ground that Mr. Mathews had worn some kind of armour to protect him, which broke Sheridan's sword.... Sheridan was taken to some hotel at Bath, where his life for some time was despaired of, but... he rallied and recovered.

He then lived for some time at Waltham Cross, and was in bad health, but used to steal up to town to see and hear Miss Lin(d)ley in publick, though he was under an engagement with her family not to pursue her any more in private. At length, however, they met, and eventually were married. Miss Lin(d)ley's reputation at this time was so great, that her engagements for the year were £5,000. This resource, however, Sheridan would not listen to her receiving any longer, altho' he himself had not a single farthing. He said she might sing to oblige the King or Queen, but to receive money while she was his wife was quite out of the question. Upon which old Lin(d)ley, her father, said this might do very well for him—Mr. Sheridan—but that for them—Mr. Lin(d)ley—it was a very hard case; that his daughter had always been a very good daughter to him, and very generous to him out of the funds she gained by her profession, and that it was very hard upon him to be cut off all at once from this supply. This objection was disposed of by Sheridan in the following manner.

Miss Lin(d)ley had £3,000 of her own, of which Sheridan gave her father £2,000. With the remaining £1,000, the only fortune Mr. and Mrs. Sheridan began the world with, he took a cottage at Slough, where they lived, he said, most happily, a gig and horse being their principal luxury, with a man to look after both the master and his horse. By the end, or before the end, of the year, the £1,000 was drawing rapidly to a finish, and then it was that Sheridan thought of play-writing as a pecuniary resource, and he wrote *The Rivals*. Having got an introduction to the theatre, he took his play there, and finally was present to see it acted, but would not let Mrs. Sheridan come up from Slough for the same purpose. *The Rivals*, upon its first performance, was *damned*; when Sheridan got to Slough and told his wife of it she said:

'My dear Dick, I am delighted. I always knew it was impossible you could make anything by writing plays; so now there is nothing for it but my beginning to sing publickly again, and we shall have as much money as we like.'

'No,' said Sheridan, 'that shall never be. I see where the fault was; the play was too long, and the parts were badly cast.'

So he altered and curtailed the play, and had address or interest enough to get the parts newly cast. At the expiration of six weeks it was acted again, and with unbounded applause. His fame as a dramatick writer was settled from that time. When it was he became proprietor of Drury Lane Theatre, or how it was accomplished, I did not learn from him, but it was the only property he ever possessed, and, with the commonest discretion on his part, would have made him a most affluent man.

Sheridan's talents, displayed in his plays, procured him very shortly both male and *female* admirers among the higher orders. The families of Lord Coventry and Lord Harrington he spoke of as his first patrons. When it was he begun with politicks, I don't recollect, but he was a great parliamentary reformer the latter end of the American war, and one of a committee of either five or seven (I forget which number) who used to sit regularly at the Mansion House upon this subject.

In 1780, the year of a general election, his object was to get into Parliament if possible, and he was going to make a trial at Wootton-Bassett. The night before he set out, being at Devonshire House and everybody talking about the general election, Lady Cork asked Sheridan about *his* plans, which led to her saying that she had often heard her brother Monckton say he thought an opposition man might come in for Stafford, and that if, in the event of Sheridan failing at Wootton, he liked to try his chance at Stafford, she would give him a letter of introduction to her brother.

This was immediately done. Sheridan went to Wootton-Bassett, where he had not a chance. Then he went to Stafford, produced Lady Cork's letter, offered himself as a candidate, and was elected. For Stafford he was member till 1806—six-and-twenty years. I remember asking him if he could fix upon any point of time in his life that was decidedly happier than all the rest, and he said certainly—it was after dinner the day of this first election for Stafford, when he stole away by himself to speculate upon those prospects of distinguishing himself which had been opened to him.

I did not hear any further of his own history from himself than this first getting into parliament. It has been a constant subject of regret to me that I did not put down at the time all he told me, because it was much more than I have stated; but I feel confident my memory is correct in what I have written.[6]

To return to Sheridan at Brighton in the year 1805. His point of difference with the Prince being at an end, Sheridan entered into whatever fun was going on at the Pavilion as if he had been a boy, tho' he was then 55 years of age. Upon one occasion he came into the drawing-room disguised as a police officer to take up the Dowager Lady Sefton[7] for playing at some unlawful game; and at another time, when we had a phantasmagoria at the Pavilion, and were all shut up in perfect darkness, he continued to sit upon the lap of Madame Gerobtzoff[?], a haughty Russian dame, who made row enough for the whole town to hear her.

[6] The inaccuracies in this account of Sheridan's career, by a friend and intimate, who on this occasion was 'writing for history,' seem to extenuate the gross or malicious falsehoods put out at the end of his life by Moore and Croker, which are still current coin despite the efforts of Rae and Sichel and a wealth of uncontrovertible documentary evidence. Made miserable all his life by calumnies, this remarkable man, whose integrity in public life has been underrated, whose genius in many fields dimmed the brilliance of contemporary genius, seems to be doomed to eternal misrepresentation. A definitive and just biography has still to be written. J. G.

[7] Isabella, daughter of 2nd Earl of Harrington, and widow of the 9th Viscount and 1st Earl of Sefton.

The Prince, of course, was delighted with all this; but at last Sheridan made himself so ill with drinking, that he came to us soon after breakfast one day, saying he was in a perfect fever, desiring he might have some table beer, and declaring that he would spend that day with us, and send his excuses by Bloomfield for not dining at the Pavilion. I felt his pulse, and found it going tremendously, but instead of beer, we gave him some hot white wine, of which he drank a bottle, I remember, and his pulse subsided almost instantly.... After dinner that day he must have drunk at least a bottle and a half of wine. In the evening we were all going to the Pavilion, where there was to be a ball, and Sheridan said he would go home, *i.e.*, to the Pavilion (where he slept) and would go quietly to bed. He desired me to tell the Prince, if he asked me after him, that he was far from well, and was gone to bed.

So when supper was served at the Pavilion about 12 o'clock, the Prince came up to me and said:

'What the devil have you done with Sheridan to-day, Creevey? I know he has been dining with you, and I have not seen him the whole day.'

I said he was by no means well and had gone to bed; upon which the Prince laughed heartily, as if he thought it all fudge, and then, taking a bottle of claret and a glass, he put them both in my hands and said:

'Now Creevey, go to his bedside and tell him I'll drink a glass of wine with him, and if he refuses, I admit he must be damned bad indeed.'

I would willingly have excused myself on the score of his being really ill, but the Prince would not believe a word of it, so go I must. When I entered Sheridan's room, he was in bed, and his great fine eyes being instantly fixed upon me, he said:—

'Come, I see this is some joke of the Prince, and I am not in a state for it.'

I excused myself as well as I could, and as he would not touch the wine, I returned without pressing it, and the Prince seemed satisfied he must be ill.

About two o'clock, however, the supper having been long over, and everybody engaged in dancing, who should I see standing at the door but Sheridan, powdered as white as snow, as smartly dressed as ever he could be from top to toe.... I joined him and expressed my infinite surprise at this freak of his. He said:

'Will you go with me, my dear fellow, into the kitchen, and let me see if I can find a bit of supper.'

Having arrived there, he began to play off his cajolery upon the servants, saying if he was the Prince they should have much better accommodation, &c., &c., so that he was surrounded by supper of all kinds, every one waiting upon him. He ate away and drank a bottle of claret in a minute, returned to the ballroom, and when I left it between three and four he was dancing.

In the beginning of November, as Sheridan was returning to London, and I was going there for a short time, he proposed our going together, and nothing would serve him but that we must be two days on the road: that nothing was so foolish as hurrying oneself in such short days, and nothing so pleasant as living at an inn; that the Cock at Sutton was an excellent place to dine and sleep at; that he himself was very well known there, and would write and have a nice little dinner ready for our arrival.

We set off in a job chaise of his, Edwards the box keeper of Drury Lane being on the dicky box, for he always acted as Sheridan's valet when he left London. Before we had travelled many miles, having knocked my foot against some earthenware vessel in the chaise, I asked Sheridan what it could be, and he replied he dared say it was something Edwards was taking to his wife. Arriving in the evening at Sutton, I found there was not a soul in the house who had ever seen Sheridan before; that his letter had never arrived, and that no dinner was ready for us. I heard him muttering on about its being an extraordinary mistake, that his particular friend was out of the way, and so forth, but that he knew the house to be an excellent one, and nowhere that you could have a nicer little dinner. He went fidgetting in and out of the room, without exciting the least suspicion on my part, till dinner was announced. Then I found his fun had been to bring the dinner with him from the Pavilion. The bowl I had kicked contained the soup, and there were the best fish, woodcocks and everything else, with claret and sherry and port all from the same place.

Among other persons who came to pay their respects to the Prince during the Autumn of 1805 was Mr. Hastings,[8] whom I had never seen before excepting at his trial in Westminster Hall. He and Mrs. Hastings came to the Pavilion, and I was present when the Prince introduced Sheridan to him, which was curious, considering that Sheridan's parliamentary fame had been built upon his celebrated speech against Hastings. However, he lost no time in attempting to cajole old Hastings, begging him to believe that any part he had ever taken against him was purely political, and that no one had a greater respect for him than himself, &c., &c., upon which old Hastings said with great gravity that 'it would be a great consolation to him in his declining days if Mr.

[8] Warren Hastings.

Sheridan would make that sentence more publick;' but Sheridan was obliged to mutter and get out of such an engagement as well as he could.

Another very curious person I saw a great deal of this autumn of 1805, sometimes at the Pavilion, sometimes at Mrs. Clowes's, was Lord Thurlow, to whom the Prince always behaved with the most marked deference and attention. I had never seen him but once before, and the occasion was an extraordinary one. Lady Oxford, who then had a house at Ealing (it was in 1801) had, by Lord Thurlow's desire, I believe, at all events with his acquiescence, invited Horne-Tooke to dinner to meet him. Lord Thurlow never had seen him since he had prosecuted him when Attorney-General for a libel in 1774 (I believe it was), when the greatest bitterness was shown on both sides, so that the dinner was a meeting of great curiosity to us who were invited to it. Sheridan was there and Mrs. Sheridan, the late Lord Camelford, Sir Francis Burdett, Charles Warren, with several others and myself. Tooke evidently came prepared for a display, and as I had met him repeatedly, and considered his powers of conversation as surpassing those of any person I had ever seen, in point of skill and dexterity (and, if at all necessary, in *lying*), I took for granted old grumbling Thurlow would be obliged to lower his topsail to him. But it seemed as if the very look and voice of Thurlow scared him out of his senses, and certainly nothing could be much more formidable. So Tooke tried to recruit himself by wine, and tho' not a drinker, was very drunk. But all would not do; he was perpetually trying to distinguish himself, and Thurlow constantly laughing at him.

In the autumn of 1805, Thurlow had declined greatly in energy from the time I refer to. It was the year only before his death. He used to read or ride out in the morning, and his daughter Mrs Brown, and Mr. Sneyd, the clergyman of Brighton, occupied themselves in procuring any stranger or other person who they thought would be agreeable to the old man to dine with him, the party being thus 10 or 12 every day, or more. I had the good fortune to be occasionally there with Mrs. Creevey.... However rough Thurlow might be with men, he was the politest man in the world to ladies. Two or three hours were occupied by him at dinner in laying wait for any unfortunate slip or ridiculous observation that might be made by any of his *male* visitors, whom, when caught, he never left hold of, till I have seen the sweat run down their faces from the scrape they had got into.

Having seen this property of his, I took care, of course, to keep clear of him, and have often enjoyed extremely seeing the figures which men have cut who came with the evident intention of shewing off before him. Curran, the Irish lawyer, was a striking instance of this. I dined with him at Thurlow's one day, and Thurlow just made as great a fool of him as he did formerly of Tooke.

Thurlow was always dressed in a full suit of cloaths of the old fashion, great cuffs and massy buttons, great wig, long ruffles, &c.; the black eyebrows exceeded in size any I have ever seen, and his voice, tho' by no means devoid of melody, was a kind of rolling, murmuring thunder. He had great reading, particularly classical, and was a very distinguished, as well as most *daring*, converser. I never heard of any one but Mr. Hare who had fairly beat him, and this I know from persons who were present, Hare did more than once, at Carlton House and at Woburn.

Sir Philip Francis, whom I knew intimately, and who certainly was a remarkably quick and clever man, was perpetually vowing vengeance against Thurlow, and always fixing his time during the autumn of 1805 for 'making an example of the old ruffian,' either at the Pavilion or wherever he met him; but I have seen them meet afterwards, and tho' Thurlow was always ready for battle, Francis, who on all other occasions was bold as a lion, would never stir.

The grudge he owed to Thurlow was certainly not slightly grounded. When Francis and Generals Clavering and Monson were sent to India in 1773, to check Hastings in his career, their conduct was extolled to the skies by our party in parliament, while, on the other hand, Lord Thurlow in the House of Lords said that the greatest misfortune to India and to England was that the ship which carried these three gentlemen out had not gone to the bottom....

...During the autumn of 1805 the Prince was a very great politician. He considered himself as the Head of the Whig Party, and was perpetually at work cajoling shabby people, as he thought, into becoming Whigs out of compliment to him, but who ate his dinners and voted with the Ministers just the same. I remember dining with him at George Johnstone's at Brighton—the Duke of Clarence, old Thurlow, Lord and Lady Bessborough and a very large party, of which Suza, the Portuguese Ambassador was one. After dinner the Prince, addressing himself to Suza, described himself as being the Head of the great Whig party in England, and then entered at great length upon the merit of Whig principles, and the great glory it was to him, the Prince, to be the head of a party who advocated such principles. Finally, he appealed to Suza for his opinion upon that subject; but the Portuguese was much too wary to be taken in. He thanked the Prince with great force, ability and propriety for his condescension in giving him the information he had done, but as, he added, the subject was an entirely new one to him, he prayed his Royal Highness would have the goodness to excuse him giving an opinion upon it, till he had considered it more maturely.

It seemed at that time the Prince's politicks were almost always uppermost with him.... Upon one occasion I remember dining with the Prince at Lady Downshire's, Lord Winslow and different people being there. After dinner he said to me privately: 'Creevey, you must go home with me.' So when he went he took me in his coach, and when he got to the Pavilion he said: 'Now Creevey, you and I must go over the House of Commons together, and see who are our friends and who are our enemies.' Accordingly, he got his own red book, and we went over the House of Commons name by name. He had one mark for a friend and another for an enemy, and of course every member of the Government who was then in the House of Commons had *the enemy's* mark put against his name.... Having made all these marks himself, he gave me the book, and told me to take it home with me. At this time Lord Castlereagh had just lost his election for the county of Down, entirely from Lady Downshire's opposition. She had gone over to Ireland expressly for that purpose.

When the Prince returned from a visit of two or three days to the King at Weymouth, he was very indiscreet in talking at his table about the King's infirmities, there being such people as Miles Peter Andrews and Sir George Shee present, in common with other spies and courtiers. So when he described the King as so blind that he had nearly fallen into some hole at Lord Dorchester's, I said—'Poor man, Sir!' in a very audible and serious tone, and he immediately took the hint and stopt.

Upon another occasion the Duke of York[9] came to the Pavilion. It was some military occasion—a review of the troops, I believe—and there was a great assemblage of military people there. Nothing could be so cold and formal as the Prince's manner to the Duke. As he was coming up the room towards the Prince, the Prince said to me in an undertone—'Do you know the Duke of York.' On my replying—'No, sir,' he said—'He's a damned bad politician, but I'll introduce you to him,' and this he did, with great form.

Having mentioned a dinner I had at Johnstone's in Brighton in 1805, I can't help adverting to what took place that day. The late King (George IV) and the present one (William IV) both dined there, and it so happened that there was a great fight on the same day between

[9] Commander-in-Chief.

the Chicken and Gully.[10] The Duke of Clarence was present at it, and as the battle, from the interference of Magistrates, was fought at a greater distance from Brighton than was intended, the Duke was very late, and did not arrive till dinner was nearly over. I mention the case on account of the change that has since taken place as to these parties. Gully was then a professional prize-fighter from the ranks, and fighting for money. Since that time, the Duke of Clarence has become Sovereign of the country, and Gully has become one of its representatives in parliament. As Gully always attends at Court, as well as in the House of Commons, it would be curious to know whether the King, with his accurate recollection of all the events of his life, and his passion for adverting to them, has ever given to Gully any hint of that day's proceedings. There is, to be sure, one reason why he should not, for Gully was beaten that day by the Chicken, as I have reason to remember; for Lord Thurlow and myself being the two first to arrive before dinner, he asked if I had heard any account of the fight. I repeated what I had heard in the street, viz. that Gully had given the Chicken so tremendous a knock-down blow at starting, that the latter had never answered to him; so when the Duke of Clarence came and told us that Gully was beat, old Thurlow growled out from his end of the table—'Mr. Creevey, I think an action would lie against you by the Chicken for taking away his character.'

Lord Thurlow was a great drinker of port wine, and Johnstone, who was the most ridiculous toady of great men, said to him that evening—'I am afraid, my lord, the port wine is not so good as I could wish;' upon which old Thurlow growled again—'I have tasted better!'

The foregoing narrative will enable the reader to understand many of the allusions in the following letters written by Mrs. Creevey from Brighton to her husband while he was attending to his parliamentary duties. It must be understood also that Creevey was quite sensible of the advantage which might be expected in regard to his own political prospects from the favour he had found in the royal leader of the Whigs. The King's madness might return on any day; the Prince of Wales would become Regent, and nobody

[10] John Gully [1783–1863], son of a publican and butcher, made his *début* in the prize-ring in 1805, and was recognised as a virtual, though not formal, champion after Pearce, the Game Chicken, retired at the end of that year. In 1808 he became a bookmaker and publican. He made a good deal of money; became a successful owner of racehorses; and, having purchased Ackworth Park, near Pontefract, represented that borough in Parliament from 1832 till 1837.

doubted that, so soon as he had the power, he would dismiss the Tory Ministers of his father. Mrs. Creevey, therefore, loyally played up to her husband's hand, and, like her lord, continued charitably blind up to the character and habits of their master. Like all who ever made her acquaintance, both Mr. and Mrs. Creevey speak enthusiastically of the unfortunate Mrs. Fitzherbert, whom the Prince had married in 1785.

Mrs. Creevey to Creevey in London

Brighton, Oct. 29th, 1805

...Oh, this wicked Pavillion! we were there till ½ past one this morng., and it has kept me in bed with the headache till 12 to-day.... The invitation did not come to us till 9 o'clock: we went in Lord Thurlow's carriage, and were in fear of being too late; but the Prince did not come out of the dining-room till 11. Till then our only companions were Lady Downshire and Mr. and Miss Johnstone—the former very goodnatured and amiable.... When the Prince appeared, I instantly saw he had got more wine than usual, and it was still more evident that the German Baron was extremely drunk. The Prince came up and sat by me—introduced McMahon to me, and talked a great deal about Mrs. Fitzherbert—said she had been 'delighted' with my note, and wished much to see me. He asked her 'When?'—and he said her answer was—'Not till *you* are gone, and I can see her *comfortably*.' I suppose this might be correct, for Mac told me he had been 'worrying her to death' all the morning.

It appears to me I have found a true friend in Mac.[11] He is even more foolish than I expected; but I shall be disappointed if, even to you, he does not profess himself my devoted admirer.

Afterwards the Prince led all the party to the table where the maps lie, to see him shoot with an air-gun at a target placed at the end of the room. He did it very skilfully, and wanted all the ladies to attempt it. The girls and I excused ourselves on account of our short sight; but Lady Downshire hit a fiddler in the dining-room, Miss Johnstone a door and Bloomfield the ceiling.... I soon had enough of this, and retired to the fire with Mac.... At last a waltz was played by the band, and the Prince offered to waltz with Miss Johnstone, but very quietly, and once round the table made him giddy, so of course it was proper for his

[11] John Macmahon, Private Secretary and Privy Purse to the Prince of Wales.

partner to be giddy too; but he cruelly only thought of supporting himself, so she reclined on the Baron.

Sunday, Nov. 3, 1805

And so I amuse you by my histories. Well! I am glad of it, and it encourages me to go on; and yet I can tell you I could tire of such horrors as I have had the last 3 evenings. I nevertheless estimate them as you do, and am quite disposed to persevere.... Mrs. Fitz shone last night very much in a sketch she gave me of the history of a very rich Russian woman of quality who is coming to Lord Berkeley's house. She has been long in England, and is I suppose generally known in London, though new to me. She was a married woman with children, and of great consequence at the court of Petersburgh when Lord Whitworth was there some years ago. He was poor and handsome—she rich and in love with him, and tired of a very magnificent husband to whom she had been married at 14 years old. In short, she *kept* my Lord, and spent immense sums in doing so and gratifying his great extravagance. In the midst of all this he return'd to England, but they corresponded, and she left her husband and her country to come to him, expecting to marry him—got as far as Berlin, and there heard he was married to the Duchess of Dorset.

She was raving mad for some time, and Mrs. F. describes her as being often nearly so now, but at other times most interesting, and most miserable. Her husband and children come to England to visit her, and Mrs. F. says she is an eternal subject of remorse to Lord Whitworth, whom she [Mrs. F.] spoke of in warm terms as 'a monster,' and said she could tell me far more to make me think so.

Wednesday, Nov. 6, 1805

I am much flatter'd, dearest Creevey, that you complain when my letters are short.... I went to the Pavillion last night quite well, and moreover am well to-day and fit for Johnstone's ball, which at last is to be. They were at the Pavillion and she [Miss Johnstone] persecuted both the Prince and Mrs. Fitzherbert like a most impudent fool. The former was all complyance and good nature—the latter very civil, but most steady in refusing to go. She said she could not go out, and Miss J. grinned and answer'd—'Oh! but you *are out* here'—then urged that it had been put off on purpose for Mrs. F., who said she was sorry for it, but hoped it wd. be put off no longer. All this Mrs. F. told me herself, with further remarks, just before I came away, which I did with Lady Downshire, and left the Johnstones with their affairs in an unsettled state, and with faces of great anxiety and misery. But the attack was renew'd, and the Prince said:—'I shall have great pleasure in looking in upon you, but indeed I cannot let this *good woman* (Mrs. F.) come: she is quite unfit for it.' And so we shall see the fun of his looking in or staying all the evening, for poor Johnstone has been running about the Steyne with a paper in his hand all the morning and invited us all.... When I got to the Pavillion last night... the Prince sat down by me directly, and I told him my headache had made me late, and he was very *affectionate*.... Harry Grey has just come in with news of a great victory at sea and poor Nelson being kill'd. It has come by express to the Prince, and it is said 20 sail are taken or destroyed. What will this do? not, I hope, save Pitt; but both parties may now be humble and make peace....

Mrs. Fitzherbert to Mrs. Creevey

Nov. 6, 1805

Dr. Madam,

The Prince has this moment recd. an account from the Admiralty of the death of poor Lord Nelson, which has affected him most extremely. I think you may wish to know the news, which, upon any other occasion might be called a glorious victory—twenty out of three and thirty of the enemy's fleet being entirely destroyed—no English ship being taken or sunk—Capts. Duff and Cook both kill'd, and the French Adl. Villeneuve taken prisoner. Poor Lord Nelson recd. his death by a shot of a musket from the enemy's ship upon his shoulder, and expir'd two hours after, but not till the ship struck and afterwards sunk, which he had the consolation of hearing, as well as his compleat victory, before he died. Excuse this hurried scrawl: I am so nervous I scarce can hold my pen. God bless you.

Yours,

M. Fitzherbert.

Mrs. Creevey to Creevey

Friday night, 12 o'clock

Dearest Creevey,

...I think you will like to hear I have spent a very comfortable evening with my mistress.[12] We had a long discourse about Lady Wellesley. The folly of men marrying such women led us to Mrs. Fox, and I saw she would have liked to go further than I dared, or than our neighbours would permit.... They were full of Prussians and Swedes

[12] Mrs. Fitzherbert.

and Danes and Russians coming soon with irresistible destruction on Buonaparte. I wonder if there is a chance of it. I don't believe it....

Nov. 7, 1805

...[The Prince's] sorrow [for Nelson's death] might help to prevent his coming to dinner at the Pavillion or to Johnstone's ball. He did neither, but stayed with Mrs. Fitz; and you may imagine the disappointment of the Johnstones. The girl grin'd it off with the captain, but Johnstone had a face of perfect horror all night, and I think he was very near insane. I once lamented Lord Nelson to him, and he said:—'Oh shocking: and to come at such an unlucky time!'...

8th Nov.

...The first of my visits this morning was to 'my Mistress.'...I found her alone, and she was excellent—gave me an account of the Prince's grief about Lord N., and then entered into the domestic failings of the latter in a way infinitely creditable to her, and skilful too. She was all for Lady Nelson and against Lady Hamilton, who, she said (hero as he was) overpower'd him and took possession of him quite by force. But she ended in a natural, good way, by saying:—'Poor creature! I am sorry for her now, for I suppose she is in grief.'

Past 4 o'clock, Monday

...Mrs. Fitzherbert came before 12 and has literally only this moment left me. We have been all the time alone, and she has been confidential to a degree that almost frightens me, and that I can hardly think sufficiently accounted for by her professing in the strongest terms to have liked me more and more every time she has seen me, tho' at first she told Mr. Tierney no person had ever struck her so much at first sight....So much in excuse for her telling me the history of her life, and dwelling more particularly on the explanation of all her feelings and conduct towards the Prince. If she is as *true* as I think she is *wise*, she is an extraordinary person, and most worthy to be beloved. It was quite impossible to keep clear of Devonshire House; and there her opinions are *all* precisely mine and yours, and, what is better, she says they are *now* the Prince's; that he knows everything—above all, how money is made by promises, unauthorised by him, in the event of his having power; that he knows how his character is involved in various transactions of that house, and that he only goes into it, from motives of compassion and old friendship, when he is persecuted to do so. In short, he tells Mrs. F. all he sees and hears, shews her all the Duchess's letters and notes, and she says she knows the Dss. hates her.... We talked of her life being written; she said she supposed it would some time or other, but with thousands of lies; but she would be dead and it would not signify. I urged her to write it herself, but she said it would break her heart.

Nov. 27, 1805

...I was very sorry indeed to go to the Pavillion, and 'my Master' made me no amends for my exertion—no shaking hands—only a common bow in passing—and not a word all night, except just before I came away some artificial stuff about the Baron, and then a little parting shake of the hand with this interesting observation—'So Creevey is gone,' and the interesting answer of—'Yes, Sir.' In short I suspect he was a little affronted by our going away the night before: but I don't mind it—he will soon come about again; or if he does not, I will make him ashamed by begging his pardon.

Nov. 29th

...Well, I am quite in favor again. When I entered Gerobtzoff's room last night Prinny was on a sofa directly opposite the door, and in return for a curtsey, perhaps rather more grave, more low and humble than usual (meaning—'I beg your pardon dear foolish, beautiful Prinny for making you take the pet') he put out his hand.... We soon went to see the ball at the Pavillion, and Mrs. Fitz selected me to go in the first party in a way that set up the backs of various persons.... We were soon tired of the amusement and sick of the heat and stink. Neither the Prince nor any one stay'd long, and the rest of the evening was horribly dull; but luckily for me, when the Prince returned I was sitting on a little sofa that wd. only hold two, and the other seat was vacant; so he came to it, and never left me or spoke to another person till within 10 minutes of my coming away at ½ past 12.... We had the old stories of Mrs. Sheridan, only with some new additions...we had Charles Grey too, and he talked of his [Grey's] dislike to him, because in the Regency he wd. not hear of his being Chancellor of the Exchequer. He talked of his bad temper and his early presumption in overrating his own talents. ...He told me that when he was king he wd. not give up his private society, and on my saying a little flattering sentence about the good I expected from him, he actually said—'he hoped I should never have cause to think differently of him.' This was going his length, so I stopt.

Dec. 2, 1805

...We have been at the Pavillion both Friday and yesterday, and Mrs. F. has desired us to come every night without invitation....Both these parties have been private and the Prince equally good and attentive to me at both.... Last night he took me under his arm through the dark, wet garden into the other house, to shew me a picture of himself. Poor little Lady Downshire push'd herself (tho' humbly) into our party, but he sent her before with Bloomfield and the lanthorn, and he and I might have gone astray in any way we had liked; but I can assure you (faithless as you are about coming back to me) nothing worse happened than his promise of giving me *the best print that ever was done of him*, and mine that it shall hang in the best place amongst my friends.

Dec. 5, 1805

...It was a large party at the Pavillion last night, and the Prince was not well...and went off to bed.... Lord Hutchinson was my chief flirt for the evening, but before Prinny went off he took a seat by me to tell me all this *bad* news had made him bilious and that he was further overset yesterday by seeing the ship with Lord Nelson's body on board. ....None of them knew Pitt was gone to Bath till I told them. I ask'd both Lord H[utchinson] and his Master if they wd. like him to die now, or live a little longer to be turn'd out. They both decidedly prefer instant death.... I think Sheridan may probably return with you on Friday if you ask him. On second thoughts—I would not have you ask him, for he will make you wait and sleep at the Cock at Sutton.

chapter three

1806–1809

PITT NEVER RALLIED from the shock of Ulm and Austerlitz. Parliament was to meet on January 21, 1806, and he travelled up from Bath by easy stages to his villa at Putney, where he arrived on the 11th, and invitations were issued for the customary official dinner of the First Lord of the Treasury on the 20th. But that dinner never took place. Lord Henry Petty had given notice of an amendment to the Address, censuring Pitt's administration; but out of respect to a disabled foe, he did not move it, and the Address was agreed to without debate.

Hon. Charles Grey, M.P., to Creevey

Howick, Jan. 13, 1806

I received your letter last night, and had from other quarters the same reports of Pitt's illness and resignation. I think you will probably find these among the false reports of the day. I cannot believe in his resigning again while he has breath; and as to his health, I shall not be surprised to see him making a speech of two hours on the first day of the Session.

Pitt expired on January 23, and the old King had at last to have recourse to all the Whigs. Lord Grenville formed a coalition Cabinet, nicknamed 'all the Talents,' in which Fox held the seals of the Foreign Office, Grey was First Lord of the Admiralty, Addington, now Lord Sidmouth, took the Privy Seal, and Erskine as Whig Lord Chancellor balanced Ellenborough as Tory Lord Chief Justice with a seat in the Cabinet. Creevey's past activity and promise of more were not overlooked, and he was appointed Secretary to the Board of Controul—a post which, as his friend Grey wrote to him, was 'better in point of emolument and of more real work' than a seat at the Board of Admiralty which was first intended for him, 'and not obliging you to vacate your seat' in Parliament. Associated with this office were the duties of party whip, which Creevey began to discharge forthwith.

It is no small tribute to Creevey that a quite important post was found for him in the Talents Ministry after less than two years of *active* participation in the House. When it is remembered that at this time aristocrats and patrons occupied ninety per cent. of the chief posts in Ministries and that men of outstanding ability, such as Brougham, Canning, Sheridan and Tierney, found obstacles of prejudice in their paths to the inner circle, it becomes clear that Creevey had impressed the House and his party with a remarkably brilliant start. As secretary to the Board of Control and a Government Whip, he made his mark in the Talents Ministry and after its collapse, still nursed hopes of the Regent favouring the Whigs and bringing still higher preferment to himself.

Six months had not gone since Pitt breathed his last, when the health of his great rival, Fox, broke down. He appeared for the last time in the House of Commons on June 10, already exceedingly ill, but determined to be at his post in order to move certain resolutions preparatory to the bill for abolishing the slave trade. This he accomplished, and the bill giving effect to these resolutions became law in the following year; but by that time Charles Fox was no more. He lingered till September 13, 1806, and every bulletin during his last illness was anxiously watched for and canvassed by men and women of both parties in the State. Assuredly no public man was ever better beloved than Fox on account of his private qualities. Notwithstanding that his great natural abilities suffered damage, and his energies were diverted and impaired by his excessive conviviality and love of gambling, even his political enemies could not help loving the man. Pitt's haughtiness repelled; Fox's simplicity and sweetness of address attracted all hearts. Pitt's talents and penetrating foresight commanded the confidence and gratitude of his followers; but it was not his lot to secure the passionate affection, approaching to idolatry, which was freely given to Fox.

Mrs. Creevey to Miss Ord

30th July

. . . On our return from walking in the Park last night at 10 o'clock we saw the Prince's chariot at Mr. Fox's door, and I find from Mrs. Bouverie that he stayed a long time, and Mr. Fox was not fatigued by it, but had a good night. . . . She has not seen him for some days, but she says that is accident, owing to Lady Holland being there whom he *will not* see; but she plants herself in one of the rooms below stairs, under pretence of waiting for Lord Holland, and so prevents his admitting any other woman.

25th August

...Mr. Creevey dined yesterday at Lord Cowper's. It was a grand dinner after the christening of his son, to whom the Prince stood god-father. The ceremony was going on in one drawing-room when Mr. Creevey arrived. After it was over, the Prince, on coming into the room where the rest of the company were assembled, said: 'Ho Creevey! you there,' and sprang across the room and shook hands with him. When he sat opposite to him at dinner he hardly spoke to anyone else, beginning directly with—'Well, tell me now, Creevey, about Mrs. Creevey and the girls, and when they come to Brighton;' and on hearing 'probably in October,' he said—'Oh delightful! we shall be *so* comfortable,' and then went over the old stories... till, as Mr. C. says, the company did not know very well what to make of it. They all adjourned to Melbourne House to supper. At 2 o'clock in the morning, that terrible Sheridan seduced Mr. Creevey into Brookes, where they stayed till 4, when Sherry *affectionately* came home with him, and upstairs to see me. They were both so very merry, and so much pleased with each other's jokes, that, though they could not repeat them to me very distinctly, I was too much amused to scold them as they deserved.

Considering how the letters even of this amiable and accomplished lady are pervaded with the fumes of wine and the aroma of broiled bones, the marvel is, not that so many men of her acquaintance suffered in their health, but why more of them did not bring their lives prematurely to a close by perpetual stuffing and swilling. Wine in excess was not only the chief cause of a disordered system, but it was made to serve as the invariable remedy, supplemented by the free use of the lancet and by drastic purges.

The constant bulletins about Fox, which it is not necessary to repeat, continued favourable till September 9, when the dropsy began to gain ground upon him.

Mrs. Creevey to Miss Ord

12 Sept., 1806

...I am going to Somerset House to enquire after poor Sheridan, who went from this house very ill at 12 o'clock last night... He complained of sore throat and shivering, and his pulse was the most frightful one I ever felt; it was so tumultuous and so strong that when one touched it, it seemed not only to shake his arm, but his whole frame.... I lighted a fire and a great many candles, and Mr. Creevey, who was luckily just come home from Petty's, began to tell him stories.... Then we sent for some wine, of which he was so frightened it required persuasion to make him drink six small glasses, of which the effect was immediate in making him not only happier, but composing his pulse.... In the midst of his dismals he said most clever, funny things, and at last got to describing Mr. Hare, and others of his old associates, with the hand of a real master, and made one lament that such extraordinary talents should have such numerous alloys. He received a note from Lady Elizabeth Forster, with a good account of Mr. Fox. It ended with—'try to drink less and speak the truth.' He was very funny about it and said: 'By G-d! I speak more truth than *she* does, however.' Then he told us how she had *cried* to him the night before, 'because she felt it her severe duty to be Duchess of Devonshire!'[1]

With Fox was extinguished the brightest of 'All the Talents.' The administration continued during the succeeding winter, but when the King, in March, 1807, demanded an assurance from his Ministers that they would bring in no measure of Roman Catholic Relief, Grenville, who, with Pitt, had resigned office in 1801 because of the King's determination on this subject, declined to continue in office on such terms, and the Cabinet resigned. Some of his colleagues disapproved highly of this course, Sheridan observing that 'he had known many men knock their heads against a wall, but he had never before heard of a man collecting bricks and building a wall for the express purpose of knocking out his own brains against it.' Probably Creevey shared this view, but there is an almost total blank in his correspondence during the year which brought his brief tenure of office to a close. The coalition of parties was at an end, and the Duke of Portland became nominal head of a Tory Cabinet.

The years 1807 to 1810 were momentous enough in the destiny of England, after the deaths of Pitt and Fox in 1806.

Those years included the abolition of the slave trade, the death of Sir John Moore at Corunna, the unhappy Walcheren expedition,

[1] The Duchess of Devonshire had died in March of this year. Lady Elizabeth married the Duke, but not till three years later, in 1809.

the decision to embark on the Peninsular war, the Duke of York's impeachment by Wardle, and Burdett's arrest and its consequences. All these matters are dealt with at length in Creevey's correspondence and he received a great number of interesting and important letters from public men of the day on all of them. He himself, under his new leader, Whitbread, found it proper to take a harsh line with the Wellesleys, and it is a measure of his worth that Wellington continued to treat him with respect all his life. In these years, Creevey was assiduous in recommending himself for higher preferment and in consequence his own contribution to his correspondence is very small.

He was in close touch with his wife who was often in Brighton and had not yet begun his correspondence with his stepdaughter. For the most part, his contribution to light on the period consists of diary fragments and memoranda. Since the object of this book is to reveal Creevey himself as a letter writer, it is therefore appropriate to pass over these years in brief.

Wellesley's expedition sailed from Cork on June 15, 1808; before the end of September the only French troops left in Portugal were the garrisons of Elvas and Almeida; General Junot, with a beaten army of 26,000 men, had been conveyed in British ships to Rochelle; the Russian Admiral Siniavin had surrendered his whole fleet in the Tagus to Sir Charles Cotton. Such were the conditions of the famous Convention of Cintra, forced upon the French by the victorious little army under Sir Arthur Wellesley. Yet was the nation almost unanimous in demanding his degradation, if not his death, with that of the two generals who successively took command over his head. They were even blamed in the King's Speech from the Throne for 'acceding to the terms of the Convention.' The sagacious Whitbread and his friends found solace in the discomfiture of the Wellesleys.

Samuel Whitbread, M.P., to Creevey

Bounds, near Tunbridge, Sept. 25th, 1808

...I conclude the same sentiment prevails all over the country respecting the Portuguese convention. Cobbet's dissertation upon it is excellent, tho' it by no means explains, nor can anything explain, the mystery. I grieve for the opportunity that has been lost of acquiring national glory, but am not sorry to see the Wellesley pride a little lowered....

Capt. Graham Moore, R.N., to Creevey

Marlborough, *Rio Janeiro, Oct. 11th, 1808*

...My whole heart and soul is with the Spaniards, and I hope and trust we shall support them and fight for them to the uttermost.... This great event in Spain must of course put a stop to any plan we may have had to emancipate the Spanish Colonies.... I hope Bonoparte has now enough on his hands without thinking of invading England. He has overshot his mark, and, I have great hopes, has done for himself. However, he will die game....I am very anxious to hear of my brother Jack[2] coming into play. I daresay he will have some Right Honble. Torpedo set over him to counteract his fire and genius; but in spite of the Devil, he is invaluable wherever he is, and the soldiers know that...

[2] Sir John Moore.

chapter three (*continued*)

1809

CANNING AND CASTLEREAGH, hitherto at one in maintaining the Continental policy of Pitt, fell at issue in 1809 as to the best means of carrying the same into effect. The seeds of their difference had been planted in the dispute about the Convention of Cintra. Canning, as Foreign Secretary, advocated a concentration of the whole military forces of Britain upon the liberation of Spain; Castlereagh, at the War Office, listened to expert advisers who had been damped by the retreat and death of Sir John Moore, and was urgent for creating diversions in other parts of Europe. Castlereagh had his way, with the result, among others, that the most powerful expedition that had ever sailed from England—40,000 troops and a splendid fleet with as many seamen and marines—were lamentably sacrificed in the swamps of Walcheren Island through the incompetence of their general; while Sir Arthur Wellesley sailed in April to assume command in a second Peninsular campaign. Great was the fury of the anti-war party in Parliament by reason of this resuscitation of the hated Wellesleys, but not greater than their rage at Lord Grenville, who, although he had acted with the Opposition until now, refused to be drawn into an unpatriotic line of conduct, or at Grey, Tierney, and other Whigs who showed scruples at embarrassing the Government in their operations.

Samuel Whitbread, M.P., to Creevey

Southill, Jan. 11, 1809

DEAR CREEVEY,

Your letter reached me at Woburn Abbey amidst rows, festivities and masquerades.... By all I can collect from the Duke of Bedford and Fitzpatrick it is not the desire of Ponsonby and the wise heads in London that any great effort should be made for an attendance....I have heard from Tierney since I saw you. He seems in flat despair about any effect to be produced by our exertions in Parlt. the ensuing session, and I am told that he wishes to abstain from *active* attendance altogether. I do not believe that any persons join with him in this feeling. I am sure I do not. It would be as unwise as impracticable to be seen and not heard in the House of Commons; and as his plan does not go the whole length of secession, it will amount in practice to nothing at all.... Lord Grenville intends to come down on the first day and make a general attack: after that, he does not at present mean to follow the matter up with the assiduity he displayed last year in the House of Lords, nor, indeed, in the absence of Grey and Holland, could it be expected.... I will only add for myself, that I have the greatest respect for Ld. Grenville, but that that respect would in no way prevent my taking any line I thought the right one....

Southill, March 31, 1809

...Do pray tell me what is said about things in general, and in particular about myself, for I fear I am but roughly handled in a *part* of the world just now.... What do you think of the Westminster meeting? I cannot say how much I was surprized by Burdett's unprovoked attack upon the great agriculturists, who are, almost without exception, real friends of Liberty and Reform—none more so than the head of them, the Duke of Bedford, who thinks parliamentary reform indispensably necessary to our existence....I am to-day working hard at the local Militia; to-morrow I intend to go fox-hunting, and on Sunday I hope to be regaled by an answer from you....

Capt. Graham Moore to Creevey

London, July 18th, 1809

...The [Walcheren] expedition is expected to sail this week. The Naval part of it is well commanded. Strachan is one of those in our service whom I estimate the highest. I do not believe he has his fellow among the Admirals, unless it be Pellew, for ability, and it is not possible to have more zeal and gallantry.

On September 21 the quarrel between Castlereagh and Canning culminated in a duel, involving the resignation of both Ministers. Lord Wellesley was recalled from Spain to succeed Canning at the Foreign Office, and Lord Liverpool took Castlereagh's place at the War Office. Another change shortly afterwards was the replacement of the Duke of Portland at the head of the Government by Mr. Perceval.

Lord Folkestone, M.P., to Creevey

Brooks's, Sept. 21, 1809

DEAR CREEVEY,

I cannot help writing to tell you what a curious scene is going on here. Old Portland is going both out of the Ministry and out of the world—both very soon, and it is doubtful which first; but the doubt arises from the difficulty of finding a new Premier, though both Perceval and Canning have offered themselves. Mulgrave is going too, they say—Castlereagh is quite gone, and Canning too, and the latter well nigh this morning quitted this sublunary globe, as well as the Foreign Office, for his friend Castlereagh on Wimbledon Common about 7 o'clock this morning as neatly as possible sent a pistol bullet through the fleshy part of his thigh. These heroes have quarrelled and fought about the Walcheren affair—Castlereagh damning the execution[1] of Lord Chatham, and Canning the plan of the planner, and being Lord Chatham's champion. Lord Chatham's friends, too, say that he is not at all to blame, that he has a complete case against Castlereagh, and further, that Sir Richard Strahan has made him *amende honorable* saying that he meant by his letter to insinuate no blame against him, and that he is ready to say so whenever and wherever called upon to do so.[2] On the other hand, Castlereagh's friends are furious too—say that never man was so ill-used, and that he never will have any more connexion with his present colleagues.

Lord Yarmouth was Castlereagh's second—Charles Ellis[3] Canning's. Castlereagh was not touched; Canning's wound is likely to be very tedious—not dangerous. In the meantime, every official arrangement is at a stand, or at least quite unknown and the whole thing appears in utter confusion.

[1] *i.e.*, the performance.

[2] 'The Earl of Chatham, with sword drawn,
Stood waiting for Sir Richard Strahan;
Sir Richard, longing to be at 'em,
Stood waiting for the Earl of Chatham.'

[3] Charles Rose Ellis, M.P. [1771–1845], created Lord Seaford in 1826.

chapter four

1810–11

ALTHOUGH THE GOVERNMENT had sustained a stunning blow in the loss of its two most prominent members, Castlereagh and Canning, the Opposition found themselves in a still more disorganised plight, so as to be quite unready to gain any advantage from the confusion of their enemies. The rising spirit of the country withdrew all attention from everything except the war; the denunciations of ministerial measures and blunders fell upon deaf ears, and the Opposition, as is commonly to be seen under similar circumstances, took to quarrelling among themselves, mistrusting each other, unable to decide upon the choice of a leader. Not from want of candidates, to be sure; it is amusing to read of the bewildering variety which was offered to them.

Samuel Whitbread, M.P., to Creevey

Southhill, Jan. 7, 1810

. . . Lord Grey passed a night here on his way to town. He was determined to be, and was, very kind, but we should not have held it long. It seems not decided that Ponsonby is not still to be continued Leader. I said 'not mine.' I had been disowned in such a manner on a topick of the greatest importance I could no longer fight under his banner. Lord Grey said if he chose to retain *his situation* he felt himself bound to support him. I could not help smiling, but I said only that I questioned much whether there would be any followers. He said he believed I was much mistaken. . . . Now write to me once more and tell me what you think of my state of mind from what I have written. I always take advice and criticism in good part from a friend—I know I do—so cut away boldly. I have no object but the publick good; I want nothing: I seek nothing. If I do wrong, 'tis because I am not wise eno' to do right. . . . All about Lord Grey is quite private.

Lord Milton, M.P., to Creevey

Milton, Jan. 8, 1810

DEAR CREEVEY,

I fully agree with you upon the trial that is about to be given to the H. of C. and lamentable indeed will it be if the issue is favourable to the Gentleman at the end of the Mall,[1] as Michael Angelo[2] calls him. It must completely damn Parliament if it takes no notice of the authors of the expedition to Walcheren, and all the disgraces and losses consequent upon their mismanagement in all quarters. . . . I am rather uneasy at hearing that the old *trader*[3] is to be the manufacturer of the amendment, but, short of a sacrifice of principle, I think a great deal ought to be done to embrace as many persons as possible; for, after all, nothing but a majority in Parlt. can lead to the practical benefit of getting rid of the present administration. . . . I trust the Marquis[4] will meet with the fate you predict for him. He is a great calamity inflicted upon England, and I heard to-day that, upon this last business with America, he has sent a proposition to her, the alternative of which is to be war. Here is the advantage of having the Conqueror of the East for our foreign secretary.

Henry Brougham, M.P., to Creevey

1810

. . . The Hon. Company are (as well as all other companies and most individuals) singularly obliged to Providence for restoring our gracious Sovereign. His death or idiocy would have been in the nature of a *quo warranto*. He is nearly recovered, and I hope to God will be able to prorogue. If a regency had been got up for a short time, with the present men as its ministers, I am confident Eldon, Perceval, &c. (who, when driven to desperation never think of violent measures, but only become more base, cunning, mean, &c.) would have licked the dust before the P. to good purpose. I wish the old ruffian,[5] however, may not have renewed his term. . . . Melville (as I learn from Scotland) wrote to Ld. Grenville urging him to *have me put out of Parliament*, on the ground that I was suspected of writing an article in the *Edinr. Review* highly disrespectful of Pitt! . . . My authority is exceedingly good—one

[1] George III.

[2] Michael Angelo Taylor, M.P., whose house in Whitehall was a constant and favourite rendezvous of the Whig party.

[3] Whitbread.

[4] Wellesley.

[5] George III.

of the law officers of Govt. in Scotland. . . . I conclude the article alluded to is Ld. Erskine's speeches; and, without saying I wrote it, I can only say I am ready to avow all it contains, in any place, and before any number of Grenvilles, Pitts or Dundasses. . . .

Memorandum

23rd January.—Parliament met. The King's speech very long, and capable of being worked to the devil. . . . Lord Barnard moved the address, Peel seconded it, and made a capital figure for a first speech.[6] I think it was a *prepared* speech, but it was a most produceable *Pittish* performance, both in matter and manner. I perceive we shall by no means cut the figure to-night that Tierney had held out. . . . Castlereagh started from under the gallery, two rows behind Canning, and everything that related personally to himself he did with a conscious sense of being right, and a degree of lively animation I never saw in him before. Base as the House is, it recognised by its cheers the claims of Castlereagh to its approbation, and they gave it. When he came to his expedition, he fell a hundred fathoms lower than the bogs of Walcheren.

Canning was sufficiently master of himself to let off one of his regular compositions, with all the rhetorical flourishes that used to set his audience in a roar; but he spoke from a different atmosphere. He was at least two feet separated from the Treasury bench, and in the whole course of his speech he could not extort a single cheer. . . . Whitbread was stout and strong—upon Wellington particularly. . . . Notwithstanding Tierney's calculations and prophecy that we should be in a majority, we were beat by 96. . . . Their strength was composed of five parties—the Government—Castlereagh's—Canning's—the Doctor's and the Saints. In looking at the majority going out, Castlereagh said with the gayest face possible:—'Well, Creevey, how do we look?' . . .

We had a grand fuss in telling the House. The Princess of Wales, who had been present the whole time, would stay it out to know the numbers, and so remained in her place in the gallery. The Speaker very significantly called several times for strangers to withdraw; which she defied, and sat on. At last the little fellow became irritated—started from his chair, and, looking up plump in the faces of her and her female friend, halloaed out most fiercely:—'If there are any strangers in the House they must withdraw.' They being the only two, they struck and withdrew. . . . In the Lords, Grey made an admirable speech, disputed the military, moral and intellectual fame of Lord Wellington most

[6] The Speaker, Charles Abbot, pronounced it to be 'the best first speech since that of Mr. Pitt.' Peel was only two and twenty.

capitally, and called loudly upon the Marquis [Wellesley], as the Atlas of the falling state, to come forward and justify the victory of Talavera.

24th.—Dined at a coffee-house: went to Brooks's at night. Lord Grey came in drunk from the Duke of York's where he had been dining. He came and sat by me on the same sofa, talked as well as he could over the division of the night before, and damned with all his might and main Marquis Wellesley, of whose profligate establishment I told him some anecdotes, which he swallowed as greedily as he had done the Duke's wine. He and Whitbread and I sat together and were as merry as if we had been the best friends in the world.... Then the Right Hon. George Ponsonby came and sat by me, and we talked over the last session a little; but I found him very sore and very bad.

25th.—Perceval has given notice of thanks to Wellington on Monday....

26th.—...On Lord Porchester's motion for an enquiry into the expedition to Walcheren, we beat the Ministers by a majority of *nine*. I did not expect it; tho' I saw that, if we could move together, our first division (of 167) on the Address must be fatal to them. It is the most perfect triumph possible, for the enquiry is to be public, like that on the Duke of York, not in a Select Committee.

On February 2 began the inquiry in Committee of the whole House into the Walcheren expedition. Witnesses gave evidence at the Bar of the House. On the motion of Mr. Yorke, the galleries of the House were cleared of strangers, in order to prevent incorrect reports of the proceedings being published in anticipation of the publication of the official minutes. During the course of the inquiry a long and detailed description was forwarded daily to Mrs. Creevey by her husband; but as the character of this famous inquiry is fully on record, it does not seem necessary to quote from it.

chapter four (*continued*)

1811

THE DEATH OF his youngest and favourite child, Princess Amelia, in the autumn of 1810 upset the poor old King's intellect for the last time. He settled into hopeless insanity, and the chief business before Parliament in 1811 was a Bill constituting the Prince of Wales Regent. Great was the stir among the Whigs, who began fitting each other into the great and little offices of the new Government; for who could doubt that the great turn of events, so long and ardently anticipated, was indeed at hand, and that the Prince, as head of the Whig party, would send his father's servants to the right about, and form a Ministry of his own friends. Judging from Creevey's correspondence, neither he nor any of his friends entertained the slightest suspicion about the sincerity of the Prince's devotion to Liberal principles, nor understood how much his politics consisted of opposition to the Court party. It was, therefore, with as much surprise as dismay that Creevey beheld the change in the Prince's attitude towards Ministers as soon as he assumed the Regency.

Creevey to Mrs. Creevey [at Brighton]

Great George St., 19th January, 1811

(For God's sake be secret about this letter.)

My hopes of seeing you to-morrow are at an end, owing to a most ridiculous resolution of our party to have another division on Monday, in which of course we shall disclose still greater weakness than on our last division. I had actually paired off with John Villiers for the week, but I am sure you will think I am right in staying over Monday, when I tell you that McMahon told me he was sure the Prince would be hurt if I was not there, and when you read the enclosed note from Sheridan. Nevertheless I give the Prince credit for not originating this business, but that it has been conveyed to him by Tierney or some such artist. I mean to be down to stay a week or ten days on Tuesday. Wm. and C.

had a very comfortable dinner again yesterday upon my mutton chops at this house, and then went to the House, and just as we had returned home again at ten o'clock, and I was beginning to dress myself to go to Mrs. Taylor's, Whitbread came and desired to have some conversation with me.... Sam's visit was to take my advice. He said things had now come to such a state of maturity that it was very necessary for him to decide (but here he has just been again, and I am afraid I shall not have time to tell).

Well—office was offered him; anything he pleased, but had he any objection to holding it under Grenville as First Lord, if he [Grenville] held as before the *two offices of First Lord and Auditor, with the salaries of both?* I know not with what disposition he came to me; he stated both sides of the question, but said his decision must be quick. I had a difficult responsibility to take upon myself, but I set before him as strongly as I could the unpopularity of the Grenvilles—the certainty of this [*illegible*] place being again and again exposed—the impossibility of his defending it after having himself driven Yorke from receiving the income of his tellership whilst he is at the Admiralty, and Perceval from receiving the income of Chancellor of the Exchequer whilst he is First Lord and Chancellor of the Dutchy—that his consistency and character were everything to him, and that, if I was him, I would compell Lord Grenville to make the sacrifice to publick opinion, and have nothing to do with the Government.

I went to him this morning, and he had done as I advised him. He had told Grey his determination and he has just been here to shew me his letter to him upon the subject—to be shewn Lord Grenville. It is perfect in every aspect, and will, whenever it is known, do him immortal honor. The fact, however, is, my lord will strike. They one and all stick to Whitbread; they can't carry on the Government without him. There is no anger—no ill will in any of them; all *piano*—all upon their knees. Is not this a triumph?'

[*Enclosure in above, from Mr. Sheridan.*

Friday night, Jany. 18th

My dear Creevey,

It is determined in consequence of the earnest Desire of *high authority* to have *a last debate and division* on the Regency bill on Monday next. Here is a Conclave mustering all Hands, and I am requested to write to you as it is apprehended you mean to leave Town to-morrow. I conjure you at any rate to be with us on Monday.

Yours ever faithfully,

Bly. Sheridan.]

Creevey to Mrs. Creevey

Great George St., Saty., Feby. 2nd, 1811

...At Brooks's I found Sheridan just arrived from Carlton House, where the conclave has just broken up, and the Prince had decided against the pressing advice of all present *not* to dismiss the Government. Sheridan was just sober, and expressed to me the strongest opinion of the injurious tendency of this resolution to the Prince's character. Lord Hutchinson said the same thing to me to-day, and added that never man had behaved better than Sheridan. I said all I thought to both Hutchinson and Sheridan in vindication of Prinny, but I presume I am wrong, as I stand single in this opinion. I went, however, to Mrs. Fitzherbert at twelve to-day, an appointment I made with her yesterday in the street, and she and I were agreed upon this subject. The Prince has written to Perceval a letter which is to be sent to-morrow, stating to him his intention, under the opinion of the physicians respecting his father, *not* to change the Government at present, and at the same time expressing the regret he feels at being thus compelled to continue a Government not possessing his confidence, and his determination of changing it should there be no speedy prospect of his Majesty's recovery after a certain time.

Now I do not see, under all the monstrous difficulties of his situation, any great impropriety of his present resolution, particularly as he means to have his letter made publick.

Mrs. Fitz is evidently delighted at the length and forgiving and confidential nature of Prinny's visits. She goes to-morrow and will tell you, no doubt, how poor Prinny was foolish enough to listen to some idle story of my having abused his letter to both Houses, and how she defended me. Poor fellow, one should have thought he had more important concerns to think of. I went from her to Whitbread, and he again conjured me to attach myself to the new Government by taking some situation, and went over many—the Admiralty Board again—Chairman of the Ways and Means, &c. I was very guarded, and held myself very much up, and said I would take nothing for which there was not service to be done—nothing like a sinecure, which I considered a seat at the Admiralty Board to be; but of course I was very good-humoured. He repeated the conversation between him and Lord Grey about me. He said my name was first mentioned by Miss Whitbread, and, having been so, Lord Grey replied—'Although I think Creevey has acted unjustly to me, and tho' in the session before last he gave great offence to many of my friends by something like a violation of confidence, yet on his own account, on that of Mrs. Creevey and of anybody connected with them,

I had always intended, without you mentioning him, to express my wishes that he might be included in the Government.' Upon which Whitbread stated from his own recollection of my speech that gave offence, his perfect conviction of its being no breach of confidence; and so the thing ended with their united sentiment in favor of my having some office.

I am affraid you will be hurt at not seeing any immediate provision for me in this new Government, should it take place; but I beg you to give way to no such sentiment.... They are upon a new tack in consulting publick opinion. *Lord Grey* and Lord Grenville have most unequivocally refused to accede to a proposal of the Prince of Wales, and which was stated to be nearest to his heart, viz. to reinstate the Duke of York as Commander-in-Chief. What think you of this in Grey? and his language to Whitbread is they must no longer be taunted with 'unredeemed pledges.' I mention these things to shew you they are on their good behaviour, and that, with such views, they must do what they ought by me. I am perfectly satisfied with the state of things—this is, supposing a Government to be formed—and perfectly secure of any wishes of mine being accomplished.

21st Jan, 1811

I am very much gratified to find you approve my counsel to Sam, and Sam for acting upon it. Every succeeding moment convinces me of the necessity there was for acting so, and of the infinite advantage and superiority it will give him over all his colleagues at starting.

What shall you say to me when I tell you I am not to vote to-night after all? Villiers won't release me from contract of pairing off; at least he consented only to stay upon terms that I could not listen to, such as —*if my being in the division might be of any use to me in the new arrangement*, that then he would certainly stay. This, as you may suppose, was enough to make me at once decline any further discussion.... However, it is universally known how I am situated, and McMahon told me just now of his own accord that the Prince had told him this morning 'that Villiers would not release Creevey from pairing off with him; that it was very good of Creevey to stay after this, and to show himself in the House, as he knew he intended.' ... Here has been Ward[1] just now to beg I would come and dine with him *tête-à-tête*, and that I should have my dinner at six precisely, as he knew I liked that: so I shall go. I know he was told the character I pronounced of him one night at Mrs. Taylor's after he was gone, upon which occasion I neither

[1] Hon. John William Ward, created Earl Dudley in 1827.

concealed his merits nor his frailties, and he has been kinder to me than ever from that time.... I don't know a syllable of what has transpired to-day between Prinny and the grandees, but I must not omit to tell you that the night before last my Lord Lansdowne for the first time condescended to come up to me at Brooks's, and to walk me backwards and forwards for at least a quarter of an hour. He asked me how I thought *we* should get on in the House of Commons (meaning the new Government), whether we should be strong enough; to which I replied it would depend upon the conduct of the Government—that if they acted right they would be strong enough, and that so doing was not only the best, but the sole, foundation of their strength, and my lord agreed with me in rather an awkward manner, and was mighty civil and laughed at all my jokes, and so we parted.

Great George St., 1st Feby., 1811

I was very much provoked at being detained so long on the road yesterday that I was just too late for the last Bill, so I eat my mutton chops and drunk a bottle of wine, and then tea, and then sallied forth to Mrs. Taylor's; but alas, she was dining out, so on I went to Brooks's, where I found Mr. Ponsonby and others; and then came Whitbread, Sheridan, and Lord Hutchinson, the latter of whom insisted upon my coming to dine with him *tête-à-tête* to-day, as he had so much to say to me. He had been dining yesterday with the Prince, and was to be with him again this morning. You may suppose I intend accepting his invitation; for to-day Whitbread was deeply involved in private conversation with these gentry; but, before he left the room, he came up to the table where I was, and said—'Creevey, call upon me to-morrow at twelve if it is not inconvenient to you;' and, having left the room, Ward, who was there, said—'There! Mr. Under-Secretary, you are to be tried as to what kind of a hand you write, &c., &c., before you are hired;' and then we walked home together, and he told me he had been offered to be a Paymaster of the Forces, and that he had refused it, and that he was sure this notice of Whitbread was to offer me an under-secretaryship in his office. I went accordingly to Sam this morning, but quite armed, I am certain, against all disappointment, and with all the air of an independent man. He began by giving me his opinion that the Prince would not change the Government, and that he was playing a false, hollow, shabby game. He said the Queen had written him a letter evidently dictated by Perceval, [*illegible*] most cursedly, and that he had been quite taken in by it. He expressed himself strongly of opinion that he [the Prince] ought instantly to change the Government; that after all that had passed between him, the Prince and Lords Grenville and Grey, it would be a breach of honour not to overthrow the ministers instantly. I confess I was more penetrated, upon this part of the conversation, with Sam's anxiety to be in office than I was with the weight of his arguments against the Prince. At the same time, it is due to him to add that Sheridan and Lord Hutchinson insist openly that the Prince, in justice to his character, is bound to make this change; and again, there certainly is nothing to make the Prince expect any rapid amendment of the King. . . . Well, this opinion of Whitbread being advanced and maintained by him as aforesaid, he proceeded to say that, in the event of the change taking place, he was very anxious to know from myself what I should look to—that he and Lord Grey had talked over the subject together—that the latter had spoken of me very handsomely, and said that, tho' I had in the session before last, fired into the old Government in a manner that had given great offence to several persons, yet that he was very desirous I should form part of the new Government. Whitbread added his own opinion that it was of great importance I should be in the Government, and then added—'The worst of it is there are so few places suited to you that are consistent with a seat in Parliament; but what is there you should think of yourself?' So I replied *that* was rather a hard question to answer; that though I was a little man compared with him in the country, yet that the preservation of my own character and consistency was the first object with me; that I could go as a principal into no office—*that* was out of the question—and I *would not* go into any office as a subaltern, where the character of the principal did not furnish a sufficient apology for my serving under him; that with these views I certainly had looked to going with him into any office he might have allotted to him. He said such had always been his wish, and then said—'You know by the Act of Parliament that created the third Secretary of State, viz., that for the Colonies, neither of the Under-Secretaries of State can sit in Parliament, and that was what I meant when I said there were so few places consistent with a seat in Parliament.' He said Grey and he had taken for granted I would not go back to my old place, or a seat at that board, after firing as I had done into the East I. Company; to which I replied they were quite right, and I added that, whenever I might be in office or out, I reserved to myself the right of the free exercise of my opinion upon all Indian subjects. He then said, with some humility, would I take a seat at the Admiralty Board; that Lord Holland would be there, and that he, of course, would have every disposition to consult my feelings. I said my first inclination was certainly against it; at the same time, I begged nothing might be done to prevent Lord Holland making an offer of any kind to me; that he was a person I looked up to greatly on his own account, as well as his uncle's;[2] that in all my licentiousness in Parliament I had never profaned his uncle's memory; it had been exclusively directed against his enemies; that I would take a thing from Lord Holland that nothing should induce me to do from any Grenvilles; at the same time, I was giving no opinion further than this, that I begged Whitbread not to prevent Lord Holland from making me an offer—let it be what it may....

How little real union there was among the various sections of the Opposition, and how greatly the Whigs dreaded the projects dearest to the Radicals, are well illustrated in the following letters.

Henry Brougham, M.P., to Creevey

April, 1811

DEAR C.,

The enclosed answer to a mutinous epistle which I fired into Holland House t'other day may amuse Mrs. C. and you. Burn it when you have read it.

Yours ever,

H. B.

[Enclosure from Lord Holland

...There is much truth in your complaints of the present state of public affairs. But how is the evil to be corrected? There is a want of popular feelings in many individuals of the party. Others are exasperated with the unjust and uncandid treatment they have received, and are every day receiving, from the modern Reformers. Another set are violent anti-Reformers, and alarmed at every speech or measure that has the least tendency towards reform. There is but one measure on which the party are unanimously agreed, and no one man in the House of Commons to whom they look up with that deference and respect to his opinion which is necessary to have concert and co-operation in a party. ...It is a state of things, however, which cannot possibly last. Before next meeting of Parliament, the Prince must either have changed his Ministers, or he must lay his account with systematic opposition to his government. Even though the old leaders of the party[3] should be willing to break with him, they will not be able to prevent their friends from declaring open hostility against his government. If such a rupture should

[2] C. J. Fox.

[3] Lords Grey and Grenville.

take place, many would of course desert the party; but those who remained, agreeing better with one another in their opinions, and consisting of more independent men, would in fact be a more formidable opposition than the present....]

Henry Brougham, M.P., to Creevey

Wed.

...I wish you would come to town and let us have a few mischievous discussions....A report is very prevalent that the siege of Badajos is raised, previous to another fight. I daresay this will prove true....*I am assured* that the Ministers have private letters from Welln., preparing them for a retreat.

As time went on, although the King's malady became confirmed, so also seemed the Regent's inclination to maintain his father's Cabinet. The irritation of the Whigs increased in proportion as their hopes sank lower. A peep down the Prime Minister's area seems to have opened Creevey's eyes for the first time to the profligacy of the Heir Apparent, to which he had been blind enough in the rousing old days at the Pavilion. So greatly may judgment vary according to the point of view!

Creevey to Mrs. Creevey

20th July, 1811

...Prinny's attachment to the present Ministers, his supporting their Bank Note Bill, and his dining with them, must give them all hopes of being continued, as I have no doubt they will....The folly and villainy of this Prinny is certainly beyond anything. I was forcibly struck with this as I passed Perceval's[4] kitchen just now, and saw four man cooks and twice as many maids preparing dinner for the Prince of Wales and Regent—he whose wife Perceval set up against him in open battle—who, at the age of 50, could not be trusted by the sd. Perceval with the unrestrained government of these realms during his father's incapacity—he who, on his last birthday at Brighton, declared to his numerous guests that it was his glory to have bred up his daughter in the principles of Mr. Fox—he who, in this very year, declared by letter to the said Mr. Perceval, and afterwards had the letter published as an apology for

[4] Spencer Perceval became Prime Minister on the death of Portland in October, 1809, and was assassinated by Bellingham in the lobby of the House of Commons, May 11, 1812.

his conduct, that he took him as his father's Minister, but that his own heart was in another quarter—by God! this is too much. We shall see whether he does dine there or not, or whether he will send word at 5, as he did to poor Kinnaird, that he can't come. I have been walking with Kinnaird, and this excuse that came too late from Prinny, the Duke of York and the Duke of Clarence has evidently made a deep impression upon his lordship's mind against the Bank Note Bill, and everything else in which the Regent takes a part.

Journal

July 12th, 1811.—...We are prorogued till the 22nd of next month *only*, but the general opinion is the King will die before that day, and then of course Parliament meets again. Publick opinion, or rather the opinion of Parliamentary politicians, is that, in the event of the King's death, Lords Grenville and Grey will be passed over and the present ministers continued, with the addition of some of the Prince's private friends, such as Lords Moira and Hutchinson and Yarmouth and old Sheridan. The latter is evidently very uneasy at the present state of things. He sat with me till 5 o'clock on Sunday morning at Brooks's—was very drunk—told me I had better get into the same boat with him in politicks—but at the same time abused Yarmouth so unmercifully that one quite perceived he thought his (Yarmouth's) boat was the best of the two. Apparently nothing can be so base as the part the Prince is acting, or so likely to ruin him....

Brighton, Oct. 30th.—The Prince Regent came here last night with the Duke of Cumberland and Lord Yarmouth. Everybody has been writing their names at the Pavilion this morning, but I don't hear of anybody dining there to-day....I presume we shall be asked there, altho' I went to town on purpose to vote against his appointment of his brother the Duke of York to the Commandership-in-Chief of the Army.

Oct. 31st.—We have got an invitation from the Regent for to-night and are going. I learn from Sir Philip Francis, who dined there yesterday, the Prince was very gay....There were twenty at dinner—no politicks—but still Francis says he thinks, from the language of the equerries and understrappers, that the campaign in Portugal and Lord Wellington begin to be out of fashion with the Regent.

Nov. 1st.—We were at the Pavilion last night—Mrs. Creevey's daughters and myself—and had a very pleasant evening. We found there Lord and Lady Charlemont, Marchioness of Downshire and old Lady Sefton. About half-past nine, which might be a quarter of an hour after we arrived, the Prince came out of the dining-room. He was in his best humour, bowed and spoke to all of us, and looked uncommonly well, tho' very fat. He was in his full Field Marshal's uniform. He remained quite as cheerful and full of fun to the last—half past twelve—asked after Mrs. Creevey's health, and nodded and spoke when he passed us. The Duke of Cumberland was in the regimentals of his own Hussars, looked really hideous, everybody trying to be rude to him—not standing when he came near them. The officers of the Prince's regiment had all dined with him, and looked very ornamental monkeys in their red breeches with gold fringe and yellow boots. The Prince's band played as usual all the time in the dining-room till 12, when the pages and footmen brought about iced champagne punch, lemonade and sandwiches. I found more distinctly than before, from conversation with the *Gyps*, that Wellington and Portugal are going down.

The Prince looked much happier and more unembarrassed by care than I have seen him since this time six years. This time five years ago, when he was first in love with Lady Hertford, I have seen the tears run down his cheeks at dinner, and he has been dumb for hours, but now that he has the weight of the empire upon him, he is quite alive.... I had a very good conversation with Lord Charlemont about Ireland, and liked him much. He thinks the Prince has already ruined himself in Irish estimation by his conduct to the Catholics.

Nov. 2nd.—We were again at the Pavilion last night.... The Regent sat in the Musick Room almost all the time between Viotti, the famous violin player, and Lady Jane Houston, and he went on for hours beating his thighs the proper time for the band, and singing out aloud, and looking about for accompaniment from Viotti and Lady Jane. It was a curious sight to see a Regent thus employed, but he seemed in high good humour.... There is nothing like a Minister about him, nor yet any of his old political friends or advisers—no Sheridan, Moira or Hutchinson. Yarmouth and the Duke of Cumberland are always on the spot, and no doubt are his real advisers; but in publick they are mute, and there is no intercourse between the Regent and them. Sir Philip Francis is the only one of his old set here, but he is not here on the Prince's invitation, nor in his suite, and is evidently slighted. Tom Stepney and I last night calculated that Francis and Lord Keith made out 150 years of age between them, and yet they are both here upon their preferment with the Regent—the first, one of the cleverest men one knows, and the other, one of the richest. What a capital libel on mankind! Francis said to me to-day:—'Well, I am invited to dinner to-day, and that is perhaps all I shall get after two and twenty years' service.' What infernal folly for such a person to have put himself in the way of making so humiliating a confession.

Nov. 5th.—We were at the Prince's both last night and the night before (Sunday).... The Regent was again all night in the Musick Room, and not content with presiding over the Band, but actually singing, and very loud too. Last night we were reduced to a smaller party than ever, and Mrs. Creevey was well enough to go with me and her daughters for the first time. Nothing could be kinder than the Prince's manner to her. When he first saw her upon coming into the drawing-room, he went up and took hold of both her hands, shook them heartily, made her sit down directly, asked her all about her health, and expressed his pleasure at seeing her look so much better than he expected. Upon her saying she was glad to see him looking so well, he said gravely he was getting old and blind. When she said she was glad on account of his health that he kept his rooms cooler than he used to do, he said he was quite altered in that respect—that he used to be always *chilly*, and was now never so—that he never had a fire even in his bedroom, and slept with one blanket and sheet only....

Nov. 6th.—We were again at the Pavilion last night... the party being still smaller than ever, and the Prince, according to his custom, being entirely occupied with his musick.

Nov. 9th.—Yesterday was the last day of the Prince's stay at this place, and, contrary to my expectation, I was invited to dinner. We did not sit down till half-past seven, tho' I went a little past six. The only person I found was Tom Stepney: then came Generals Whetham, Hammond and Cartwright, Lords Charlemont, Yarmouth and Ossulston, Sir Philip Francis, Congreve, Bloomfield and others of the understrappers, and finally the Regent and the Duke of Cumberland. We were about sixteen altogether. The prince was very merry and seemed very well. He began to me with saying very loud that he had sent for Mrs. Creevey's physic to London.... At dinner I sat opposite to him, next to Ossulston, and we were the only persons there at all marked by opposition to his appointment of his brother the Duke of York, or to the Government generally, since he has been Regent. He began an old joke at dinner with me about poor Fonblanque, with whom I had dined six years ago at the Pavilion,... [when] the Prince and we all got drunk, and he was always used to say it was the merriest day he ever spent. However, it was soon dropped yesterday.

The Duke of Cumberland and Yarmouth never spoke. The Prince was describing a pleasant dinner he had had in London lately, and was going over each man's name as he sat in his order at the table, and giving each his due in the pleasantry of the day. Coming to Col. [Sir Willoughby] Gordon he said: 'To be sure, there's not much humour in him!' upon which Ossulston and I both gave a kind of involuntary laugh, thinking the said Gordon a perfect impostor, from our recollection of his pompous, impudent evidence before the House of Commons in the Duke of York's case; but this *chuckling* of ours brought from the Prince a very elaborate panegyric upon Gordon which was meant, most evidently, as a reproof to Ossulston and myself for quizzing him.

We did not drink a great deal, and were in the drawing-room by half-past nine or a little after; no more state, I think, than formerly—ten men out of livery of one kind or other, and four or five footmen. At night everybody was there and the whole closed about one, and so ended the Regent's visit to Brighton.

And so, it may be added, ended Creevey's intimacy with the Regent. Henceforward he acted in constant opposition to his future monarch's schemes.

'Robeing the Regent; or, the road to preferment'
(From left to right: Whitbread, Grenville, Sheridan, Geo. Bloomfield, the Regent, Col. McMahon, Adam, Perceval)
Published February 1st, 1811, by Walter and Knight, Cornhill

chapter five

1812

THE MARQUESS WELLESLEY, who had joined Perceval's Cabinet in 1809 on the resignation of Castlereagh and Canning, himself resigned in February, 1812, partly owing to dissatisfaction at the manner in which the Government supported the Peninsular war, but chiefly because of the Regent's persistence in refusing to listen to any proposals of Roman Catholic relief. The King's recovery being now considered out of the question, it was fully expected that the Regent would avail himself of the occasion of a reconstruction of the Cabinet to put his own political friends in power. However, instead of dismissing Perceval, he invited Grey and Grenville to join his administration, which they refused to do so long as Catholic Emancipation was a forbidden subject. The Regent bitterly resented their conduct, and continued Perceval in office, until that Minister was assassinated in the lobby of the House of Commons on May 11. Meanwhile, another and a striking personality had appeared in Parliament, Henry Brougham, to wit. Elected for Camelford for the first time in 1810, he had registered a vow not to open his mouth in the House for the first month; which vow he kept, indemnifying himself for his self-control by incessant oratory ever after. George Ponsonby was still leader of the Whigs in the Commons; but Brougham's energy and eloquence were so striking that he had not been four months a member before he was reckoned as one of the most formidable of the many candidates for the first place. His letters to Creevey during the early months of 1812 are very numerous; but it is difficult to fix the exact stage of proceedings to which they refer, owing to his omission to date them except by the day of the week.

Henry Brougham, M.P., to Creevey

Saturday, 6 o'clock [*May? 1812*]

The intriguing is going on briskly. Wellesley has seen P., and then Wellesley saw Grey. Grey says all is afloat and nothing settled, but that all will be settled before Monday. This shows a *nibble* at least, and I lament it much. To be in the same boat with W. and Canning is pretty severe. I see no chance of their making such a thing as one *can* support; indeed I feel in opposition to them already, should they agree about it. . . . Holland and Wellesley are at the bottom of it all, and have been together to-day, and at York House. The Spanish madness and love of office of Lady H[olland] is enough to do all the mischief we dread. Anything without the country is real madness or drivling.

In the Comee. on Orders in C[ouncil] we sat this morning till *four*, and I have been all day at a Sheriff's Jury on damages, so am knocked up and can add no more.

H. B.

H. of Coms. [in pencil] Friday, 22nd May, 1812

They are all out. The answer of Prinny is short—that he is to comply immediately with the address to form a Govt. I had no hand in this bad work. I would not vote. It is the old blunder of 1804—acting at Canning's benefit. The old rotten Ministry was to my mind.

Creevey had a safe seat at Thetford, one of the Duke of Norfolk's boroughs, but his ambition was fired by an invitation to contest one of the seats for his native Liverpool. Brougham, at the same time, having received notice to quit from a new proprietor of Camelford, determined to stand for the other Liverpool seat; and, on the dissolution taking place, these two gentlemen went down to fight Mr. Canning and General Gascoigne.

Henry Brougham to Creevey

Brougham, Friday, [May] 1812

On my return from a visit to the Jockey[1] I received yours. While there, I passed my time as you might suppose—drinking in the evening, and in the morning going thro' *tête-à-tête* with him the red book and other lists of boro's. It was quite a comedy. I believe I can almost come up to the never-to-be-forgotten or surpassed night enjoyed by Ld. S[efton] and yourself with that venerable *feudal* character. We had women—and speeches—in the first style: the subjects infinitely various, from bawdy to the depth of politics, and this morning at breakfast he was pleased to enter largely on the subject of the *Daiety* and his foreknowledge; settling that question as satisfactorily as if it had been one touching *the Gairter*, which he likewise discussed at length. I assure you I have had two choice

[1] The 11th Duke of Norfolk.

days, and there wanted only some one Xianlike person to enjoy it with, and the presence also of a few comforts—such as a necessary, towels, water, &c., &c., to make the thing compleat. He goes up to-morrow to *Airundel*, and he is coming here on his way (to talk about the dissolution), which will give me a more quiet slice of his humours; for there was rather a crowd of parasites....

There follows here a long discussion of the question whether Creevey and Brougham—either of them, both, or neither—should stand for Liverpool. Then he continues—

... As to being out of Parlt.—don't laugh at me if I say I really should submit to such a fate with composure, indeed with cheerfulness. I am fond of my profession, which you'll say is a queer taste; but I really do delight in it more and more every day. I see also how greatly I might rise in it by this means, and how infallibly I should command anything parliamentary that I might chuse, after a few years. This is clear, and I might be as much of a *demagogue* as I thought fit to be—I mean, in a good sense—and these times require looking *outside* of Parlt., in my opinion, as much as any we have lived in.

Creevey to Mrs. Creevey

House of Commons, (May) 25th, 1812

Oh dear! I have been waiting for Whitbread's latest intelligence, till I have little time left. First then, when Prinney sent for Wellesley, the latter began by mentioning some of the Opposition as persons to be consulted with; to which the former replied—'Don't mention any names to me *now*, my lord, but make an Administration for me.' To which the other says—'In a business of such nicety I trust your Royal Highness will not press me for time.'—'Take your own time,' says Prinney, 'tho' there is not a shilling left in the Exchequer.' Well, off sets Wellesley, calling at the doors of the Opposition—Grey, Grenville, Holland and Moira; and yesterday some minutes of their conversations were made that had taken place between Wellesley, Grey and Grenville about the Catholic question and the war in Spain. There is some vague kind of coincidence of sentiments expressed between them on these subjects—no other subject mentioned. With this first fruit of his expedition Wellesley went to Carlton House last night at seven, and just as he was beginning to dilate upon his success, Prinney told him he was *busy*, and that he must call again to-day.... This I know to be quite true; it comes from Grey through Whitbread to me.

This is the whole effect of the defeat of the old Government, and in the meantime the said old Government have one and all contracted with each other in writing never to act with such a villain as Wellesley again; in which they are quite right, but what think you of such a patron for our friends? Well: we had Whitbread and Lady Elizabeth at Holland House yesterday, Milton, Althorp, Lord John Russell, Sheridan, Lord Ossory, Fitzpatrick, Horner, Bennett and many more, and we had a very merry day, occasioned by my jokes about our new patron the Marquis [Wellesley]. Poor Holland was quite inimitable, but I will tell you more about it to-morrow. They will be all ruined: *they have flung Whitbread overboard*; he has just told me so himself, and that Lord Grey had just told him so in the coolest manner. Not a word of this! but it is *death* to them. He told me yesterday his fixed determination to have nothing to do with Wellesley and Canning, and they have anticipated him....

House of Commons, Tuesday, 26th

...Well: nothing is known to-day except that Prinney saw both Eldon and Liverpool yesterday for a long time before he saw Wellesley, and that a Cabinet Council of the old Ministers was summoned to Liverpool's office last night, and sat for a long time.... Well, the jaw is over. Castlereagh says the old Government is still out, and he knows nothing of any new one. It is *true* that Prinney told Wellesley that Grey and Grenville were a couple of scoundrels, and that Moira was a fellow no honest man could speak to. Wellesley then told him the danger he was exposed to, both himself, his throne and his country, washed his hands of him and his concerns, and is actually gone out of town. Ferguson told me he *knew* all this, and of course Moira is his authority. Canning will have nothing to do with the old Government, and has just renewed his motion about the Catholic question. Prinney must be stark raving mad, by God! ... The projected exclusion of Whitbread from the new Cabinet is spreading like wildfire against Grey and Grenville.

Brooks's, 27th

Well, after all that passed between Prinney and Wellesley on Monday night after all the foul language about Moira, &c., late last night Prinney sent for Moira and flung himself upon his mercy. Such a scene I never heard of; the young monarch *cried* loud and long; in short he seems to have been very nearly in convulsions. The afflicting interview was entirely occupied with lamentations over past errors, and delight at brighter prospects for the future under the happier auspices of his old and true friend now restored. Moira told him generally the terrible state of the country, which the other said had been concealed from him by his Ministers, and that he had not seen a paper these three or four weeks. Moira suggested to him that perhaps he would wish to be more *composed* before they went further into detail, and this was agreed to, so he has been there again to-day for three hours. I saw him come away at a little before four, and Lord Dundas called with me at his door and found he had gone off to Lord Wellesley's, where Grenville and Grey now are hearing the substance of this long interview of Moira with his Master.... My jokes about Wellesley are in great request. Lady Holland said to me on Sunday in the drawing-room after dinner—'Come here and sit by me, you *mischievous toad*, and promise that you won't begin upon the new Government with your jokes. When you do, begin with those Grenvilles.' I dined at old Tankerville's yesterday, who said—'Creevey, never desert Wellesley! give it him well, I beg of you.' Sefton asked me to dine there to-day, evidently with the same view. Sheridan is more base in his resentment against Whitbread than you can imagine, and all from Drury Lane disappointment.

House of Commons, 28th

...Just after I finished my letter yesterday, I met Sheridan coming from a long interview with the Prince, and going with a message to Wellesley; so of course I walked with him and got from him all I could. ...He described the Prince's state of perturbation of mind as beyond anything he had ever seen. He conceives the different candidates for office to be determined upon his ruin; and, in short, I begin to think that his reign will end in a day or two in downright insanity. He first sends for one person, then another. Eldon is always told everything that passes, and the Duke of York (Lord Grey's friend and slave) is the unalterable and inveterate opposer of his brother having anything to do with the Opposition. He and Eldon work day and night to keep Prinney in the right course. Melville is a great favorite too. To-day he (Prinney) has seen the Doctor and Westmorland, Buckinghamshire, and now Moira is with him. Canning has been found out in some intrigue with Liverpool already. There has been some explanation between Grey and Whitbread, certainly creditable to the former. He has admitted to the fullest extent the importance of the Brewer and his own unalterable and unfavorable opinion of Canning. He maintained this opinion to his friends as strongly as he could, and pressed them, as they valued able and upright men to shuffling rogues, to stand by Whitbread and abandon Canning. In this proposition, however, he *stood alone*. Petty and Holland even were against him. Grey pronounced that tho' he was bound by this decision, he knew such decision must inevitably be their ruin. He has told all this to Brougham, as well as to Whitbread, and you know he always at least tells the truth. Of course you will not quote this . . . From Lisbon the accounts are very unfavorable. The American embargo has produced the greatest consternation, and our Commissariat is utterly destitute of money or credit. In addition to this, General officers write home that the ravages of the late sieges and other things have made a supply of 30,000 men from this country absolutely necessary, if Portugal alone is to be kept.

York St., Monday, 1st June

As Folkestone, Bennett and I are to go from the H. of Commons this afternoon to dine at Richmond, I begin my dispatch here, lest I should have no time to do it at the House. Folky and Bennett return at night, but I shall sleep there . . . The more one sees of the conduct of this most singular man [the Prince Regent], the more one becomes convinced he is doomed, from his personal character alone, to shake his throne. He is playing, I have no doubt he thinks, some devilish deep game, from which he will find he is utterly incapable of extricating himself without the most serious and lasting injury to himself and character. . . . I dined at Taylor's last night with that excellent young man Lord Forbes,[2] and I have never seen a greater appearance of worth and honor in any young man in my life. Besides being Moira's nephew, he is an aide-de-camp to the Regent, and he has received such usage from his Master, either on his uncle's account or his own voting in Parliament, that he won't go near him, and greatly to the horror of Taylor, he came to dine yesterday with the yellow lining and the Prince's buttons taken away from his coat. He said never again would he carry about him so degrading a badge of servitude to such a master. To Taylor, who was done up in the neatest edition of the said badge, this was too much.

House of Commons

Well, now we have made a start. Mr. Canning has got up with due pomp and dignity, and has declared he has full authority to state from his noble friend Lord Wellesley that he, Lord Wellesley, has this morning received from the Regent his Royal Highness's commands to form an administration. So much for this first official act of the new Whig Government! . . .

Richmond Hill, June 2nd

Very large paper this, my precious, but we must see what we can make of it. As the day is so charming and the country so inviting, I have

[2] The eldest son of the 6th Earl of Granard by a daughter of the 1st Earl of Moira.

resolved to stay over the day, and accordingly my cloaths have gone to be washed. I leave, therefore, this eventful day in London to all the heart-rending anxieties of politicians, who, I think, have as hopeful a prospect of disappointment as ever politician had. I cannot bring myself to regret that I am not to serve under Marquis Wellesley or Mr. Canning.... We shall now see what this singular association of statesmen will be able to do. Canning is *for* Orders in Council, Grenville considers them as the source of all the existing national distress. Grenville thinks the country incapable of sustaining the expenditure of the war: Wellesley thinks such war to be starved by our penury. Grey is against all secret influence; Prinney says he will part with his life rather than his household. Prinney, Wellesley and Canning have each betrayed everybody they have had to do with—pretty companions for a man of honor like Grey!... Prinney will not strike yet to Grey and Grenville without conditions to which they will not submit.... I flatter myself both Tierney and Huskisson are to be Cabinet Ministers, which, considering that Burke and Sheridan, Dunning and [*illegible*] used to be considered as not elevated enough in rank to be admitted into such high company, will be well enough.

I must, upon the whole, condemn Grey as acting most unwisely in putting himself forward as a candidate for power under all the circumstances of the country. He would have done much better to wait till Grenville's death or some other event dissolved the fatal connection with that family. He ought to have let Wellesley and Canning perish in their own intrigues, and he ought to have permitted the old and feeble Government to conduct the country so near its ruin that men could no longer doubt either its condition or the authors of its calamities. In such a case, which would have inevitably arrived, the country and the Crown would have called for his assistance, and in such case only, my belief is, could he have done a permanent good to the country with honor to himself.... Grenville I consider a dead man, and Prinney, Wellesley and Canning are both madmen and villains.... In the meantime, we must have sport. Amongst other things, we must have the Bank made to pay us in specie... which would give you and me £700 per annum more than we have. This would be something like, so we shall see what we shall see.

Richmond Hill, Wednesday, 3rd

I have dilly-dallied so long here that if I don't set out directly I shall not get in time to write you a word, my precious, so I will first fire a little shot at you before I leave this place. William brought us last night just such intelligence as I was prepared to expect from Petty that the

Marquis [Wellesley] had been with Earl Grey and had offered him and his friends *four* seats in the Cabinet; that he himself had condescended to become First Lord of the Treasury, that there must be some limitations of concession to Ireland, with a great variety of other restraints upon the four poor Foxite and Grenville Ministers, the whole of which induced the Earl to give the Marquis the most unqualified rejection of these proposed indignities. Ha! ha! ha! or Oh dear me! which of these exclamations is best suited to the occasion? Is one to laugh at our poor foolish party having so obviously and so fatally for themselves played the game of these villains Wellesley and Canning, or is one to cry at the never-failing success of rascality in this country? Oh how glad I am that I had no hand in making this madman Wellesley preside over the destinies of this country, to sacrifice the thousands of brave lives that he will assuredly do in Spain and Portugal, and to torture by poverty and privations the thousands that will feel the effects of his extravagance in England.

York St., Saturday, June 6th

...In coming up from the House I was much surprised to meet Sam (Whitbread) covered with smiles. He was enquiring where he could find Sheridan....I presumed his trip to town was merely upon private business, and in this persuasion I remained till almost 3 o'clock this morning, when old Sheridan became drunk and communicative. He then told me he had sent an express for Sam, and that the said Sam had been dining at Moira's, with him Sheridan. Further than this he did not tell me, excepting the expression of his own conviction that Sam was the man both for the Prince and the People, and that Wellesley, Canning and Grenville must all be swamped and flung overboard. Was there ever anything equal to this?...If Sam does come in, it must now be upon his own terms, and I cannot think, after all my honest conduct to him, he could desert me....The Whigs evidently know of an offer made to Whitbread, and are as civil to-day as be damned....

Brooks's, Monday, 8th

...I found from Sheridan yesterday just before dinner that Moira was First Lord of the Treasury, and that it was expected that the writs of Canning and others would be moved for to-night in the Commons.... He said he and Whitbread were to dine at Moira's yesterday, and he concluded with his regret that Whitbread was not Chancellor of the Exchequer....I came, of course, here in the evening, and I soon found there was a meeting of the party at Ponsonby's to which, as I had no summons, of course I did not go. I found from people as they returned from this meeting that Whitbread had given great offence by giving his opinion that Grey and Grenville had pushed the thing too far in insisting, under all circumstances of the case, upon the surrender of the household.... This morning brought to my bed a note from Whitbread desiring to see me, which of course I instantly complied with, and from himself I learnt all the particulars of his intercourse with Moira.... Moira produced his plan for revoking Orders in Council, conciliating America by all manner of means, the most rigid economical reform, nay, parliamentary reform if it was wished for: in short every subject was most agreeable and satisfactory.... So far so good... but I have such a devil of new matter pressing upon me I must be off. Huskisson has just announced to people in the streets that Moira's powers are revoked, and that a message is coming from the Prince saying he (Moira) cannot form a Government, and that he has ordered his old servants to proceed with public business.

House of Commons. Same date.

Well, this is beyond anything. Castlereagh has just told us that Moira resigned the commission this morning, and that His Royal Highness had appointed Lord Liverpool Prime Minister. Was there ever anything equal to this? ...

House of Commons, Tuesday, 9th

... There has been a meeting of Government members at Lord Liverpool's house to-day, and he has declared to them the intention of the Government not to oppose the Catholic question as a Government measure, but everybody is to do as he pleases. Of course the measure will now take place and it will be done by Liverpool, Eldon,[3] &c. This convinces me more than ever of the great fault committed by Grey and Grenville in letting their negociations go off about the Household ... but they are all at once so prodigiously constitutional, one almost suspects one's own judgment. They are, at all events, dished for the present, and most lucky will they be to be so, if anything like a rupture with America is now determined upon by that country, because that event, I am positive, gives check-mate at once to the revenue of this country.[4]

House of Commons, Wednesday, 10th

Well, the Doctor succeeds Ryder as Secretary of State for the Home Department; Lord Harrowby succeeds the Doctor; Lord Bathurst suc-

[3] It was done by their party, but not until sixteen years had passed; Liverpool was dead, and Eldon as strongly opposed as ever to emancipation.

[4] War with the United States began exactly nine days after these words were written.

ceeds Lord Liverpool, Bragge Bathurst is Chancellor of the Dutchy—such is the worthy *new* Administration. Is it not capital? so much for 'No predilections' nor yet 'resentments.'

Sydney Smith to Creevey (who had written at Lord Grey's request to desire him to vote for Lord Milton)

June 6th, 1812

Your letter followed me here, where I had come after voting for Lord Milton, one of the most ungainly looking young men I ever saw. I gave my other vote for Wilberforce,[5] on account of his good conduct in Africa, a place returning no members to parliament, but still, from the extraordinary resemblance its inhabitants bear to human creatures, of some consequence. An election out of Westminster is sad work—at the moment of the greatest ferment, York was, in the two great points of ebriety and pugnacity, as quiet as average London at about 3 o'clock in the morning.

Unpleasant rumours began to fly about presently concerning the intentions of the Duke of Grafton, who owned the second seat for Thetford, the Duke of Norfolk and Lord Petre owning the other. Creevey had become the guest of Mr. Bernard Howard at Fornham, near Bury, pending a summons to Liverpool. He was getting nervous about the tricks his colleague in that candidature might play him, for he had learnt already to regard Brougham with considerable distrust.

...Forster speaks very mysteriously about Ossulston's having the Duke's seat (for Thetford) again, which alarmed me not a little. Our neighbour, Marchioness Cornwallis, was passing in her barouche, and calls Howard to the carriage, who was alone in the road.

'And so,' says she, 'the Duke of Grafton turns Mr. Creevey out of Thetford at last.'

'Upon your soul!' says Barny, 'then there's a volley for you, for Mr. Creevey is now at my house, and is to be member for Thetford next Thursday, and for Liverpool the week after.'

So the Gordon *chienne*[6] went off as grumpy as be damned!... Howard is very good to me and I amuse him very much. He is confidential

[5] William Wilberforce [1759–1833], M.P. for Hull, 1780, and for Yorkshire, 1784. An active philanthropist, his name must ever be associated with the suppression of the slave trade.

[6] The Marchioness Cornwallis was daughter of Jane, Duchess of Gordon.

about young Harry and the dukedom, which he evidently expects to be in possession of before long. I see he means never to sell his seats. Jockey does.

Fornham, Sunday, 4th October

Diddy[7] has no letter again to-day from Roscoe,[8] but he expects one by express in the course of the evening. I should not be least surprised if the Liverpool election did not take place to-morrow week, and that in that event I might safely stay over the Thetford one on Thursday.... This express, whenever it comes from Roscoe, will bring with it, of course, some of Brougham's ingenuous remarks.... Bernard Howard is deeply affected with the apparent treachery of my *colleague* [Brougham], and his evident wishes to give me the go-by; but we shall see what we shall see.

The express came that night; a note from Brougham, and a letter from Roscoe with news from Liverpool.

... Gascoigne and Tarleton[9] came here to-day, both indifferently supported, particularly the latter, who came on horseback with only two friends. They are neither of them popular.... Canning, it is said, will make his appearance on Monday.... Gladstone is his commander-in-chief. Believe me, our prospects are very flattering.

Creevey, therefore, had to set out for Liverpool post haste, but found time at every stopping-place to write to his wife. He was duly elected without opposition for Thetford on October 8.

Cambridge, Monday, 5th Oct.

You will be somewhat surprised to see Diddy's handwriting from his favorite University. The accompanying letter from Wm. Roscoe will explain this movement.... Bernard Howard has been as good to me as possible, and *you* would delight in his suspicions of Brougham.... Come, Mr. John Horn, where are my eels and mutton-chops?—Here they are, by Jingo, and the said John, who is an old friend of mine of five and twenty years' standing, says he can give me an excellent bottle of port.—No such thing: I never tasted worse. The chops were, however, damned fair.... I send for the approbation of yourself and my dears, Diddy's colours at Thetford.... To Diddy himself they produce most

[7] Creevey's pet names among his family were Diddy and Mr. Nummy.
[8] William Roscoe [1753–1831], historian, &c.; represented Liverpool in 1806, but lost his seat in 1807.
[9] The old members for Liverpool. Tarleton retired in favour of Canning.

agreeable sensations; they constitute to him a certain seat in parliament, and they remind him of a connection really virtuous, without propitiating a capricious bitch, and without Villain [Brougham] always frightful. So I am as happy as a grig with little *Thet*, and don't care a damn for Liverpool my little *Pet*.

Arrived in Liverpool, Creevey was plunged into the thick of a hot contest, the details whereof are of little interest at this day. At that period, the poll remained open for many days, generally a fortnight, and Creevey reported progress every night to his wife at Brighton. Brougham succeeded at first in reassuring him as to his good faith.

Liverpool, 11th Oct.

...I must say Brougham behaves as well as a man can possibly do, and I am every day more struck with the endless mine of his intellectual resources. Nevertheless his speech to the crowd yesterday was thought not near so good as mine.... The people *pet* me in a way that is, upon my soul, affecting....

14th October

...We had an excellent day yesterday: Sefton, Stanley, Brougham, Roscoe, Ashton, Heywood, &c., &c. To be sure it is quite astonishing to see the superiority of our friends over those of the enemy as to rank and good manners and then they do behave so perfectly to one, it is quite beautiful...Sefton has really been most interesting to me since breakfast in discussing the education of his son, Lord Molyneux, who is sixteen years of age, at Eton and a tutor with him. Who would think that these people (meaning him and my lady), in the midst of their eating and drink and play and racing, &c., &c., are eternally at work in the education of their children?...My lady is greatly touched at my writing to you every day, and praises me much for it....

Thursday, 18th Oct.

Well, my pretty, Diddy and Brog-ham are fairly done—beat to mummy; but we are to take the chance of some miracle taking place in our favor during the night, and are not to strike till eleven or twelve or one to-morrow. We had to do with artists who did not know their trade. Poor Roscoe made much too sanguine an estimate of our strength....

Creevey and Brougham withdrew from the contest next day, Creevey being at the bottom of the poll with 1,060 votes, but claiming a moral victory.

Croxteth Park, 17th Oct., 1812

Now for the first time since Diddy left home, can he sit down in quietness to write to his pretty.... As to the result of the campaign, disastrous as it is in the extent of the defeat, it is impossible to consider the whole as unfavorable to me. In the first place, my friends will have no occasion for their *compassion* for my being out of parliament. This is everything to begin with. Then I have begun a connection with the town of Liverpool to be used or not at my discretion on future occasions.... Canning, in the present state of things, *must* be shortly in office, and then he vacates, and I never will believe that as a Minister of State he will submit to the club canvassing.... You never saw a fellow in your life look so miserable as he has done throughout.... I have been perfectly amazed during this campaign at the marvellous talent of Brougham in his addresses to the people. He poured in a volley of declamation against the *immortal memory of Pitt* the day before yesterday, describing his immortality as proclaimed by the desolation of his own country and the subjugation of mankind, that, by God, shook the very square and all the houses in it from the applause it met with. Yesterday he renewed the subject by a comparison of Fox with Pitt, that was done with equal skill and success. Still, I cannot like him. He has always some game or underplot out of sight—some mysterious correspondence—some extraordinary connection with persons quite opposite to himself.

Knowsley, 19th Oct.

...We are all mighty gracious here. My lady [Derby] told me before we went in to dinner yesterday to sit with my best ear next to her.... We sat down 22 to dinner, all of them Hornbys, except 4 Hortons, 2 Ramthornes, young Ashton and myself. My lord was in excellent spirits, and, for *such* company, it went off all very well.... I never saw Lady Stanley looking so well, or in such good spirits. She and her lord are damned attentive to Diddy, so upon the whole, you know, it is very well he came.... I won a shilling last night, I'd have you know, and then ate some shrimps, and Lady Derby would have some negus made for me alone; and all the toadys laughed very much, because my lady did, so it was all very well....

There is beginning to be damned distress in Liverpool already, and if the Americans will but continue the war for a twelvemonth, Masters Canning and Gascoigne and their supporters will have enough of it.

...Let me not omit to mention to you that Col. Gordon,[10] who you

[10] Alexander Gordon, brother of the 4th Earl of Aberdeen. He was aide-de-camp to the Duke of Wellington, and was killed at Waterloo.

know is with Wellington, is in constant correspondence with both Grey and Whitbread, and that his accounts are of the most desponding cast. He considers our ultimate discomfiture as a question purely of time, and that it may happen on any day, however early; that our pecuniary resources are utterly exhausted, and that the [*illegible*] of the French in recovering from their difficulties is inexhaustible; that Wellington himself considers this resurrection of Marmont's broken troops as an absolute miracle in war, and in short Gordon considers that Wellington is in very considerable danger.[11] Of course you will not use this information but in the most discreet manner.

Brougham to Creevey[12]

Nov. 4

Pray did it strike you that Sam [Whitbread] is *well pleased* at all of us being out? Among other marks, I was with him about a week and he never said a syllable by way of condolence or regret at my being out, or Romilly &c.

The Holland House folks, I plainly perceive from some things, don't relish attacks on Pitt....

Creevey took his defeat with equanimity, falling back upon his seat at Thetford. Not so Brougham, who could not but feel sore at his exclusion from an arena where he felt so well qualified to excel. And when Brougham felt sore, he made it his business to make others smart also; never did he forgive Grey for the philosophy with which that gentleman accepted Brougham's departure from Parliament.

Henry Brougham to Creevey

The Hoo, 1812

...Should I (being quite certain that I am *out* for good, inasmuch as I see no possible seat and have received from all the leaders, except Grey, regular letters of dismissal, thanking me for past services, &c.) *should I take parliamentary practice or not?* My first intention was quite clear agt. it; for, tho' I don't affect to say a large bit of money would be dis-

[11] Marmont having been defeated at Salamanca on July 22, Wellington occupied Madrid. But on October 21 he was forced to raise the siege of Burgos and begin his retreat upon the Portuguese frontier, which partook more of the nature of disaster than any operation ever undertaken by him.

[12] Taken in from *Creevey's Life & Times*, p. 65. J. G.

agreeable, yet gold may be bought too dear, and I don't like to lower myself, either in Parlt. or the country, to Adam's level. I never hesitated on this till I began to get angry with the leading Whigs for their cool way of taking leave [of me]; as much as to say—it is out of the question our ever bringing you in again. This has rather raised my spleen, and given me an inclination to go into that line and make enough to buy a seat (with what I can afford to add, viz. £2000 or £2500), and then come in and enjoy the purest of all pleasures—at once do what I most approve of in politics and give the black ones an infernal licking every other night! Now really this is my only inducement, and I am half doubting about it. My judgment tells me *not* to go into Committee practice; but what do you think? I own I shall be pleased if you are as clear agt. it as I feel; but pray give your opinion *with dispatch*....

chapter six

1813–1814

THE TORIES CAME back triumphant from the polls in 1812. Lord Liverpool had succeeded Perceval as Prime Minister; although Canning remained still an ominous, brooding figure on the skirts of the party. Castlereagh had succeeded Wellesley at the Foreign Office, and his charming manner and amiability stood him in far better stead as leader of the House of Commons than greater rhetorical gifts could have done. Moreover, his able and far-sighted conduct of foreign policy, coupled with the favourable progress of the Peninsular campaign, impressed men at last with the conviction that Napoleon had overshot his mark, and that the will of England was to be enforced. Under these depressing circumstances, the old Whigs inclined to withdraw from active hostilities in Parliament; while the Radicals—'the Mountain,' as they delighted to call themselves—cast about for some new weapon of offence against the hated Administration. There was one ready to their hand—one that was to serve them for many a year to come; and it was Brougham, though without a seat in Parliament, who best saw its value and how it was to be wielded.

It were an unpleasant and unnecessary task to repeat the unlovely story of the Prince Regent's married life. It is enough to remember that, in order to please his father, George III, and induce him to pay his debts, the Prince married Princess Caroline of Brunswick in 1795. She never was an agreeable woman; there never was the slightest affection between them, and, after the birth of their only child, Princess Charlotte, they separated; and the Prince, among many other less venial loves, returned to Mrs. Fitzherbert, whom he had solemnly married in 1786 and for whom, as Creevey has already explained in these papers, he maintained a remarkable establishment at Brighton and in London. Meanwhile, the Princess of Wales resided at Blackheath, and the profligate life of her husband sufficed to attract to her a large share of popular commiseration.

In 1806, owing to manifold indiscretions of this unfortunate Princess, a Commission of twenty-three Privy Councillors was appointed, at her husband's instance, to inquire into her conduct. She was acquitted on the charge of having borne an illegitimate child, though censure was passed upon her mode of life. George III refused to allow Princess Charlotte to be taken out of her mother's custody, but when the kindly old King became hopelessly mad, the power passed into the hands of the Regent, who forbade his wife to see her daughter more than once a fortnight.

After the general election of 1812, it was obvious that the Opposition had no further grounds for hope from their ancient friendship with the Prince Regent. He had thrown them overboard, as he never hesitated to do anybody who had ceased to be useful or amusing to him. Brougham, therefore, who had been presented to the Princess of Wales in 1809, and who perceived how the sympathy excited by her unfortunate position might be made to reflect odium upon Ministers, and at the same time to injure the Prince Regent, proffered his legal services to the Princess. Associated with him was Whitbread, who, however little may be thought of his discretion, was probably perfectly disinterested and sincere in desiring that justice should be done. Acting under the advice of these counsellors, after waiting in vain for an answer to her letter to her husband, the Princess caused the said letter to be published in the *Morning Chronicle*. The result was the appointment of another commission of three and twenty Privy Councillors, who, by 21 votes to 2, supported the Prince's decree about the intercourse that should be permitted between his wife and daughter. From this time forward Brougham, receiving the means of avenging the treatment of the Whigs by the Prince Regent and, at the same time, making political capital out of the Princess's wrongs, became indefatigable in the cause. He and Whitbread drew to themselves the cordial support of the Radicals, who waxed indignant with the old Whigs by reason of their constitutional scruples in taking action against the Regent. Thus the schism in the Opposition grew ever deeper; nor was it any part of Brougham's plan that it should be healed, so long as he should be out of Parliament. He wrote incessantly to Creevey about the varying phases of the case, which it would be wearisome and unprofitable to follow in detail.

Lady Holland to Mrs. Creevey

Holland House, Wednesday.

...Lord Darlington is to marry his *bonne amie* Mrs. Russell, *alias* Funnereau, this week;[1] and his daughter has chosen Mr. Forester. Neither of these alliances are brilliant. Mme. de Stael continues to be an invariable topick. The servants at assemblies announce her as *Mrs. Stale*. Her daughter, the *seduisante Albertine*, is very much relished by those who know her well.

Holland House [*no date, 1813*]

...I have seen few people and heard no news....Lt. Clifford (the Dss. of D.'s son[2]) is to marry Lord John Townshend's 2nd daughter: Ld. Clinton Miss Poyntz. The report at Windsor is that Princess Charlotte is in a bad state of health—a fixed pain in her side, for which she wears a perpetual blister; and she is grown very large and is generally unwell. The Duke of York was so tipsy at [*illegible*] that he fell down and was blooded immediately, and whilst the Queen was delivering her warlike manifesto, the little Pss. was making game and turning her back upon her....Poor Courtenay has had a paralytick stroke, and Nollekens the sculptor is very ill from the same dreadful visitation. Ld. Lauderdale's eldest daughter was 8 days in labour of a dead child, and was not out of danger when he wrote.

Henry Brougham to Creevey

Brougham, Sept. 15, 1813

...Your account of the Brighton festivities is invaluable. I am glad to be prepared for the Jockey, with whom I shall certainly take the earliest opportunity of beginning the subject, in order to make him admit before witnesses his having had his journey to Brighton for his pains, and thus to confirm his hatred of P....I beg to remind you of my predictions, viz. Wellington's retreat in Novr. or Decr., and a separate peace on the continent before Xmas, tho' he clearly will never make such terms now as he used to do formerly.[3]...

[1] They were married on July 28. Lord Darlington was created Duke of Cleveland in 1833.

[2] Admiral Sir Augustus Clifford, Bart., C.B., died in 1877.

[3] The prediction was not fulfilled. Soult was driven across the Pyrenees on August 2; San Sebastian fell on the 31st; the battle of the Nivelle was fought on November 10; Wellington went into winter quarters early in December on French soil; Napoleon abdicated on April 6, 1814.

Hon. H. G. Bennet, M.P., to Creevey

Chillingham, 24th Sept., 1813

I have been looking out for a letter from you to tell me all the news of the south, and your *fêtes* at the Pavilion, at which I conclude you were, being in such favour with our magnanimous Regent! In the 1st place—is it true that Parliament is to be assembled on the 4th of November? If so, I am in despair, as in town I cannot be, and to be out of it will drive me wild. Money, I conclude, is the want, and as I feel disposed to have a fight for every shilling, and to state a grievance for each vote in supply, I am miserable at the chance of the campaign opening without me. To be sure, affairs look better on the Continent, and the capture of St. Sebastian is of the greatest importance to the safety of our army. We grumblers can have nothing to say, but the question of expence nothing can stave off.... To-day Ld. Grey was to have been in the chair at the Fox dinner at Newcastle: this kept me from the dinner, as Ld. Grey and the principles of Mr. Fox have long ago parted company....

The year 1814 was one of great excitement, political and social, in London. In early spring the Russian, Prussian, and Austrian armies entered France, the British army having been already established on the north side of the Pyrenees since the previous autumn. The Allies entered Paris on March 31; a few days later Napoleon abdicated and was allowed to retire to Elba; Louis XVIII was restored to the throne of France, and visited London in May, to be followed in June by the Emperor of Russia, the King of Prussia, and other royalties. The proclamation of peace on May 6 marked the beginning of a series of *fêtes* and rejoicings, which continued at intervals all through the summer. Unfortunately, they served to bring into harsher relief than before the scandalous relations between the Prince Regent and the Princess of Wales. The Queen having commanded two drawing-rooms to be held in June in honour of the foreign royalties, the Princess intimated her intention to appear at one of them; whereupon the Queen wrote to the Princess, informing her that she had received a communication from her son, the Prince Regent, stating that it was necessary he should be present at her court, and that he desired it to be understood, for reasons of which he alone could be the judge, that it was his 'fixed and unalterable determination not to meet the Princess of Wales upon any occasion, either public or private.'

One hundred and fifty years have passed since these events, and what a distance have we travelled in the development of popular judgment! It would not be possible for any prince in these days to trample thus upon public opinion, and to treat in this tyrannical manner a wife whom it had been proved impossible to convict of infidelity. The offence thus offered to public morality and self-respect goes far to account for the profound apprehensions for the monarchy which men of all parties began to entertain in view of the great increase in popular power which parliamentary reform, not to be staved off much longer, must necessarily entail.

Lady Holland to Mrs. Creevey [at Brighton]

Holland House, Saty.

...The great wonder of the time is Mme. de Stael. She is surrounded by all the curious, and every sentence she utters is caught and repeated with various commentaries. Her first appearance was at Ly. Jersey's, where Lady Hertford also was, and looked most scornfully at her, pretending her determination not to receive her as she was an *atheist!* and immoral woman. This harsh resolve was mitigated by an observation very agreeable to the observer—that her personal *charms* have greatly improved within the last 25 years. She (Mme. de Stael) is violent against the Emperor, whom she says, is not a man—'ce n'est point un homme, mais un système'—an Incarnation of the Revolution. Women he considers as only useful 'pour produire les conscrits;' otherwise 'c'est une classe qu'il voudroit supprimer.' She is much less ugly than I expected; her eyes are fine, and her hand and arm very handsome. She was flummering Sheridan upon the excellence of his heart and moral principles, and he in return upon her beauty and grace. She is to live in Manchester Street, and go occasionally to breathe the country air at Richmond Inn.

During the debate on the Swedish treaty, Mr. Ward[4] came into the Coffee House, assigning for his reason that he could not bear to hear Ld. Castlereagh abuse his *Master*; upon which Jekyll said—'Pray, Ward, did yr. *last* Master give you a *character*, or did this one take you without?' Those present describe Ward as being overwhelmed, for, with all his talent, he is not ready at *repartee*, tho' no doubt by this time he has some neat epigrams upon the occasion. Lady Jane has had a return of spitting of blood, and she was blooded twice last week; the pain in her breast is very troublesome, and I much fear she is fast approaching to

[4] Afterwards Lord Dudley.

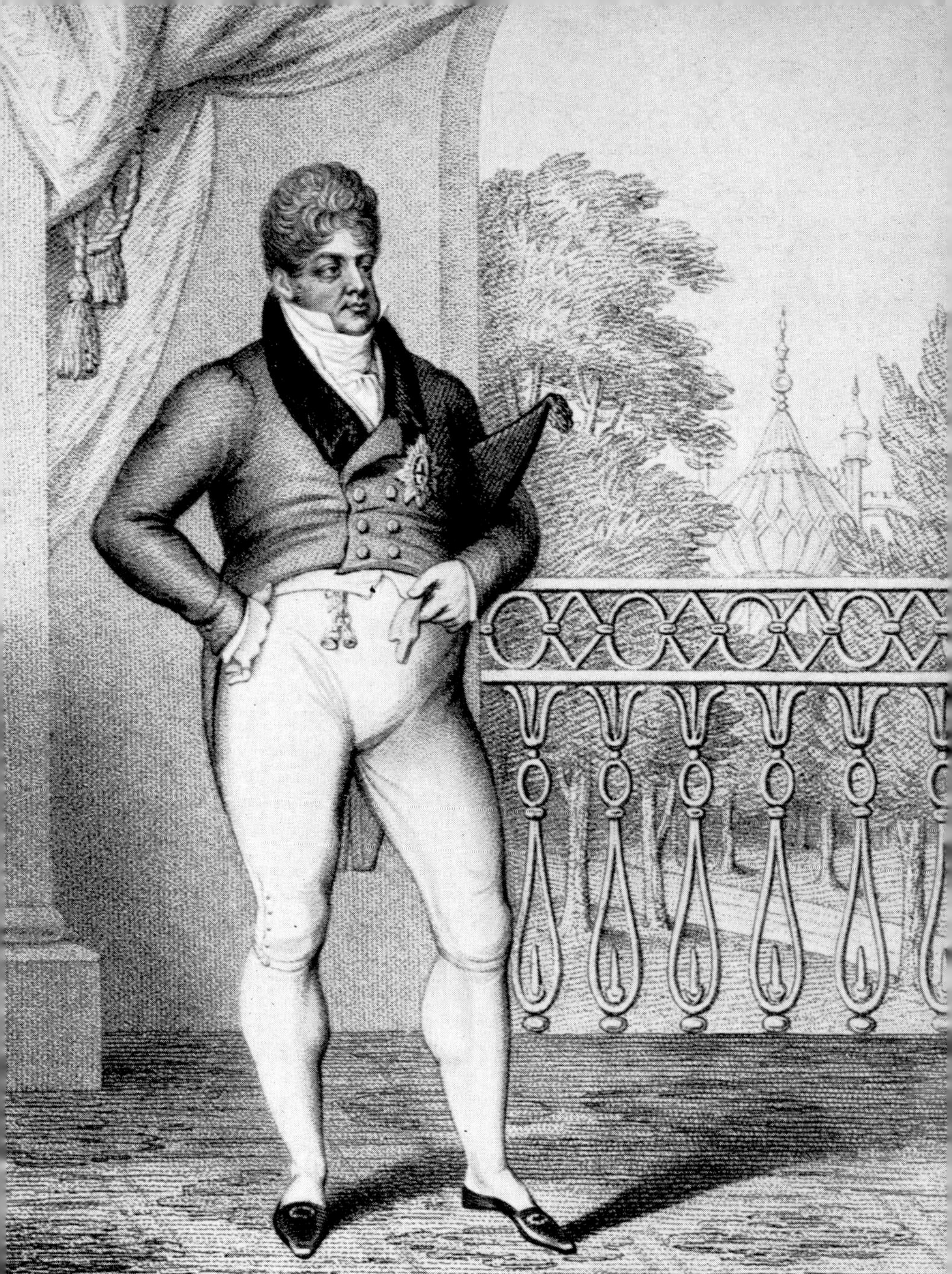

The Prince Regent at the Brighton Pavilion

From a drawing by Isaac Cruikshank

Mrs. Fitzherbert

From a miniature by Richard Cosway

Queen Caroline

From the portrait by James Lonsdale

an untimely close of her innocent and valuable life.[5] There are reports, but I believe idle ones, of marriages between Lady Mildmay and Ld. Folkestone, and Sir Harry [Mildmay] and Miss Thayer. Ld. H. Beauclerk is certainly to marry Miss Dillon. The Greys... are not invited to the *fêtes* at C[arlton] House, nor any more of the Opposition than usual....

Lord Folkestone to Creevey

April 5, 1814

...If you should happen to hear in the world that I am going to be married to Mildmay's *sister*, you need not put yourself to the trouble to deny it. I have not any pretensions to suppose that Mrs. Taylor interests herself enough about me to presume to write to her, but I wish you would tell her from me that I should have been glad to have had an opportunity of informing her in person how immutable with me is the power of *black eyes*.[6]...

Thomas Sheridan[7] to Samuel Whitbread, M.P.

[*April, 1814*]

Bonaparte has signed his resignation—Bourbons proclaimed—Victor, Ney, Marmont, Abbé Sieyes, Caulincourt, &c., &c., &c., have sign'd. The Emperor has a pension of 200,000 per ann.: and a retreat in the Isle of Elba.... There are to be immense rejoicings on Monday—white cockades and tremendous illumination. Carlton House to blaze with fleurs de lis, &c. The royal yacht is ordered to take the King (Louis)—the Admiral of the Fleet, the Duke of Clarence to command her—all true, honor bright—I am just come from the Prince. TH. S.

Samuel Whitbread, M.P., to Thomas Sheridan

Cardington, April 10, 1814

MY DEAR SHERIDAN,

I thank you for your letter, and I daresay you will not be surprized when I tell you that the Circumstances which have led to, and attend upon, this great Event, are such as to enable me to contemplate it with entire satisfaction.

A Limited Monarchy in France, with Religious Liberty, a Free Press and Legislative Bodies such as have been stipulated for before the Recognition of the Bourbons, leave their Restoration without the possibility

[5] It had been strange if life had long endured in a patient treated for phthisis by blood-letting!

[6] The marriage took place in 1814. Miss Mildmay was Lord Folkestone's second wife.

[7] Son of R. B. Sheridan by his first marriage to Miss Linley.

of Regret in the Mind of any Man who is a Lover of Liberty and a friend to his kind. Paris safe, Bonaparte suffered to depart, after the experiment had been fully tried of effecting a Peace with him, upon terms such as he was mad to reject—'Tis more than I dared to hope!

Then the great Example set of the Fidelity of all His Generals, and of the Armies they commanded, up to the very Moment that He himself gave all up for lost and opened his own Eyes to the consequences of His own desperate Folly, must surely have its effect on the World, and redeems many of the Treacheries Men have committed against their Leaders. I confess it pleases me beyond measure.... God grant us a long and glorious Peace.

If the Regent had but a true friend to tell him that he had only two things to do at home to complete the Happiness and Splendour of this Epoch![8] I hear He says I am the worst Man God Almighty ever formed, except Bonaparte! but I could tell him how to be as justly popular as Alexander himself.[9] ... No Murders, No Torture, No Conflagration—how will the pretty Women of London bear it?

Hon. H. G. Bennet, M.P., to Creevey

Brooks's, 1814

DEAR C.,

Nothing new. The Boneys & Co. are understood to have left Fontainbleau on the road to Italy. What a fall! and what a triumph for sound doctrines of freedom! The Coles look very low. Their chance of office is at 100 per cent. discount, and the Holland Housians are in a sad quandary. Our dinner was good and well managed, and a good spice of Whiggism.... The Duke of Sussex talked very sad stuff: his last feat was the following toast—'Respectability to the Crown, durability to the Constitution and independence to the People!' He talked of the Stuarts and made an odd allusion to their fate and the Bourbons. The King of France is to make his palace at Grillons. He comes to-morrow. ... It is pleasing to see so many happy faces.

Henry Brougham to Creevey

Temple, 1814

DEAR C.,

I write to congratulate you on this most speedy and compleat, as well as favorable termination of the Revolution. I pass over the reasons for approving of it as regards France. These are many—but I

[8] One was the rehabilitation of the Princess of Wales, the other, probably, Roman Catholic Emancipation.

[9] The Emperor Alexander I of Russia, at that time in high favour with the English Whigs.

look chiefly to England. . . . It really appears to me that the game is in the hands of the Opposition. Every charge will now breed more and more of discontent. The dismissal of officers and other war functionaries will throw thousands out of employ, who will sooner or later ferment and turn to vinegar. All this will tell agst. Govt. and the benefits of the peace. The relief from taxes, &c., will never be able to tell much for them.

One should think these things evident enough, and yet the Cole school, and Holland House above all, are in perfect despair. I am, however, glad to find Grey as right and factious as can be. . . . Thanet is exactly in the same spirit tho' he expects nothing from the *folly and moderation* of our friends and their fear of annoying Prinnie. By the way, Ld. Grey dines with Mother P. on Wednesday next to meet the D. of Glo'ster, to the no small annoyance of the Coles.

Lancaster, 1814

. . . As for a seat in Parlt. generally, I should feel that the use of it is nearly gone if the peace is made and discussed. Allow me just to observe in passing (a subject I don't think I have ever alluded to before) the great use of Whig boro's; for, without any extravagant pretensions, I can't help thinking it a little strange that my being left out permanently is, to all appearance, now a settled matter. This is the more odd, because Grey is so decidedly anxious for my coming in. Were I, by any chance, once again in that place, I certainly have some little arrears to settle with more folks than one.

Hon. H. G. Bennet, M.P., to Creevey

Brooks's, Saturday.

. . . The Kings dine with Liverpool to-day—Prinny to-morrow, and with Ld. Stafford on Monday; a review on Tuesday and I believe to Oxford afterwards. Alexander grumbles at the long dinners of the Regent's. I like the Prussians very much; they are the best.

Samuel Whitbread, M.P., to Creevey

June 11, 1814

. . . The Emperor [of Russia] has as yet returned no answer nor returned any civility to the Pss.'s message and letter by St. Leger. *They* [the Princess of Wales, &c.] go to the Opera to-night, and if you were here she would be sure to be well received. Why the Devil are you not here? Brougham will, I suppose, certainly stand for Westminster, which will be favourable to him in the Cry that will be raised for him. You must come and stop as long as you are wanted. The Pss. shall not compromise anything. She is sadly low, poor Body, and no wonder. What a fellow Prinny is!

Brougham entertained the idea of standing for the vacancy in Westminster, but Sheridan was already in the field.

Henry Brougham to Creevey

Temple, 29 June, 1814

Dear C.,

As you may be amused to hear the infinite follies of mankind, I write to say that the Whigs have just discovered Old Sherry to be 'an old and valued friend and an ancient adherent of Fox.' They therefore support him. To be sure, he has ratted and left them—he kept them out of office twice—and he now openly stands on Yarmouth's influence and C[arlton] House, and Ld. Liverpool is supporting him! ...

Creevey to Mrs. Creevey

14 June, 1814

... The Emperor of Russia sent for Lord Grey, Lord Grenville, Lord Holland, Lord Lansdowne and Lord Erskine, and had long conversations with all of them. Lord Grey represents him as having very good opinions upon all subjects, but quite royal in having all the talk to himself, and of vulgar manners. He says the Emperor was much indebted to his sister the Dutchess of Oldenburg for keeping him in the course by her judicious interposition and observations. In truth he thinks him a vain, silly fellow, and this opinion is much confirmed by what the Austrian who is in London now, and who went with Buonaparte to Elba, states to be Buonaparte's opinion as he (the Austrian) heard him deliver it. It seems there is no subject more dealt in by Buonaparte than criticism upon people. He said to this Austrian:—

'Now I'll tell you the difference between the Emperor of Russia and the King of Prussia. The Emperor thinks himself a very clever fellow, and he is a damned fool; whereas the King of Prussia thinks meanly of his own talents, and he is a very sensible man.'

Grey, Holland, &c., &c., agree in their opinion of Buonaparte, in that Buonaparte seems the most popular person possible with all parties, both foreigners and our own grandees. Blücher is a very nice old man, and so like your old friend Lord Grey[10] that Lady Elizabeth Whitbread cried

[10] The 1st Earl.

when she met him at Lady Jersey's. Platoff is so cursedly provoked at the fuss made that he won't accept an invitation to go out. To be sure, as Russ. is the only language he speaks, I don't much wonder at his resolution. They are all sick to death of the way they are followed about, and, above all, by the long dinners. The King of Prussia is as sulky as a bear, and scarcely returns the civilities of the populace.

Prinny is exactly in the state one would wish; he lives only by protection of his visitors. If he is caught alone, nothing can equal the execrations of the people who recognise him. *She*, the Princess, on the contrary, carries everything before her, and had it not been for an accident in her coming into the opera on Saturday night, whilst the applause of the Emperor and King was going on, by which means she got no *distinct and separate applause*, tho' certainly a great deal of what was going on was directed to her. By the bye, I called on her this morning, and saw very different names in her calling book from what I had ever seen before. Lord Rivers was the first name, Lady Burghersh the second, and so on, which, you know, is capital. All agree that Prinny will die or go mad. He is worn out with fuss, fatigue and *rage*. He came to Lady Salisbury on Sunday from his own dinner beastly drunk, whilst her guests were all perfectly sober. It is reckoned very disgraceful in Russia for the higher orders to be drunk. He already abuses the Emperor lustily, and his (the Emperor's) walzing with Lady Jersey last night at Lady Cholmondeley's would not mend his temper, and in truth he only stayed five minutes, and went off sulky as a bear, whilst everybody else stayed and supped and were as merry as could be.

June 21, 1814

Well, my pretty, I hope you admired our little brush last night in the presence of all the foreign grandees except the Emperor.[11] It was really very capitally got up, and you never saw poor devils look so distressed as those on the Treasury Bench. It was a scene well calculated to make the foreign potentates stare as they did, and the little Princes of Prussia laugh as they did.... We have now, however, a new game for Master Prinny, which must begin to-morrow. Whitbread has formal authority from young Prinny[12] to state that the marriage is broken off, and that the reasons are—first, her attachment to this country which she cannot and will not leave; and, above all, her attachment to her mother, whom in her present distressed situation she likewise cannot leave.

[11] The 'brush' was that, knowing the foreign potentates were to be in the Gallery of the House of Commons, Sir M. Ridley was put up by the Opposition to move a resolution respecting the marriage of Princess Charlotte of Wales to the Prince of Orange.

[12] Princess Charlotte.

This is, in short, her letter to the Prince of Orange in taking leave of him, and a copy of this letter is in Whitbread's possession. What think you of the effect of this upon the British publick?

Since writing the last sentence Whitbread has shown me Princess Charlotte's letter to the Prince of Orange. By God! it is capital. And now what do you suppose has produced this sudden attachment to her mother? It arises from the profound resources of old Brougham, and is, in truth, one of the most brilliant movements in his campaign. He tells me he has had direct intercourse with the young one; that he has impressed upon her this fact that, if her mother goes away from England, as she is always threatening to do from her ill usage in the country, that then a divorce will inevitably take place, a second marriage follow, and thus the young Princess's title to the throne be gone. This has had an effect upon the young one almost magical.

Although there is no reference in these papers to the scene in the House of Commons when the Duke of Wellington was admitted to receive the thanks of the House, still it is agreeable to remark that, while Mr. Whitbread and his party had not scrupled to avail themselves of the difficulties of the campaign in the Peninsula as the means of bringing reproach upon the Government and their officers in the field, it was Mr. Whitbread who now objected that the grant to the Duke moved by the Speaker, viz. £10,000 a year, commutable for £300,000, was too small.

Three days later a debate, in which Whitbread took a leading part, arose upon Lord Castlereagh's motion to increase the allowance to the Princess of Wales from £35,000 to £50,000 a year. This was moved and carried in the earnest hope that the Princess would carry out her wish to go to the Continent, and that she would stay there. The removal of this rock of offence to the Ministry was by no means to the liking of the Opposition.

Henry Brougham to Creevey

Temple, 1st July, 1814

Dear C.,

I suppose you have heard of Mother P. bungling the thing so compleatly—snapping eagerly at the cash, and concluding with a civil observation about unwillingness to 'impair the Regent's tranquillity!!' &c. This was all done on the spot and in a moment, and communicated to Sam and me next day, 'that we might be clear of all blame in advising it.' We are of course fully justified in giving her up. I had written a proper letter to the Speaker, refusing, which would only have made the House certain to give it [the grant to the Princess]. The intelligence came before my letter reached her.

However, tho' she deserves death, yet we must not abandon her, in case P. gets a victory after all, therefore I have made her send St. Leger to the Bp. of Lincoln (Dean of St. Paul's) to notify her intention of going in state on Thursday, and demand proper seats for her and her suite. They are trying to fight off, but tho' they may dirty themselves, nothing shall prevent her from going. This is a healing and a good measure.

Again—there is a second letter from Castlereagh, mentioning a bill to 'confirm the arrangement of 1809;' and as this involves separation, it has (as well it may) alarmed her, and now she is all for asking our advice! They *may* make such a blunder, as all along they have blundered; if they do, we are *all alive* again, and shall push it. Say how it strikes you.

As for Westr.—it now appears that Ald. Wood is only making a catspaw of old C[artwright][13] and that he counts on his dying, and leaving a place for him—the Alderman. He has avowed that he would rather see Sheridan, or any court tool, returned than a *Whig in disguise*, viz., me; and he asserts plainly that, on the comparison, 'more is to be hoped from Cart.'s parliamentary talents than from B.'s—the former being greater.' This has opened some eyes—for they justly conclude he can't be really speaking his mind. . . . I can't help fearing Burdett is doing something, but I don't know for certain. Holland House from *personal hatred* [*i.e.* of Brougham] supports Sherry; the Russells and Cavendishes, I understand, quite the contrary. . . .'

The next stage in this intolerable scandal was the refusal to the Princess of a seat in St. Paul's Cathedral on the occasion of the national thanksgiving for peace on July 7.

To the chagrin of the irresponsible members of the Opposition, the Princess of Wales, having declined the increase to her allowance voted by Parliament, left the country in August, for which Brougham bitterly blames Whitbread—unjustly, as far as one can see.

9th Aug., 1814

. . . By G—d, Sam is incurable—all this devilry of Canning, &c., and Mrs. P. bolting, &c., is owing to his d——d conceit in making her give up the £15,000—*of himself*, without saying a word to any one.

[13] John Cartwright [1740–1824], the 'Father of Reform.'

chapter seven

1814–1815

THE PEACE HAVING reopened the Continent to English travellers, Creevey took his wife, who was in failing health, in the autumn of 1814, to spend the winter at Brussels; than which, as affairs turned out, he could scarcely have chosen a less tranquil resting-place for an invalid. There is evidence from his correspondence that Creevey, as a result of his failure at Liverpool and his conviction in the libel action which followed, lost interest in party politics for several years. He was to hunt bigger game in Brussels.

Lord Holland to Creevey [at Brussels]

Holland House, 17th Oct., 1814

The peace, as it is with some stretch of courtesy called, satisfies no one class of people. Those who hate France think enough has not been done to reduce her power of mischief, and those who feel some little sympathy with her from a recollection of the original cause in which she engaged, and to which late events have in some degree brought her back, lament her humiliation, and resent yet more the triumphs of her enemies. When a male child is born, every woman in the house looks an inch higher; and when a legitimate King is restored, every sprig of Royalty in Europe becomes more insolent and insufferable.... I have, I own, a little *tendresse* for the Dutch King whom you laugh at. It does not seem that the Flemish have any....

Brougham to Creevey

Temple, Nov. 24, 1814

DEAR LORD CREEVEY,

I beg to begin by informing you that Lord Binning, the Canningite, is extremely angry to find persons who are *not* lords getting the title in France just as if they were. To learn that this delusion extends to Brussels must drive him mad. As for ... Prinnie, he has been ill in the bladder, on which Sam [Whitbread] said—'God make him worse!'

but this prayer was rejected. Young P.[1] is as ill off as ever—no money, sale of trinkets to pay pensions, &c., an old lady sleeping in the room, &c., &c. The Party are no longer as averse to the subject as Lauderdale would wish and Ly. Holland.... I mentioned above my Paris trip having been most agreeable. I say, after seeing all the rest of Europe from Stockholm to Naples, nothing is to be named in the same year with Paris for delights of every kind and sort.... It is the place to go to and live at: be sure of that.

Temple, 15 Dec., 1814

I delayed writing last Friday in hopes of having better news to give you of Sefton, who had been dangerously ill of an inflammn. of the bladder.... To-day came a letter from himself, which is a picture of the man, to be sure, but gives rise, nevertheless, to much alarm. He concludes by saying he had had a relapse, and been in great jeopardy, and that he had lost 140 ounces of blood in five days. This was in addition to 40 the first attack, besides every sort of discipline—calomel, hot baths, antimony, &c., &c.... After such evacuation by bleeding, I know the cursed effects upon the system, and want him to have the best advice.... My own complaints came, I believe, wholly from the infernal bleeding I had in that country of broken bones and traders and voices—Northumberland; and tho' I bled about a bucket full, it was nothing to this late performance of the Earl.

I put all private feeling out of the question (tho' I don't know why one should, considering the d——d country we have to deal with), and I say that no loss I know would annoy me more at present than his. If he was invaluable before, now that everything like discipline is at an end he is 1000 times more so. You cannot easily conceive... how he rallied, animated, stirred, supported—in short, did all that a man could do who absurdly chose to be silent when he might have done great things in speaking. He was once or twice even on the point of doing *this* also, and I *know must* have succeeded.... I dined yesterday at Coutts's. The last time I had that pleasure (Erskine being there) a difficulty arose about thirteen persons at table; to prevent which, E. being there likewise yesterday, twenty guests were provided; among them Lauderdale, Warrender[2] and his wife. I learnt from W. (and L. seemed to agree), that Prinnie is in a bad way. They have positively ordered him to give up his stays, as the wearing them any longer would be too great a sacrifice to ornament—in other words, would kill him....

[1] Princess Charlotte of Wales.
[2] Sir John Warrender, 5th Baronet of Lochend.

The D. of York dined t'other day at Holland House, and was very gracious. Whether any attempt at getting £200,000 to pay his debts will succeed, is another matter.... A breach between Prinnie and him seems unavoidable, sooner or later, tho' the D.'s discretion will make it more difficult to P. to bring him to a quarrel than most people.

As for Mrs. P., I never for a moment have doubted that a divorce is as impossible as ever. They may buy her; but even that will take time, for we were prepared for such a purpose 3 years ago, and steps were taken to create delays, which must be effectual. However, I don't expect to see the Ministers do such an act of folly, not to mention the situation of the Chancellor, and Canning, and the interests of Hertford House.

As the session approaches, it is natural to feel anxious for your return. It will be a session of detached and unexpected affairs, and full of sport and mischief, after a dull commencement.... Don't believe those who say nobody will come up. Everybody will. Curiosity and idleness will also make everybody attend from 4 to 7 daily,[3] and when have they done more? ... Your coming is indispensable. I could give so many reasons, that I shall give none. You must be over before the 27th Jany.—that is quite certain.... I shall only say everything will depend on a little exertion soon after the meeting. When I tell you that Bennet almost gave up attendance, because Mrs. B. would not allow him to remain later than 6 any night, you will conclude that there are two fools in the world; and, strange to tell, one is a brother of O[ssulston]—the other a Russell.[4] *She* is really too bad. I used to think her a model, till marriage brought her out: *now* she exceeds all belief....

Southill, 28 Dec., 1814

... C. Stuart[5] will do whatever he can to make himself useful to you. ... He is a plain man, of some prejudices, caring little for politics and of very good practical sense. You will find none of his prejudices (which, after all, are little or nothing) at all of an aristocratic or disagreeable kind. He has no very violent passions or acute feelings about him, and likes to go quietly on and enjoy himself in his way. He has read a great deal and seen much more, and done, for his standing, more business than any diplomatic man I ever heard of. By the way—as for *diplomacy*, or rather its foppery, he has none of the thing about him; and if you

[3] In those days the sittings of the House of Commons began at 4 p.m.

[4] The Hon. Henry Bennet, 2nd son of the 4th Earl of Tankerville, and an active member of 'The Mountain,' married, in 1816, Gertrude Frances, daughter of Lord William Russell.

[5] Sir Charles Stuart, G.C.B., British Minister at Brussels, created Baron Stuart de Rothesay in 1828.

ever think him close or buttoned up, I assure you he had it all his life just as much. He has no nonsense in his composition, and is a strictly honorable man, and one over whom nobody will ever acquire the slightest influence. I am so sick of the daily examples I see of havoc made in the best of men by a want of this last quality, that I begin to respect even the *excess* of it when I meet it. I thought you might like to be forewarned of your new Minister, and therefore have drawn the above hasty sketch....

Hon. H. G. Bennet, M.P., to Creevey [at Brussels]

Whitehall, 2 Feby., 1815

Our partys at Taylor's[6] are very flourishing—the veal tree in full fruit—and I go there every night. All the party (tree as well) send their remembrances to you. Taylor is steady with Prinny for the session, as he has been told that Py. said the other day—'he loved no man so well.' Is not this provoking? that so good a man shd. be so duped.

Henry Brougham to Creevey

Temple, Jan. 17, 1815

...Liverpool (the town) is all in an uproar (indeed I might say the same of the man of that name) about the property tax. *We* shall do them to a certainty. Our friends are in much force on the American peace and renewal of their trade, and the Scotchman (Gladstone) at a woful discount, having become odious to all parties. His letters in the newspapers boldly denying the receiving a communication from Jenky[7] on the property tax (and which he now explains away, I understand, by a quibble) are quite fatal with a 'generous and open-hearted publick,' who never understand special pleading, and are very ready to confound it with lying. Accordingly, I expect to see severe handling at the approaching meeting called by a large requisition, at the head of which are 'Earl of Sefton and W. Roscoe, Esq.' S. will be good on the *backbone*, and the *pautriot* will have much to urge....Erskine is K.T., and says he passes the happiest hours of his life at the Pavillion, which is like enough, if his w——e knocks him down before his son as she lately did.

March 8, 1815

...I must repeat my intreaties that if *you can* at all make it convenient to come even for a fortnight *this* session after Easter, you should

[6] Michael Angelo Taylor's, a constant rendezvous of the Whig party. Mr. Taylor was an importunate candidate for a peerage.

[7] The Premier, Lord Liverpool.

do so. *Whitbread cannot* tell you how much you are wanted, because he is quite satisfied all is right when he is there himself....

The deliberations of the Congress of Vienna, where Wellington was British Plenipotentiary, were verging upon violent rupture, owing to the anxiety of every Continental Power either to increase its own dominions or to diminish those of its neighbour. The disputants had gravitated into two hostile groups, wherein Russia and Prussia, supporting Murat, King of Naples, in his aggression on the Papal States, were ranged against Great Britain, France, and Austria. Suddenly, at the beginning of March, all these disputes were hushed to silence in the imminence of common peril. Napoleon had escaped from Elba and landed in France. The Hundred Days had begun.

Hon. H. G. Bennet to Creevey [at Brussels]

Upper Brook St., 3rd April, 1815

...You are at the fountain head of all the continental projects. Here we are certainly for war: the old doctrines of there being no security for peace with Napoleon are again broached, and you hear all repeated, which one had almost forgot, of the nonsense of 1793. Parties are making on these subjects, and they are as you may imagine. Ld. Grenville started furious for war, or at least declaring there was no chance of avoiding it. A correspondence has taken place between him and Grey, who is anxious for peace, which has considerably softened the Bogey, and now he [Grenville] declares that his opinions are not made up, but that he shall await further information. So much is gained by Grey's firmness, who is behaving very well.... Prinny, of course, is for war: as for the Cabinet, Liverpool and Ld. Sidmouth are for peace; they say the Chancellor[8] is not violent the other way; but Bathurst, Castlereagh, &c., &c., are red hot, and if our allies will concur and the plans do not demand too much money, war we shall have. Sam is all for Boney, and the Slave Trade decree has done something. We consider here that the Jacobins are masters at Paris, and let them and the free press and the representative government come from that source. Leave them to themselves, and quarrel they will; but war will unite every soul, particularly if upon the cursed motives of the high party.... However, all the world of all parties speak of Ney with abhorrence, as his offers to the King—from whom he got everything, double the money he demanded, &c.—

[8] Lord Eldon.

were all made with a firm determination to betray him. He said, among other things, that he would bring Napoleon in a cage: to which the King replied—'Je n'aimerais pas un tel oiseau dans ma chambre!' Chateaubriand has also declared for Napoleon, and made a speech in his favour in the same style of nonsense and blasphemy for which the Bourbons had named him Minister to Sweden.

Most brilliant court at the Tuilleries, and the French say 'L'Empereur est la bonté même.' They would say the same of the devil; but if I was a Frenchman, I should be all for Napoleon.... The Guards have marched this morning to embark at Deptford for Ostend. I consider they will be there in two days. The fellows went off in high spirits, as it is known here that beer, bread, meat and gin are cheap in Flanders....

From Creevey's Journal

Brussels, Sat., April 22, 1815. I met this night at Lady Charlotte Greville's, amongst various other persons, the Duke of Wellington, and he and I had a conversation to which most of those present became parties. He maintained that a Republick was about to be got up in Paris, by Carnot, Lucien Buonaparte, &c., &c., &c. I asked if it was with the consent of the *Manager* Buonaparte, and what the nature of the piece was to be. He said he had no doubt it would be *tragedy* for Buonaparte, and that they would be at him by stiletto or otherwise in a very few weeks. I, on the contrary, thought the odds were in favor of the old performer against the new ones, but my Lord would have it B. was to be done up out of hand at Paris: so *nous verrons*. I thought several times he [Wellington] must be drunk; but, drunk or sober, he had not the least appearance of being a clever man. I have seen a good deal of him formerly, and always thought the same of his talents in conversation. Our conversation was mightily amicable and good, considering our former various sparring bouts in the House of Commons about Indian politics.

Hon. H. G. Bennet, to Creevey [at Brussels]

May 31, 1815

...We, the Mountain, are in hopes the Grenvilles are about to part company. Ld. Buckingham holds very warlike language abroad and is for peace against the Ministers, so we are not to be fettered or controuled; and this even on Althorpe's motion about Prinny's [*illegible*] the £100,000 outfit. The Grenvilles swear either to vote against us or not to attend. I mean one of these fine days to fire a shot at them when they are sheering off, and I cannot tell you how joyful I feel at the chance of it. You may depend upon it the Marquess wishes to be a Duke,[9] and he is looking sharp after Stafford's patent, with which Ld. G. Leveson's earldom is soon to come forth;[10] but I don't think that the Government are at all pleased at our division. They put off the debate till that of the Lords was over to try the effect of Bogey's speech;[11] but it had but little, and so far from it lessening Sam's minority, you see we rose from 72 to 92. The Treasury Bench thought we might divide 80, but none calculated on more. We hope it may tell with the foreigner: it does much here. Grattan, after all, was no great thing—full of wit and fire and folly—more failures than success in his antithesis, and his piety and religious cant was offensive, as, after all, whatever may be its merit in an individual, it is only used in a speech for the worst of purposes.

Enclosed in this letter was the following list of 'the Mountain':—

Milton.	Wynn, Sir Watkin.
Balem.	Mallem.
Plunket.	Fremantle.
Pelham.	F. Lewis.
Grattan.	Gower, Lord.
Baring.	Calvert.
Baring, Sir T.	Knox.
Wrottesley.	S. Smith.
Carew.	Smith.
Wynn.	

Bennet to Creevey

Whitehall, June 13

Why, what a fellow you are! have you not received my two last letters that you complain so? Sam complains too, and he sends you his *respects*, for you never write to him, and he says you ought to do so, for you have nothing to do but to lounge. He has not been well—his old attack, but he looks better, and is so. I hope soon he will get out of town, and we shall have our release from that damned place the H. of C., where we spend our time, health and fortunes.... We all congratulate you at the recovery of your senses, as we thought the Great Lord[12] had bit you, and that he, [*illegible*] and the Frog[13] had got you quite over, and that you

[9] The 2nd Marquess of Stafford, created Duke of Sutherland in 1833.

[10] Lord Granville Leveson-Gower, created Viscount Granville August 12, 1815, and Earl Granville in 1833.

[11] Lord Grenville's.

[12] Wellington.

[13] The King of Holland.

really believed Boney was to be eat up alive; but from all we hear from Paris he has a great army, and that things are disturbed in La Vendée, &c., &c. Yet I put my confidence in the Jacobins, and if they act, all the youth of France will come out with them, and then let me see the state your Kings will be in. For my part, if I thought they [the Kings] could succeed, I shd. be miserable; it is only their entire failure that keeps me in tolerable humour.... It is quite impossible but that our finances must, if Boney be not overthrown this year, give way, and our dividends cease.... The Loan is taken this day, I hear, at 54, so you see to what a state our finances have sunk.

The agony of apprehension—the scuffle of preparation—which swept over Europe during the terrible Hundred Days, when, regiment by regiment, the French army rallied to the returned Emperor, can never lose their hold upon the reader of history. The dismay among English residents and holiday-makers in Brussels, their precipitate flight, and the scenes of undignified confusion and panic which accompanied it, can never be more vividly or more truthfully depicted than in the pages of *Vanity Fair*. Still, Thackeray wrote from hearsay. Distant though that day may be from our own, it has lost little of its interest for us of the present. One is grateful to one who, like Creevey, actually witnessed the mighty drama, and was at the pains to record his experiences. From the moment when, on April 5, the Duke of Wellington arrived in Brussels from Vienna to take command of the allied forces in Belgium, it was apparent that these must act on the defensive, much as their commander desired to take the initiative. Of the 700,000 troops of which he had written on March 24 to his brother, Sir Henry Wellesley, as ready to be massed on the French frontier 'in about six weeks,' none were yet at hand. The Russians were advancing slowly through Poland; the Austrians had their hands full with Murat in Italy; of the Prussians, only 30,000 were near enough to co-operate with the Duke's composite array of 24,200, whereof but 4,000 were British, mostly recruits. The choice of battleground, then, lay with Napoleon, not with the Powers. Everything depended upon how soon he could make ready to strike.

He wasted no time. It was not his custom to squander that priceless element of successful war. Entering Paris on March 20, he had at his disposal in the first week of June a regular army of 312,400, and an auxiliary force of 222,600—in all, 535,000 men. By that time Wellington's forces also had been considerably augmented; but how different was their quality from the army he had dispersed in the south of France the year before—the army of which he proudly said in after-years it was 'fit to go anywhere, and do anything'! The actual composition of his force in Belgium on June 13 was this:

British	31,253
King's German Legion	6,387
Hanoverians	15,935
Dutch-Belgians	29,214
Brunswickers	6,808
Nassau Contingent	2,880
Engineers, Staff Corps, etc.	1,240
	91,717

Napoleon left Paris on June 12 to join his army on the Belgian frontier. On the 14th his headquarters were at Beaumont, about sixteen miles south of Charleroi, with his five *corps d'armée*, numbering 126,000 of all arms, well within reach of his personal command.

Thus much to show the position outside Brussels. Creevey and his correspondents throw some light upon the aspect of affairs within that capital. Doubtless he would have removed his wife from a scene so little suited to an invalid, and have joined the stream of migrating English before the French crossed the frontier, had not Mrs. Creevey's state of health made it the lesser of two evils to remain where she was.

First come a series of hurried, clandestine notes from Major Hamilton, who married the eldest Miss Ord, and was on General Barnes's staff.

Major Hamilton to Creevey

Brussels, Thursday, 4 p.m. [*about 18th March*]

MY DEAR MR. CREEVEY,

If you will not blab, you shall hear all the news I can pick up, bad and good, as it comes. I am sorry to tell you bad news to-day. General Fagal writes from Paris to say that Bonaparte may be in that capital ere many days. His army encreases hourly; and as fast as a regiment is brought up to the neighbourhood of Lyons, it goes over to its

Mrs. Creevey

From a contemporary miniature

Thomas Creevey

From a contemporary watercolour drawing

Place Royale, Brussels

From an engraving by A. Cruse after J. Fussel

Regent Street

From a contemporary print

old master. Soult is said to have promised not to act *against* the King, but that his obligations to Bony would not allow him to take part against the latter. Thus saying, he resigned to Louis the office of War Minister, and the man who now holds it said he would only do so so long as the Chamber of Deputies were in favor with the nation. Fagal, take notice, is an alarmist, and I hope our next accounts will not be so gloomy a nature.

Yours,
A. H.

March 20th, 1 o'clock

Bonaparte is at Fontainebleau with 15,000 men, every man of whom he can depend upon, because every man is a volunteer, and they have risked all for his sake. The Royal army is at Melun, consisting of about 28,000 men, National Guards, &c., &c., included—not a man of whom can be relied on. This is the critical moment; for if they allow him to enter Paris without a battle, all is over. I feel that I am not acting imprudently in thus stating facts, which naturally Mrs. Creevey must be made acquainted with.... Wherever we may be ordered to bend our course, I shall always have it in my power to give you such information as you may see necessary to ask for.

March 22nd

There is no news this morning. All communication with Paris is at an end, and we now look with anxiety for the arrival of Lord Wellington.

March 22, 11 p.m.

...The unfortunate Louis 18th was at Abbeville yesterday, and has sent to the General commanding at Lille to know if it would be safe for him to go there. Baron Trippe has gone off to Lille to ascertain the answer....2000 men still remain with Louis.

Friday, 4 p.m.

I am sorry my news still continues bad, indeed worse to-day than ever. The people of Paris seem to think all is lost, and await the entry of Bonaparte as a circumstance not to be prevented. Marshal Macdonald has acted with the utmost loyalty, but all his influence and exertions have been unavailing. His men have told him to 'go back to the King, to remain faithful to him if he pleases, but that they would go over to the Emperor.' The troops have refused on every occasion to fire at Bonaparte's force, or to make any resistance. He has gone to Dijon. The

Government has no good information, for the very persons who are sent to gain intelligence go over to the enemy.

Matters are not so well with ourselves here as they might be, inasmuch as the Belgians at Mons evince a bad spirit. Dorneburg, who commands that garrison, is a determined and good officer, and has a corps of the German Legion near him should circumstances require aid. A letter from Lille speaks favorably of the good spirit prevailing amongst the inhabitants; but alas! if the soldiers do not hold to their allegiance, what can be expected? Pray do not blab; for although all this may have come to your knowledge through other channels, yet it would not do for *me* to have the name of a news-giver.

In haste, much yours,

A. H.

10 p.m., Saturday

The only good news is the spirit which seems to prevail amongst the people, particularly at Marseilles.... Everything looks gloomy; I fear that my dispatch of to-morrow will announce Bony to be not many leagues from Paris. The big-wigs are now together, and I shall have more to tell you at 12 o'c.

Sunday, 2 p.m.

Old Fagal seems to have recovered very much from his fright. He now says Bony is still at Lyons—that the best spirit prevails throughout France, and that affairs seem to wear a brighter aspect. 3000 Dutch troops are on their march to reinforce this army.

[No date], 5 o'clock

The Prince [of Orange] is just now returned, you shall know what news he brings from Tournay.

Dorneburg is a good officer, and has much judgment and experience. He commands at Mons.

Halket commands at Courtray; has a fine British brigade and is a gallant soldier.

Old Alten has the Cavalry at Ypres, with the 52nd and 69th British, and 4 of the Hanoverian battalions: all good stuff. 7000 Royalists from France, first to bleed, are outside the Belgic frontier; and will give us notice, *by their running away*; but until WE begin to run, Mrs. Creevey need not fancy the French are in Bruxelles; and, *for her sake*, may they never be is the very sincere wish of

Yours,

A. H.

Saturday

Headquarters remain here for the present. The Prince [of Orange] brings no news. All is quiet. Lord March was sent to find out where the King was on the 24th. His Majesty was not at Bruges, and *the Earl returned*. If Lord Wellington comes in a day or two *or three*, how Mrs. Creevey will crow over all the world! For, rest satisfied, if Bony does not push to-morrow (which he *cannot* do) his game for the present is up, and a stand can be made on the ground we occupy, with the troops hourly expected from Ostend, *and with the Patrone*![14]

26th, 10 p.m.

A Russian general arrived this day at Mons who left Paris on the 24th. Bonaparte was to review *his* troops on this day. The General saw no troops on the road but one regiment, and it was marching on Paris. A General from the Prussian army (Röder) has been sent here by Kliest to remain at our headquarters. A great deal of *talk*, much communication, aides-de-camp from the Duc de Berri—from the King—from Victor; in short, all parties seem to have lost their heads, and instead of getting troops together, they *talk* about it. It is hoped that Dunkirk is not yet in Boney's possession. If not, it will form a good flanking position in case of Boney not succeeding in his first attack on our line.

Wellington took up the command of the allied forces in Belgium on April 5. There is nothing from Creevey's pen until the crisis of the campaign was upon Europe.

From Creevey's Journal

June 16. Friday morning, ½ past two.—The girls just returned from a ball at the Duke of Richmond's. A battle has taken place to-day[15] between Buonaparte and the Prussians: to what extent is not known; the result is known, however, to be in favour of the French. Our troops are all moving from this place at present. Lord Wellington was at the ball to-night as composed as ever.

Reminiscences, written in 1822

A number of incidents contained in Creevey's letters and journals of this period were afterwards thrown into a consecutive form by him, together with many not elsewhere recorded.

[14] Wellington.

[15] Writing early in the morning of the 16th, he refers to Napoleon's passage of the Sambre on the 15th and the capture of Charleroi.

Cantley, July 28, 1822.—I became a member of the House of Commons in 1802, and the moment a man became such then, if he attached himself to one of the great parties in the House—Whigs or Tories—he became at once a publick man, and had a position in society which nothing else could give him. I advert particularly to such persons as myself, who came from the ranks, without either opulence or connections to procure for them admission into the company of their betters.

The account of Buonaparte's conversation with O'Meara at St. Helena, which is just published, is so infinitely curious and interesting that they present a very favorable occasion to me for committing to paper general facts within my own knowledge, more or less connected with some of the events to which he refers. Most of these facts I have already recorded, either in letters to my friends at the time, or by occasional journals; but they are all as distinctly in my recollection at present as if they had happened yesterday.

In the autumn of 1814, Mrs. Creevey, her two eldest daughters (the Miss Ords) and her second and young son, Mr. Charles Ord, and myself went to Brussells, where we took a house for a term.... We found Brussells full of our London Guards; our cavalry and other troops were quartered up and down the country. Having spent our winter very merrily with our English officers, and others who had arrived there in great abundance, about the 8th of March, 1815, I think it was, we first heard of Buonaparte's escape from Elba. At the time the young Prince of Orange was Commander-in-Chief of our forces in Brussells; General Sir Edward Barnes was Adjutant General of the army, and Sir Hudson Lowe Quartermaster General. We remained nearly a fortnight in great suspense as to what was to be the result of this enterprise of Buonaparte. Since our arrival in Brussells I have formed a sufficiently intimate acquaintance with General Barnes to be quite sure of learning from him the earliest intimation of any movement of our army. One of the aides-de-camp, too, the late Col. Hamilton, had already formed an attachment to Miss Ord, which in 1815 ended in their marriage.... It was on the 24th March, I think, in the morning, that he came to tell us that in all probability Buonaparte had passed the preceding night at Lille, and might be reasonably expected at Brussels in two days' time, and that we ought to lose no time in leaving the place. Mrs. Creevey at this time was a great invalid, quite lame, and only to be removed with very great pain and difficulty to herself. Upon consulting with some people of the place, therefore, as to the supposed conduct of the French if they arrived, and knowing from Barnes that our troops were to retire without fighting, we resolved to stay.

During the whole of this day—the 24th—the English were flying off in all directions, whilst others were arriving from Paris; and in the night the Guards all marched off to Ath, Enghien, &c., &c. On one of these days, I forget which, I saw arrive on the same day from Paris the old Prince de Condé and all his suite, who went to the Hotel Bellevue—Marmont, who went to the Hotel d'Angleterre—Victor to the Hotel Wellington, and Berthier to the Duc d'Aremberg's. On Easter Monday, I think it was, I was sitting at Charlotte Greville's, when the Duc de Berri came to call upon her, and expressed his great astonishment that any English should remain there, as Buonaparte was certainly at Lille and would no doubt be here on the Wednesday following, and that he himself, in consequence, was going to Antwerp.... We soon found there was no foundation for the report of an early invasion of Belgium by Buonaparte, and a good many of our people returned to Brussells, and other new ones came there. In April the Duke of Wellington arrived (I forget what day[16]) at Brussells from Vienna; and it was the 22nd, I think, I met him at Lady Charlotte Greville's in the evening; she was having a party of all the principal persons then in Brussells of all countries every evening.

I had seen a good deal of the Duke of Wellington in 1806, and in a very amicable way. He was then just returned from India, and [was] brought into the House of Commons to defend his brother Ld. Wellesley's Indian government. I was Secretary of the Board of Controul at the time, so that all Indian papers moved for on either side came thro' me; and this brought me very much in contact with Sir Arthur Wellesley personally, as well as with Paull, who was attacking his brother.[17] Afterwards in 1807–8 and –9 I took a very decided part in Parliament against Lord Wellesley, which produced such angry words between Sir Arthur and myself that I was quite prepared for there being no further intercourse between us. To do him justice, however, he not only did not seem to resent or recollect these former bickerings, but from the first moment he saw me at Lady Charlotte's (where he put out his hand to me) till he quitted France finally in the end of 1818, he behaved with the most marked civility and cordiality to myself and to all who were connected with me.

[16] It was the 5th.

[17] Among Creevey's papers are many letters from this Paull, who was the son of a Perth tailor, was educated in an Edinburgh writer's office, and was a trader for some years in India. Expelled by the Nawab from the Dominion of Oude, he was reinstated by Lord Wellesley's influence, made a large fortune, and was returned to Parliament, where he exerted himself to obtain his benefactor's impeachment. Having taken to gambling and lost heavily, he cut his throat in April, 1808.

The first occasion when I met him at Lady Charlotte's was so curious a one that I took a note of it when I returned home, and this I now have by me. We had much conversation about Buonaparte, and the Duke would have it that a Republick was the thing which he was sure to be got up at Paris—*that it would never come to fighting with the Allies*—that the Republick would be all settled by Carnot, Lucien Buonaparte, &c., &c.—*that he was confident it would never come to blows*. So he and I had a good deal of joking, and I asked him what he thought the old manager Buonaparte would say to this new *piece*, and whether it was with his consent it was got up, and whether it would in truth turn out a tragedy, comedy or farce. He said he had no doubt it would be a tragedy for Buonaparte, and that they would beat him by stilleto or otherwise in a very few weeks.

I retired with the impression of his (the Duke) having made a very sorry figure, in giving no indication of superior talents. However, as I said before, he was very natural and good-humoured.

I continued to meet him both at Lady Charlotte's and other places repeatedly, and he was always equally communicative—still retaining his original opinion. I remember his coming in one day to Lady Charlotte's in great glee, because Baron Lories, the Finance Minister, had fled from Paris to join the French King at Ghent.—'The old fox,' he said, 'would never have run for it, if he had not felt that the house was tumbling about his ears.'

Then he was always expressing his belief that the then approaching fête at Paris in the Champ de M[ars] would be fatal to Buonaparte—that the explosion would take place on that occasion, and that Buonaparte and his reign would both be put an end to on that day. So when we knew that the day had passed off in the most favorable manner to the Emperor, being that night at a ball at the Duke's house, I asked him what he thought of things now at Paris; upon which he laughed and seemed not in the least degree affected by the event. But when on the same evening I made a remark about the Duke's indifference to Sir Charles Stuart,[18] our ambassador, the latter said in his curious blunt manner:—'Then he is damned different with you from what he is with me, for I never saw a fellow so cut down in my life as he was this morning when he first heard the news.'

The Duke during this period was for ever giving balls, to which he was always kind enough to ask my daughters and myself; and very agreeable they were. On one occasion, having been at a ball in his house on a Saturday night, old Blucher and his staff came over to the

[18] Nephew of the 1st Marquess of Bute, created Lord Stuart de Rothesay in 1828.

town on the next day—Sunday, and the Duke sent out instantly to all who had been there on the preceding evening to come again that night to meet Blucher, and he kept making everybody dance to the last. Amongst others, I remember his bringing up General [*illegible*], who has since been so conspicuous in France, to dance with Miss Ord, which he did.

Some short time before the battle of Waterloo—a fortnight, perhaps, or three weeks—the two Miss Ords and myself were walking in the Park at Brussells. When opposite the Ambassador's house (now the Prince of Orange's) the Duke of Wellington and Sir Charles Stuart, having been engaged in conversation, parted, and the Duke joined us. It was the day the papers had arrived from England, bringing the debates in Parliament where the question is the war. So he began to me by observing:—'What a good thing it is for Ministers that Grattan has made a speech in favor of the war.'—To which I replied that all Ministers were always lucky in finding some unexpected support: and then I added the question was a nice one.—'A question of expediency,' said the Duke.—'Granted,' I replied, '*quite*; and now then, will you let me ask you, Duke, what you think you will make of it?' He stopt, and said in the most natural manner:—'By God! I think Blucher and myself can do the thing.'—'Do you calculate,' I asked, 'upon any desertion in Buonaparte's army?'—'Not upon a man,' he said, 'from the colonel to the private in a regiment—both inclusive. We may pick up a marshal or two, perhaps; but not worth a damn.'—'Do you reckon,' I asked, 'upon any support from the French King's troops at Alost?'—'Oh!' said he, 'don't mention such fellows! No: I think Blucher and I can do the business.'—Then, seeing a private soldier of one of our infantry regiments enter the park, gaping about at the statues and images:—'There,' he said, pointing at the soldier, 'it all depends upon that article whether we do the business or not. Give me enough of it, and I am sure.'

About a week before the battle, he reviewed three regiments of our infantry, and three Hanoverian ones, in the Allée Verte, and I stood in conversation with him as they passed. They were some of our best regiments, and so he pronounced them to be. As the Hanoverians passed he said:—'Those are very good troops too, or will be so when I get good officers into them.'

On Wednesday evening the 14th June, having had daily rumours of the approach of the French, I was at Lady Conyngham's, where there was a party, and it was confidently stated that the French had reached or crossed the frontier. The Duke presently came in and said it was so.[19]

[19] Napoleon did not cross the frontier till the morning of the 15th.

On the 15th there was a ball at the Duke of Richmond's, to which my daughters, the Miss Ords, and their brother went; but I stayed at home with Mrs. Creevey. About half-past eleven at night, I heard a great knocking at houses in my street—la Rue du Musée—just out of the Place Royale, and I presently found out the troops were in motion, and by 12 o'clock they all marched off the Place Royale up the Rue Namur. ... I sat up, of course, till my daughters and their brother returned from the Duke of Richmond's, which they did about two o'clock or half after. I then found that the Prussians had been driven out of Charleroi and other places by the French, and that all our army had been just then set in motion to meet them. The Duke had been at the ball—had received his intelligence there, and had sent off his different orders. There had been plenty of officers at the ball, and some tender scenes had taken place upon the ladies parting with them.

I saw poor Hamilton that night; he came home in the carriage with the Miss Ords and their brother.

On Friday the 16th the Duke and his staff rode out of the Namur gate about nine,[20] and we were without any news the best part of the day. I dined at Mr. Greathed's in the Park. ... In walking there between 4 and 5, poor Charles Ord and I thought we heard the sound of cannon; and when we got to Greathed's we found everybody on the rampart listening to it. In the course of the evening the rampart was crowded with people listening, and the sound became perfectly distinct and regular.[21]

Just before we sat down to dinner, Greathed saw Col. Canning, one of the Duke's Aides-de-camps, walking by the window, and he called him up to dine. He had been sent by the Duke on a mission to the French King at Alost, and was then on his return. He was killed two days afterwards at Waterloo.

In the evening—or rather at night—Colonel Hamilton rode in to Brussells, to do some thing for General Barnes, and to see us. We found from him that the firing had been the battle of Quatre-Bras. He was full of praise of our troops, who had fought under every disadvantage of having marched 16 miles from Brussells, and having neither cavalry nor artillery up in time to protect them.[22] He was full, too, of admiration of the talent of Buonaparte in this daring attempt to get between

[20] Other witnesses say 8 a.m.

[21] The action at Quatre-Bras began about 3 p.m. and lasted till 9 o'clock.

[22] The Allies began the action with 7,000 infantry and 16 guns. Van Merlen's horse, 1,200 strong, joined them before 5 o'clock, but Lord Uxbridge's division of cavalry halted on the Mons–Brussels road, through a mistake in their orders.

the English and Prussian armies.... Hamilton had seen the Duke of Brunswick killed at the head of his Brunswickers,[23] and represented the grief of these soldiers as quite affecting. Two of our young Brussells officers and friends had been killed, too, in the action—Lord Hay, aide-de-camp to General Maitland, and a brother of Jack Smyth's. Upon one occasion during the day, Hamilton stated, Wellington and his whole staff had been very nearly taken prisoner by some French cavalry.[24]... Hamilton returned to headquarters about 12 at night.

On Saturday the 17th I remember feeling free from much alarm. I reasoned with myself that as our troops had kept their ground under all the unequal circumstances of the day before, surely when all the Guards and other troops had arrived from Ath and Enghien, with all the cavalry, artillery, &c., they would be too strong for the French even venturing to attack again. So we went on flattering ourselves during the day, especially as we heard no firing. About four o'clock, however, the Marquis Juarenais [?], who I always found knew more than anybody else, met me in the street and said:—'Your army is in retreat upon Brussels, and the French in pursuit.' He quite satisfied me that he knew the fact; and not long after, the baggage of the army was coming down the Rue de Namur, filling up my street, and horses were bivouacked [picketed?] all round the park.

At night Hamilton came in to us again, and we learnt from him that Buonaparte had beaten Blucher so completely the night before that all communication between the latter and Wellington had been cut off, and that, under such circumstances, Wellington had been obliged to fall back and take up another position.

It was now clear there was going to be a desperate battle. Hamilton said so, and we who knew the overflowing ardent mind, as well as the daring nature, of his General (Barnes) well knew the danger his life would be exposed to next day. He returned to headquarters, according to custom, at midnight.

Sunday, June the 18th, was of course a most anxious day with us. I persuaded poor Charles Ord to go that day to England. Between 11

[23] Their black uniform, with silver death's-head and cross-bones, commemorated the death of the Duke's father at the head of his Brunswicker Hussars at Jena.

[24] This happened just after the Duke of Brunswick fell. The Brunswick infantry giving way before a charge of French cavalry, Wellington rode up with the Brunswick Hussars to cover them; but these also fell into disorder under a heavy fire of musketry, and were then driven off by Piré's Red Lancers. Wellington galloped off, closely pursued. Arriving at a ditch lined by the Gordon Highlanders, he called out to them to lie still, set his horse at the fence, and cleared it, bayonets and all.

and 12 I perceived the horses, men, carts and carriages of all description, laden with baggage, which had filled every street all night, had received orders to march, and I never felt more anxiety than to see the route they took; for had they taken the Antwerp or Ostend road, I should have concluded we were not to keep our ground. They all went up the Rue de Namur *towards the army*.

About three o'clock I walked about two miles out of the town towards the army, and a most curious, busy scene it was, with every kind of thing upon the road, the Sunday population of Brussells being all out in the suburbs out of the Porte Namur, sitting about tables drinking beer and smoking and making merry, as if races or other sports were going on, instead of the great pitched battle which was then fighting.

Upon my return home about four, I had scarcely got into my own room to dress for dinner, when Miss Elizabeth Ord came running into the room saying:—'For God's sake, Mr. Creevey, come into the drawing-room to my mother immediately. *The French are in the town*.'—I could not bring myself to believe that to be true, and I said so, with my reasons; but I said—'Let all the outside blinds be put to, and I will come in an instant.'—So having remained five to ten minutes in the drawing-room, and hearing nothing, I went out; and then I found the alarm had been occasioned by the flight of a German regiment of cavalry, the Cumberland Hussars, who had quitted the field of battle, galloping through the forest of Soignes, entering the Porte Namur, and going full speed down the Rue de Namur and thro' the Place Royale, crying out the French were at their heels. The confusion and mischief occasioned by these fellows on the road were incredible, but in the town all was quiet again in an instant.

I then sat down to dinner, in the middle of which I heard a very considerable shouting near me. Jumping up to the window which commanded the lower part of the Rue de Namur, I saw a detachment of our Horse Guards escorting a considerable body of French prisoners, and could distinctly recognise one or two eagles. I went into the Place Royale immediately to see them pass, and then returned to my dinner. Their number was said to be 1500. In half an hour more I heard fresh shouting, and this proved to be another arrival of French prisoners, greater in amount—it was said 5000 in all had arrived.

About this time, in looking out of my window I saw Mr. Legh, of Lyme, M.P. for Newton, arrive on horseback at his lodgings, which were next to my house; and finding that he had been looking at the battle, or very near it, I rejoiced with him upon things looking so well, which I conceived to be the case from the recent arrivals of prisoners.

My surprise, therefore, was by no means small when he replied that he did not agree with me: that from his own observation he thought everything looked as bad as possible; in short, that he thought so badly of it that he should not send his horses to the stable, but keep them at his door in case of accidents.

After this I went out to call on the Marquis Juarenais in the Park, to collect from him what news I could; and in passing the corner of the Hôtel Bellevue I came in contact with one of our Life Guards—a soldier who had just come in. I asked him how he thought the battle was going when he left the field; upon which, after turning round apparently to see if anybody could hear him, he said:—'Why, sir, I don't like the appearance of things at all. The French are getting on in such a manner that I don't see what's to stop them.'

I then got to Juarenais's, and was shown into a drawing-room, in the middle of which I saw a wounded officer of our Foot Guards (Griffiths, his name was, I knew afterwards) sitting in apparently great pain—a corporal on one side picking his epaulet out of the wound, and Madame de Juarenais holding a smelling-bottle under his nose. I just heard the officer apologise to Madame de Juarenais for the trouble he was giving her, observing at the time that he would not be long with them, as the French would be in that night, and then he fainted away.

In going out of the drawing-room into the balcony commanding the Park, the first thing I saw was General Barnes's chaise and four going as fast as it could from his own house in the Park towards the Porte Namur and, of course, the field of battle; upon which I went immediately to Barnes's to see what intelligence I could pick up there; when I found a foreign officer of his staff—I forget his name—who had just arrived, and had sent off the General's carriage. His information was that General Barnes was very badly wounded—that Captain [*illegible*] [25] Erskine of his staff had lost an arm—that Major Hamilton was wounded but not severely, and that he thought everything was going as badly as possible.

With this intelligence I returned to Mrs. Creevey and my daughters between 8 and 9, but I did not mention a word of what I had heard, there being no use in my so doing. About ten o'clock, however, or between that and 11, Hamilton entered the room, and then the ladies and myself heard from him that Genl. Barnes had been shot through the body by a musquet ball about 5 o'clock—that his horse having just previously been killed under him, the general was on foot at the time—that Hamilton and the orderly sergeant had put him immediately upon

[25] [Perhaps Hon. E. S. Erskine, D.A.A.G.—J. G.]

Hamilton's horse, and that in this manner, one on each side, they had walked these 12 miles to Bruxelles, tho' Hamilton had been wounded both in the head and in one foot. *Observe*—the road had been so choaked by carts and carriages being overturned when the German regiment[26] ran away, that no carriage could pass that way for some time.

Well—Hamilton had put his general to bed, and was then come to give us the opinion, both of the general and himself, that the battle was lost, and that we had no time to lose in getting away. Hamilton said he would immediately procure horses, carriages or anything else for taking us from Brussels. After a very short consultation, however, with Mrs. Creevey, under all the circumstances of her ill health and helplessness, and the confusion of flying from an army in the night, we determined to remain, and Hamilton returned to his general.

The young ladies lay down upon their beds without undressing. I got into my own, and slept soundly till 4 o'clock, when, upon waking, I went instantly to the front windows to see what was passing in the Rue Namur. I had the satisfaction of seeing baggage, soldiers, &c., still moving *up* the street, and towards the field of battle, which I could not but consider as very favorable. Having dressed and loitered about till near six, I then went to the Marquis Juarenais's, in pursuit of news; and, upon the great court gate being opened to me, the first person I saw was Madame de Juarenais, walking about in *deshabillé* amidst a great bivouack of horses. She told me immediately that the French were defeated and had fled in great confusion. I expressed so much surprise at this, that she said I should learn it from Monr. Juarenais himself; so she took me up to his bed, where he was fast asleep. When he woke and saw me by his bedside in doubt about the truth of the good news, he almost began to doubt himself; but then he recollected, and it was all quite right. General Sir Charles Alten, who commanded the Hanoverians, had been brought in to Juarenais's late at night, very badly wounded; but had left particular orders with his staff to bring or send the earliest accounts of the result. Accordingly, one of his officers who had been on the field about 8 o'clock, when the French had given way, and who had gone with the Duke in the pursuit as far as Nivelles,[27] had brought all this intelligence to Alten at Juarenais's about 3 o'clock.

I went in the first place from Juarenais's to General Barnes's; where, having entered his bedroom, I found him lying in bed, his wound just dressed, and Hamilton by his side; and when I told him the battle was

[26] The Cumberland Hussars.

[27] Wellington did not follow as far as Nivelles, but handed over the pursuit to Blücher at La Belle Alliance.

won (which he did not know before), and how I knew it, he said:—'There, Hamilton, did not I say it was either so or a drawn battle, as the French ought to have been here before now if they had won. I have just sent old [*illegible*] (one of his staff) up to headquarters for news.'

I then returned directly home, and of course we were all not a little delighted at our escape.

About eleven o'clock, upon going out again, I heard a report that the Duke was in Bruxelles; and I went from curiosity to see whether there was any appearance of him or any of his staff at his residence in the Park. As I approached, I saw people collected in the street about the house; and when I got amongst them, the first thing I saw was the Duke upstairs alone at his window. Upon his recognising me, he immediately beckoned to me with his finger to come up.[28]

I met Lord Arthur Hill in the ante-room below, who, after shaking hands and congratulation, told me I could not go up to the Duke, as he was then occupied in writing his dispatch; but as I had been invited, I of course proceeded. The first thing I did, of course, was to put out my hand and congratulate him [the Duke] upon his victory. He made a variety of observations in his short, natural, blunt way, but with the greatest gravity all the time, and without the least approach to anything like triumph or joy.—'It has been a damned serious business,' he said. 'Blücher and I have lost 30,000 men. It has been a damned nice thing—the nearest run thing you ever saw in your life. Blücher lost 14,000 on Friday night,[29] and so got damnably licked I could not find him on Saturday morning; so I was obliged to fall back to keep up [regain?] my communications with him.'[30]—Then, as he walked about, he praised greatly those Guards who kept the farm (meaning Hugomont) against

[28] It may seem improbable that the Duke should have made himself so accessible to a mere civilian on such a momentous morning; but there is ample confirmation of Mr. Creevey's narrative from the Duke's own lips. In 1836 he described the circumstance to Lady Salisbury, who noted it in her journal (unpublished) as follows:

' "I was called," said the Duke, "about 3 in the morning by Hume to go and see poor Gordon" (in the same inn at Waterloo), "but he was dead before I got there. Then I came back, had a cup of tea and some toast, wrote my dispatch, and then rode into Brussels. At the door of my own hotel I met Creevey: they had no certain accounts at Brussels, and he called out to me:—'What news!' I said:—'Why I think we've done for 'em this time.' " '

The dispatch was begun at Waterloo and finished at Brussels, evidence of which remains in the draft of the original now at Apsley House, which is headed first 'Waterloo'; that is struck out and 'Bruxelles' substituted.

[29] At Ligny.

[30] Napoleon had detached the column of Maréchal Grouchy, 34,000 men with 96 guns, on the 17th to pursue the Prussians to Namur.

the repeated attacks of the French; and then he praised all our troops, uttering repeated expressions of astonishment at our men's courage. He repeated so often its being *so nice a thing—so nearly run a thing*, that I asked him if the French had fought better than he had ever seen them do before.—'No,' he said, 'they have always fought the same since I first saw them at Vimeira.'[31] Then he said:—'By God! I don't think it would have done if I had not been there.'[32]

When I left the Duke, I went instantly home and wrote to England by the same courier who carried his dispatch. I sent the very conversation I have just related to Bennet.[33] I think, however, I omitted the Duke's observation that he did not think the battle would have been won had he not been there, and I remember my reason for omitting this sentence. It did not seem fair to the Duke to state it without full explanation. There was nothing like vanity in the observation in the way he made it. I considered it only as meaning that the battle was so hardly and equally fought that nothing but confidence of our army in himself as their general could have brought them thro'. Now that seven years have elapsed since that battle, and tho' the Duke has become—very foolishly, in my opinion—a politician, and has done many wrong and foolish things since that time, yet I think of his conversation and whole conduct on the 19th—the day after the battle—exactly the same as I did then: namely—that nothing could do a conqueror more honor than his gravity and seriousness at the loss of lives he had sustained, his admission of his great danger, and the justice he did his enemy.

I may add that, before I left him, I asked whether he thought the French would be able to take the field again; and he said he thought certainly not, giving as his reason that every corps of France, but one, had been in the battle, and that the whole army had gone off in such perfect rout and confusion he thought it quite impossible for them to give battle again before the Allies reached Paris.

On Tuesday the 20th, the day after this conversation with the Duke, Barnes and Hamilton would make me ride over to see the field of battle, which I would willingly have declined, understanding all the French dead were still on the field—unburied, and having no one to

[31] In 1808.

[32] Captain Gronow, to whom Creevey gave an account of this interview, remarks: 'I do not pretend to say what the Duke meant in his conversation with Mr. Creevey, who was truth itself' [*Reminiscences*, vol. i, 212].

[33] Hon. H. G. Bennet, M.P. [Creevey had the originals of this and other of his letters to Bennet and to Charles Ord before him at Cantley when he wrote this memorandum in 1822. See *Creevey's Life and Times*. His recollection therefore was 7 *hours*, not 7 years, old. J. G.]

instruct me in detail as to what had passed—I mean as to the relative positions of the armies, &c. However, I was mounted, and as I was riding along with Hamilton's groom behind me about a mile and a half on the Brussells side of the village of Waterloo, who should overtake me but the Duke of Wellington in his curricle, in his plain cloaths and Harvey by his side in his regimentals. So we went on together, and he said as he was to stop at Waterloo to see Frederick Ponsonby and de Lancey, Harvey should go with me and shew me the field of battle, and all about it. When we got to Waterloo village, we found others of his staff there, and it ended in Lord Arthur Hill being my guide over every part of the ground.

My great surprise was at not being more horrified at the sight of such a mass of dead bodies. On the left of the road going from Waterloo to Mont St. Jean, and just close up to within a yard or two of a small ragged hedge which was our own line, the French lay as if they had been mowed down in a row without any interval.[34] It was a distressing sight, no doubt, to see every now and then a man alive amongst them, and calling out to Lord Arthur to give them something to drink. It so happened Lord Arthur had some weak brandy and water in his holster, and he dismounted to give some to the wounded soldiers. It was a curious thing to see on each occasion the moderation with which the soldier drank, and his marked good manners. They all ended by saying to Lord Arthur:—'Mon général, vous êtes bien honnête.' One case in particular I remember, on the other side of the road near the farm at Hugomont, a remarkably fine-looking man reared himself up from amongst the surrounding dead. His aiguilette streaming down his arm, Lord Arthur asked him if he was an officer, to which he replied no, but a sergeant of the Imperial Guard. Lord Arthur, having given him some drink, said he would look about for some conveyance to carry him off (his thigh being broken), and apologised for its not being sooner done, on account of the numbers of our own men we had to take care of. The Frenchman said in the best manner possible:—'O mon général, vous êtes bien honnête: après les Alliés.'

I rode home with Hume the physician at head quarters, who said there were 14,000 dead on the field; and upon my expressing regret at the wounded people being still out, he replied:—'The two nights they have been out is all in their favor, provided they are now got into hospitals. They will have a better chance of escaping fever this hot weather than our own people who have been carried into hospitals the first.'

[34] Where Picton's 5th Division repulsed d'Erlon's corps in the morning. The ragged hedge has now disappeared.

Lord Arthur Hill to Creevey

Mons, 25th June, 1815

DEAR CREEVEY,

The King entered Le Cateau yesterday and was very well received. I was sent off from thence here with letters from the Duke to Talleyrand, who is here, with the news that Nap had abdicated in favor of his son. There is a provisional government formed. I don't suppose we shall have any more fighting. Hd. quarters advanced to-day however, but I don't know where to. I shan't be able to reach them to-night—roads horrible. Cambray was taken last night by storm: the Governor still in the Citadel—can't last. Inhabitants illuminated and received our troops with joy—Genl. Colvill's brigade. Let me hear of Harris and other wounded.

Yours,
ARTHUR HILL.

My wounded mare is in the Duke's stable under care of Percy's servant. Will you visit her?

chapter eight

1815–1816

AFTER THE STERN realities of war, home politics and social gossip read flat enough. The crowning victory of Waterloo brought no strength to the Opposition. There were troubles enough ahead for the Government, arising out of the fall in prices consequent on the peace and the thousands of idle hands thrown on the labour market following on reduction of the forces; but, meanwhile, the country was aglow with enthusiasm for the Government and the army. It was when their prospects were at the lowest that the Liberals received a cruel blow in the suicide of one of their chief representatives in the Commons, Samuel Whitbread.

Hon. H. Bennet to Creevey [at Brussels]

Whitehall, July, 1815

...Nothing could be more droll than the discomfiture of our politicians at Brooks's. The night the news of the battle of Waterloo arrived, Sir Rt. Wilson and Grey demonstrated satisfactorily to a crowded audience that Boney had 200,000 men across Sambre, and that he must then be at Brussels. Wilson read a letter announcing that the English were defiling out of the town by the Antwerp gate; when the shouts in the street drew us to the window, and we saw the chaise and the Eagles. To be sure, we are good people, but sorry prophets! The only consolation I have is in peace, and that we shall have, and have time, too, to look about us, and amend our system at home, and damage royalty, and badger Prinny. I will venture to say he will long again for war abroad, as we will give him enough of it at home in the H. of Commons, so I beg you will be preparing for battle in the ensuing campaign.

...You will be sorry to hear that Sam looks and is very ill. He has lost all spirits, and cannot speak. I hear he vexes himself to death about Drury Lane. I am told a bill is filed against him to the tune of £25,000. ...I hope it is Drury Lane and not bad health that destroys his spirits.

Whitehall, July 7

My dear Creevey,

It is with a heavy heart that I write to tell you that you have lost your friend Whitbread; and though I hardly know how to name it, yet I must add that he destroyed himself in a paroxysm of derangement from the aneurism in the brain. He had been for the last month in a low and irritable state. The damned theatre and all its concerns, the vexatious opposition he met with, and the state of worry in which he was left—all conspired together to [*illegible*] his understanding as to lead to this fatal step. On Wednesday night the 5th I had a note from him written in his own hand, and as usual. He spoke on Tuesday in the H. of Commons more in his usual style than of late.... On Wednesday he passed all the evening with Burgess the solicitor, discussing the theatre concerns—walking up and down the room in great agitation, accusing himself of being the ruin of thousands. As you may well imagine, he did not sleep, but got up early on Thursday in a heated and flurried state—sat down to dress after breakfast about 10, and, while Wear was out of the room, cut his throat with a razor. When Wear returned, he found him quite dead. Is it necessary to say what the blow is to us all? To lose him in any way, at the maturest age, would have been a cruel loss, but in this manner—one feels so overpowered and broken down that the thing seems to be but a frightful dream. To me, the loss is greater than that of Fox, for the active, unwearied benevolence—both public and private—of our poor friend surpassed all the exertions of any one we ever knew. He lived but for mankind—not in showy speeches and mental exertions alone, but there was not a poor one or oppressed being in the world that did not consider Whitbread as his benefactor.... I never heard of his equal, and he was by far the most honest public and private man I ever knew....

July 11

...I am not astonished at Grey's losing his heart, as this day he is to attend Sir W. Ponsonby's[1] funeral, and at night he is to go down to Southill to attend our poor friend's to-morrow....

12th

...I delay sending this to say that Tavistock moved yesterday the writ in the most perfect and [*illegible*] manner: there was not a dry eye in the House. Wilberforce said he always considered Whitbread as the

[1] Major-General the Hon. Sir William Ponsonby [1772–1815] commanded the 'Union' brigade at Waterloo, and was killed in their famous charge upon d'Erlon's column.

true [*illegible*], possessing all the virtues of the character, tho' with its foibles, and that he was one of the public treasures. Vansittart deeply regretted his loss, and allowed that, when most in opposition to them, he was always manly, honest, [*illegible*] and true, and that he was an ornament to his country. Thus ended the saddest day I have yet seen in the House of Commons. Tierney sobbed so, he was unable to speak; I never saw a more affecting scene....

Henry Brougham to Creevey [at Brussels]

Friday, July 14, 1815

The message I sent you by C. Grey three weeks ago must have prepared you for this dreadful calamity which has befallen us, though nothing could reconcile you to it. Indeed one feels it more, if possible, as a private than a publick loss.... It seems as if the Opposition lay under a curse at this time—not merely politically, but physically. Romilly last winter was *bled out* of a violent inflammation of the lungs, and I think him damaged by it, next winter will show whether permanently or not, but at 58 such things are not safe, and he continues to work as hard as ever.[2] Ossulston has been most dangerously ill.... The anxiety and labour Grey has lately had make one fear a severe attack of his spasms—indeed he had one a few nights ago, having been on Monday at Sir W. Ponsonby's funeral, and having to set off for Whitbread's at 4 the next morning. The attack was in the night, and he went notwithstanding.

I hardly can venture to mention myself after these cases, but I have been very ill for 4 or 5 months, hardly able to go through common business, and now forced to give up the circuit.... I can only give you a notion how much I am altered by saying that I have not made such an exertion in writing for three months as this letter is, and that I already *ache all over* with it.... To continue my catalogue, Lord Thanet has been alarmingly ill, tho' now somewhat better; and such dismal accounts of the Hollands are daily arriving that one of my chief reasons for writing to you now is to ask you how the poor boy is.... In this state of affairs and of my own health, when there seems nothing to be done, and when, if there were, I am not the man now to do it, you will marvel at my coming into Parlt., which I have been overpersuaded to do, and which will have happened almost as soon as you receive this.[3]

[2] He committed suicide in 1818.

[3] Brougham remained out of Parliament after his defeat at Liverpool in 1812, until returned for Winchelsea, a borough of Lord Darlington's, in 1816.

The usual and unchangeable friendship of Ld. G[rey] obtained the seat, but I am not at all satisfied that I have done wisely in accepting it, for the reasons just hinted at. All I can say to myself is that I *may* recover and be again fit for service, in which case I should think myself unjustifiable had I decided the other way. But 20 years hard work have produced their effect, I much fear, and left little or nothing in me....

Lord Ossulston, M.P., to Creevey in Brussels

Walton, July 31, 1815

...Buonaparte still remains at Plymouth, but it is expected that the ship which is to convey him will sail very shortly. I believe he is allowed to take 3 persons (besides servants) with him, excepting those who are named in the list of proscribed. The general feeling, I think, here is that he ought to be placed out of the reach of again interfering in the concerns of the world, tho' it is difficult not to feel for a man who has played such a part, if he is destined to end his days in such a place as St. Helena. Seeing the other day a list of intimate friends invited to meet the P. Regent at Melbourne House—viz. Jack Manners, Ld. Headfort, &c., I could not help thinking what a strange fortune it was by which Buonaparte shd. be at that moment at Torbay, waiting his destiny at the Prince's hands.... Kinnaird is in town. His accounts of his arrest by Buonaparte is that, hearing of the battle of Waterloo, he had said in society—'Now the French have nothing to do but to send for the D. of Orleans;' which being reported to Buonaparte on his return, he sent to Kinnaird to quit Paris in 2 hours, and France in 2 days. Kinnaird upon this asked leave to go to Fouché, who told him not to stir, for that in two hours he would hear something which wd. surprise them—that was Buonaparte's abdication.... Whitbread's eldest son comes into not less than £20,000 per ann.—so Brougham told me. Whitbread, however, in the last year had outrun his income by £14,000—probably the theatre....

Henry Brougham to Creevey

London, Nov. 7, 1815

...What chiefly moves me to write is some conversation that Ossulston and I have had concerning the state of the Party in one material point. The Jockey is gone—you may lay that down. It is a question between days and weeks, and he cannot possibly see the meeting of Parlt. Baillie says if things go favourably he *may* last six weeks, but that he won't insure him for ten days. In short, it is a done thing.

Now upon your friend B[ernard] Howard's succession to this most important publick trust (for so I consider it), it is plain beyond all doubt that old Mother Stafford[4] will be working by every means to touch him —at all events to neutralize him. She will make the young one[5] turn Protestant—a most improper thing in his station; for surely his feeling should be—'I *will* be in Parlt., but it shall be by force of the Catholic emancipation;' and, viewing this as a personal matter to himself, he should shape his political conduct mainly with reference to it. But I fear that is past praying for, and all we can hope is that the excellent father should remain as steady in his politics as he is sure to be in his adherence to his sect.... Now what strikes both O. and myself is—that at such a critical moment your friendly advice might be of most material use towards keeping the newcomer on his guard against the innumerable traps and wiles by which he will assuredly be beset, and if you intend (which of course you do) to come over this session, perhaps it would be adviseable to come a little sooner so as to be here before the Jockey's death, for the above purpose.

Creevey, however, continued to live in Brussels for the sake of his wife's health, resisting many pressing entreaties from his friends to come over and rouse the flagging spirits of the Opposition. He and Mrs. Creevey received many letters from London containing the gossip and speculations of the day.

Lady Holland to Mrs. Creevey [in Brussels]

Holland House, 1st Jany., 1816

...According to the song, 'London is out of town;' the country houses are overflowing. The love of tennis is come so strongly upon Lord Holland that he has persuaded me rather reluctantly to go once more to Woburn for 3 or 4 days, in order that he may play a few setts. The plea which makes me yield is that I believe exercise keeps off the gout.

The most violent people here even rejoice at poor La Vallette's escape. What an abominable proceeding it has been. That tygress the Duchess of Angoulême in talking of Madame de la Bedoyère observed—'Elle a été elevée dans des bons principes, mais *elle nourrit* le fils d'un traitre'— an envious reproach from her sterile Highness, who can never enjoy the poor widow's maternal felicity. There is a strong feeling getting up in the country at our permitting the capitulation to be broken, altho' none

[4] Wife of the 2nd Marquess of Stafford, who was created Duke of Sutherland in 1833, she having been Countess of Sutherland in her own right.

[5] Eldest son of Bernard Howard; became Earl of Arundel on his father succeeding to the dukedom.

are sorry Ney suffered.[6] . . . Lady Waldegrave is dying of water in the chest. Her death will cause the disclosure of the secret whether Lord Waldegrave is married or not. . . . I want a handsome Valenciennes *collerette*, either made up, or lace to make it. Remember, my throat is *thick*, and it is to wear over the collar of a pelisse. . . . Sir Hudson Lowe has married a beautiful and for him a young, widow. She is the niece of Genl. Delaney—quite a military connexion. . . .[7]

The following refers to the speech on the Treaty of Paris, whereby, on February 9, Brougham marked his return to the House of Commons.

Mr. Western, M.P., to Creevey [in Brussels]

9th Feb., 1816

. . . I have often marvelled at the *want* of sense, discretion, judgment and common sense that we see so frequently accompany the most brilliant talents, but damn me if I ever saw such an instance as I have just witnessed in your friend Brougham. By Heaven! he has uttered a speech which, for power of *speaking*, surpassed anything you ever heard, and by which he has damn'd himself past redemption. You know what my opinion of him has always been: I have always thought he had not much sound sense nor too much political integrity, but he has outstripped any notion I could form of indiscretion; and as to his politicks, they are, in my humble opinion, of no sterling substance (but that between ourselves). He has been damaging himself daily, but to-night there is not a *single fellow* that is not saying what a damn'd impudent speech that of Brougham's—four or five driven away—even Burdett says it was too much. He could not have roared louder if a file of soldiers had come in and pushed the Speaker out of his chair. Where the devil a fellow could get such lungs and such a flow of jaw upon such an occasion as this surpasses my imagination.

Mr. J. Whishaw, M.P., to Creevey

Lincoln's Inn, Feb. 10th, 1816

. . . We have had two distinguished foreigners for some time in London—General de Flahaut[8] and Genl. Sebastiani. The former was one

[6] Such was not Lord Holland's sentiment. Among Creevey's papers is a very long letter from Lord Holland to Kinnaird, declaiming against Wellington for permitting the execution of Ney and Labedoyère.

[7] [She was Mrs. Johnson, daughter of Stephen de Lancey. J. G.]

[8] [Flahault. He married the heiress, Baroness Keith. J. G.]

of Napoleon's chief favourites, and is the reputed son of Talleyrand by the present Madame de Souza, formerly Madame de Flahaut. He does not inherit the talents of his parents, but is a handsome, accomplished and very agreeable officer, a flattering specimen of the manners of the Imperial Court, which assuredly could not boast of many such ornaments. Sebastiani is nearly the reverse of all these, with somewhat of an air of pedantry and solemn importance, of which you may recollect some traits in his famous dispatch. It is a little curious to sit at table with a person formerly so much talked of, and who contributed so much to the war of 1803. You may remember that he was one of Pitt's principal topics on that occasion....

Henry Brougham to Creevey [in Brussels]

Temple, Thursday [*May, 1816*]

Dear C.,

I think it better to trust this to the post than to any of their d——d bags. [Here follow some minute details concerning Creevey's seat at Thetford, which he seemed to be in some danger of losing, owing to changes of plan on the part of the Duke of Norfolk and Lord Petre, who had the disposal thereof]....All I desire is that you put *me* personally wholly out of your view. I am worked to death with business, and, for my own comfort, care little whether I remain out this session or not. The labour would be a set off agt. the pleasure of revenging myself agt. certain folks, and even the sweets of that revenge would be dashed with bitterness, for I forsee a rupture with Grey as by no means an unlikely result of doing my duty and taking my swing....I have served Prinny with a formal notice from his wife that in May she returns to Kensington Palace....

1816

If Mrs. C. can possibly let you come for a few weeks, for God's sake do come! It is morally certain you can come in for L'pool....If you don't come in there, you are out altogether, with some other good men—as Mackintosh, Ossulston, &c., and, for anything I know to the contrary, myself. For who can answer for a county like Westmorland, where there has been no contest for 50 years? and where I have all the parsons, justices, attorneys, and nearly all the resident gentry (few enough, thank God! and vile enough) leagued agt. me, besides the whole force of the Government. The spirit of the freeholders, to be sure, is wonderful, and in the end we *must* beat the villains. Govt. complain of L[onsdale] for getting them into it, and he complains of them for not dissolving. My satisfaction is that he is now bleeding at every pore—all the houses open

—all the agents running up bills—all the manors shot over by anybody who pleases.

Lady Holland to Mrs. Creevey

Holland House, 21st May, 1816

. . . Lord Kinnaird carried over the singular libel published by Lady C. Lamb against her family and friends.[9] It is a *plaidoyer* against her husband addressed to the religious and methodistical part of the community, accusing him of having overset her religious and moral (!) principles by teaching her doctrines of impiety, &c. The outlines of few of her characters are portraits, but the *amplissage* and traits are exact. *Lady Morganet* is a twofold being—Dss. of Devonshire and her mother: *Lady Augusta* Lady Jersey and Lady Collier: *Sophia* Lady Granville, who had 6 years ago a passion for working fine embroidery, and she marks most *atrociously* her marriage with Lord Granville. *Lady Mandeville* is Ly. Oxford: *Buchanan* is Sir Godfrey Webster: *Glenarvon* and *Vivian* are of course Lord Byron. Lady Frances Webster is sketched and some others slightly. Lady Melbourne is represented as bigotted and vulgar. The words about Mr. Lamb are encomiastick, but the facts are against him, as she insidiously censures his not fighting a duel which her fictitious husband does. The bonne-bouche I have reserved for the last—myself, where every ridicule, folly and infirmity (my not being able from malady to move about much) is portrayed. The charge against more essential qualities is, I trust and believe, a fiction; at least an uninterrupted friendship and intimacy of 25 years with herself and family might induce me to suppose it. The work is a strange farrago, and only curious from containing some of Lord Byron's genuine letters—the last, in which he rejects her love and implores an end to their connexion, directed and sealed by Lady Oxford, is a most astonishing performance to publish. There is not much originality, as the jokes against me for my love of *aisances* and comforts she has heard laughed at by myself and *coterie* at my own fireside for years. The invasion of Ireland is only our own joke that when we were going out of Bruxelles with such a cavalcade, the inhabitants might suppose we were a part of the Irish Army rallied. The *dead* poet is Mr. Ward's joke at Rogers having cheated the coroner. I am sorry to see the Melbourne family so miserable about it. Lady Cowper is really frightened and depressed far

[9] Lady Caroline Ponsonby [1785–1828], only daughter of the 3rd Earl of Bessborough, married in 1805 the Hon. W. Lamb, afterwards Viscount Melbourne and Prime Minister, but was separated from him in 1825. *Glenarvon*, the romance referred to in the text, was published anonymously in 1816, and reissued in 1865 under the title of *The Fatal Passion*.

beyond what is necessary.... The work has a prodigious sale, as all libellous matters have.

I know Lord Kinnaird also took over the *Antiquary* and the new play, otherwise I would send them to you; but if Moore's poem is good you shall have it.

We have been returned to our delicious old mansion above a week. Foliage and birds are the only demonstration of a change of season from December, as the cold, piercing easterly winds are still dreadful....

Holland House, Tuesday

I take the opportunity of Lady Lansdowne's departure to send you a small parcel of rubbish for your friend Gina, and, what is *not* rubbish, some verses by Mr. Rogers to add to his poems.... The town has been much occupied by a very strange affair which led to a duel between Ld. Buckingham and Sir Thos. Hardy. It is a mysterious business, but I sincerely hope quite over for ever. It was the charge of Ld. B. being the author of some very scandalous, offensive anonymous letters to, and about, Ly. Hardy. You would naturally suppose that the character of a gentleman, which Ld. B. has never forfeited, would have been a sufficient guard to have repelled such a charge; but the Lady was angry. There are various conjectures about the writer of these letters; but, except just the angry parties, the world generally does justice to Lord B., from the impossibility of a man of character and in his station of life being capable of such an abominable proceeding. It is not the mode of revenge which a man takes, however he may have been jilted, or believed himself as so. But all these stories you will have heard from the Tierneys, who meant to spend some days at Bruxelles....[10]

Hon. H. G. Bennet, M.P., to Creevey

Whitehall, July 12 [1816]

Now a word or two about poor Sheridan. One does not feel the loss of so great a creature as one ought to do, for, after all, he is the last of the giants, and there is no one to take the chair he leaves. I believe there is no doubt that his death was hastened, if not caused, by his distress—by his fear of arrest—and if he had been in Parliament he would probably have been alive. His dread was a prison, and he felt it staring him in the face.... The funeral takes place on Saturday. Peter Moore invites people to attend, and several are going. I have heard of Ld. Guildford and Thanet. I shd. like to do what was right, but I do not think ceremony at all wise or in good taste.

[10] [See my *Nelson's Hardy and his wife* for the Hardy side of this curious affair, pp. 48–52. J. G.]

From Henry Brougham, M.P., to Creevey [in Brussels]

Aug. 15, 1816. Geneva (uninhabitable)

Dear C.,

...I have been here for some time and in the neighbourhood. It is a country to be in for two hours, or two hours and a half, if the weather is fine, and no longer. Ennui comes on the third hour, and suicide attacks you before night. There is *no resource whatever* for passing the time, except looking at lakes and hills, which is over immediately. I should except Mme. Stael, whose house is a great comfort.

You may wish to know the truth as to Mother P. They resolved, under Mrs. Leach's auspices, to proceed. I rather think the Chancellor and ministers were jealous of Mrs. L.; at any rate they were indisposed to the plan, but on it went, and a formal notification was made to little P.'s husband[11] and herself. I believe they were to have begun in Hanover, to have something to show to Bull and his wife and daughter. But *steps were also taken in England*. Being advised of this *from the best authority*, I deemed it proper, according to the tacticks we have always adopted, *not* to wait to be attacked, but to fire a shot of some calibre, and you will by this time have seen more of it, tho' you may not have guessed whence it came....As for Mrs. P. herself, she won't do any more; but the daughter is a stronge force and will carry the old lady through. Mrs. P. is, I believe, among the Ottomans, but I have no sort of communication with her....Tell Kinnaird that Lord Byron is living here, entirely cut by the English.

Rome, 14 Nov., 1816

...I agree in your view of the high importance of this session. Lord [*illegible*],[12] who is here, holds that it will be one of expedients and shifts, and that the grand breakdown won't happen yet. I don't much differ from him; but still it will be *the* session, for their shifts and struggles and agonies will be the very time for work. The illustrious Regent meantime has been suffering in the flesh as well as the spirit, and I rejoice to find that his last defeat (which was a *total* one) has greatly annoyed him. I suppose you are aware of the secret history of it, and of Mother P. having miraculously been found fit for service once more. However, this time I must say she was rather a name than anything else, and little P. in reality bore the brunt of the day. I rejoice to say that Lord Grey views the divorce question in its true light, as do the

[11] In May of this year Princess Charlotte of Wales had married Leopold, Duke of Saxe-Coburg-Saalfeld.

[12] [? Lansdowne. J. G.]

party generally, *i.e.* in its connection with little P. and upon more general grounds. Both Carlton House and Hertford House now say the matter is finally at rest.... There are too many of the party abroad this session. Lord Lansdowne is here and remains all the winter in Italy, unless some very imperious call should take him home. The Jerseys and Cowpers come in a few days with the same plans.... Lady Jersey's absence is very bad for the party. She alone had the right notion of the thing, and her great influence in society was always honestly and heartily exerted with her usual excellence of disposition. Ill as we can spare speakers, we can still less afford such a loss as this.... All this brings me to my text. You *must* come over; it won't do to be absent any longer, therefore make up your mind to take the field. Meet me at Paris or Calais, if I can't come to Brussels, and I can take you easily if you don't fear the squeeze of three in a carriage.... When you get to London, if you please you may have my chambers, for as a long as you stay, with the laundress and man. I take lodgings in Spring Gardens during the session, and only am in chambers now and then for half an hour to look at the statutes....

Mr. Allen to Creevey[13]

Maidenhead, Nov. 20th

Dear Sir,

Lord and Lady Holland are in very great affliction, and you who knew the dear little girl they have lost and how much they were attached to her, will not wonder at their sorrow.... It is a satisfaction to hear that Lord Derby's fears are subsiding, and from what I observed before I left town I think several others who were in the same predicament are recovering from their alarm. This mud bespattering of the extra Radicals at their last meeting has made people ashamed of their fears, and if the Whigs most inclined to popular courses adhere steadily to their determination of having no communication with the Radicals of any description, I trust the session may pass over without any schism among Opposition, and that ministers will have revived this alarm to very little purpose. But all depends on the discretion of the two or three first days of the session. One violent speech, received with approbation by the more eager members of the party, would cause the same break-up as in 1792, and give Jenky and the Duke of Wellington the same despotic authority that Mr. Pitt exercised from that period to the end of his administration....

[13] John Allen, M.D. [1771–1843], political writer, a regular inmate of Holland House; of whom Byron said that he was 'the best-informed and one of the ablest men' that he knew.

chapter nine

1817–1818

IN 1817 THE CREEVEYS continued in Brussels. Apparently the hopeless disorganisation of the Opposition in Parliament deterred Creevey from coming home; at least, there are no indications of his having availed himself of any of the numerous and pressing invitations he received. His friends, however, still kept him well supplied with gossip, and Brussels at that time was the centre of much political activity, so Creevey had no want of occupation for his thoughts, his tongue, and his pen.

Henry Brougham, M.P., to Creevey

London, April 1, 1817

...I am glad you and Kinnaird approved of my broadside on the 13th March.[1] ...I knew that Govt. would be taken by surprise, and had told Sefton so, for Ward and others had said to me some days before that they took it for granted I was to give them, as they were pleased to say, 'a most valuable speech,' on the plan of my last year's on Agricultural distress—a sort of pair or pendant to that. I answered I meant no such matter, and should divide at all events, and regarded it as a hostile occasion. They did not believe it—had no guess of attacks on *foreign* policy, and looked innocent and astonished as I went on. I was very much tickled, and really enjoyed it, for I began quietly to the greatest degree, and only flung in a stray shot every 20 minutes or ½ hour by way of keeping them on the alert and preserving attention; and when, at the end of the first hour and a half, I opened my first battery, I do assure you it had a comical effect.... Still, it was not quite personal to Castlereagh, and when it was over, I changed my plan, in order to get breath, and play with them a little longer, and give my other fire more effect—that is, I went back to general, candid and speculative observations, and at large into the taxation part of the subject, and having prepared them by a few more random shots for a factious conclusion, I

[1] He had spoken vehemently against the Property Tax and in favour of retrenchment in various departments.

then opened my last battery upon C., to see whom under the fire was absolutely droll. He at first yawned, as he generally does when galled—then changed postures—then left his seat and came into the centre of the bench—then spoke much to Canning and Van, and at last was so d——d fidgetty that I expected to see him get up. It ended by his not saying one word in his own defence, but *appealing to posterity*. . . . We really want you more than words can describe. You positively *must* come, if but to show. . . .

Lord Holland to Creevey

Holland House [*No date*]

Dear Creevey,

I have put off answering your very entertaining letter and interesting communication to the last moment, and unfortunately to a moment when I am full of business—trying to get up a Middlesex meeting and to bring the great guns, called Dukes, to bear upon the question of Habeas Corpus. That cursed business of Reform of Parliament is always in one's way. With one great man nothing is good unless that be the principal object, and with another nothing must be done if a word of Reform is even glanced at in requisition, petition or discussion. . . . They say the Prince has left off his stays, and that Royalty, divested of its usual supports, makes a bad figure. . . . I wish I had politics, tittle-tattle or book-news to send you. Of the latter, Llandaff's memoirs are empty, but cursed provoking to the Court and the Church. Franklin's life will be curious, both for its information and style. *Rob Roy* is said to be good, but falls off at the end. . . .

Hon. H. G. Bennet to Creevey

Oakley, July 20, 1817

. . . I rejoice at the prospect of your return home, as not only I want you, but we all require your counsel and aid. . . . Your friends the Grenvilles are not only nibbling, but biting at us once more, but I trust we shall have nothing to do with them. Have you heard of our plan for a leader? Some persons last year thought of one of straw, such as Althorpe or Ld. G. Cavendish, but that wd. not do, and we, the Mountaineers, resented the scheme. At present we all concur in the necessity of some one, and, taking all circumstances into consideration, Tierney is the man selected in this choice. Romilly and Brougham cordially concur, and I do so likewise: not that Mrs. Cole has not many grievous faults, but there is no one else who has not more. Romilly cannot, from his business; and Brougham cannot from his unpopularity and want of discretion. I think that the good old lady can be kept in order, and tho' she be timid and idle, yet she is very popular in the House, easy and conciliatory; in no way perfect—in many ways better than any other person. The proposition takes immensely, and at present between 60 and 70 persons have signified their adherence. Let me know your opinion....

Lady Holland to Mrs. Creevey

Holland House, Friday, September, 1817

...We staid a short time at Edinburgh and made a long visit of a fortnight at Howick, where I had the delight of seeing Lord Grey all the time in the most perfect health and spirits, his countenance exhibiting gaiety and smiles which never are seen on this side of Highgate Hill.... Lady Louisa is very handsome, the others are very tolerably well-looking, but not equal to her, but graceful in dancing and riding, and excellent musicians. Some of the boys are uncommonly promising, especially the 2nd son Charles, and little Tom. The House is made one of the most comfortable mansions I know, and the grounds are as pretty as they can be in the ugliest district in the Island. I never expected to be so long in a country house, and yet leave it with regret, which was the case in this instance. We made a visit to Lambton, which is a magnificent house, everything in a suitable style of splendor. He is an excellent host: his three little babies are his great resource, tho' I hope he is recovering his spirits; and as he has no son, the sooner he decides upon taking another wife, the happier it will be for all parties. He is full of good qualities, and his talents are very remarkable.

London is very deserted: only a few stragglers, and those are not likely to encrease; as September is invariably the most empty month. Lawyers and sportsmen are always absent, and they are a numerous part of the community.

We have been near losing our Regent, and as the physicians mistook his disorder, they have probably curtailed his length of life, for the disease was treated at first as inflammatory, and they took 60 ounces of blood. When Baillie saw him he declared it to be spasm, and gave laudanum and cordials. The consequences are likely to produce dropsy. His disinclination to all business is, if possible, encreased, and there have been serious thoughts of a council of Regency to assist in the dispatch of affairs. Pss. Charlotte is going on in her *grossesse*, but there are some strange awkward symptoms.[2] They are living at Claremont. Ld. Castlereagh is supposed to have entire influence over the Prince Leopold.

[2] Princess Charlotte died in childbirth the following year.

What think you of the pamphlet on the divorce? It is most artfully done. The appeal to the shabby ones in the H. of Commons will have its weight, and perhaps the threat of recrimination may startle the party at Ragley. This skilfull work is supposed to come from the borders of the Lake of Geneva.[3]

In the *beau monde* I hear of Ly. C. Cholmondeley's marriage with Mr. Seymour, a son of Lord Hugh's; his brother and Miss Palk; Lord Sunderland and Ly. E. Conyngham. The Duke of Marlborough gives him £5000.

You heard of Lady L [*illegible*] from a ceremonial depriving herself of the pleasure of seeing Napoleon. The Govt. are displeased that the determination of Napoleon's adherents to continue with him should be known, and more strictness is adopted in the correspondence with the Island [of St. Helena]. As you will see from many idle paragraphs that the impression to be given in this country is that all belonging to him hate and abhor him, and wish to be quit of him; whereas the fact is notoriously the contrary. It is rather mortifying to see this country become the jailors and spies for the Bourbon Govt.; for to that condition Ld. Castlereagh has brought it.

The following notes of a conversation with H.R.H. the Duke of Kent remain in Creevey's handwriting, apparently as they were written down immediately after the event. Previous to this year, there is no indication that Creevey ever entertained the notion of collecting or publishing anything from his papers; but after his wife's death, which occurred in 1818, time hung more heavily on his hands, and he conceived the idea, which he discussed frequently with his stepdaughter, Miss Ord, of compiling a history of his own times. This never took shape, further than that his letters to Miss Ord were carefully preserved by his desire, along with much other correspondence. Upon this occasion, H.R.H. the Duke of Kent happened to be in Brussels, shortly after the death of Princess Charlotte of Wales. He desired Creevey, whom he had known familiarly in former times at the Pavilion and Carlton House, to call upon him; when, after discussing some trifling matter relating to the appointment to a chaplaincy, he broached a subject which evidently was weighing upon his mind. It must be confessed that his Royal Highness was not very discreet in choosing Creevey as the repository of his confidence in such a delicate matter. Creevey seems to

[3] *i.e.* from the pen of John Cam Hobhouse.

have had no scruple in communicating the tenor of the conversation to some of his friends. He certainly told the Duke of Wellington, and on December 30 Lord Sefton wrote from Croxteth, acknowledging Creevey's letter with its 'most amusing contents. Nothing could be more *apropos* than its arrival, as it was put into my hand while a surgeon was sounding my bladder with one hand and a finger of the other, to ascertain whether I had a stone or not. I never saw a fellow more astonished than he was at seeing me laugh as soon as the operation was over. Nothing could be more first-rate than the Royal Edward's ingenuousness. One does not know which to admire most—the delicacy of his attachment to Mme. St. Laurent, the refinement of his sentiments towards the D. of Clarence, or his own perfect disinterestedness in pecuniary matters.'

Notes of a Conversation with H.R.H. the Duke of Kent at Brussels, Dec. 11, 1817

... The Duke began, to my great surprise, a conversation upon the death of the Princess Charlotte, and upon an observation from me upon the derangement of the succession of the throne by this event, and of the necessity of the unmarried Princes becoming married, if the crown was to be kept in their family; and having in addition asked him, I believe, what he thought the Regent would do on the subject of a divorce, and whether he thought the Duke of Clarence would marry, the Duke of Kent, to the best of my recollection, and I would almost say word for word, spoke to me as follows.

'My opinion is the Regent will not attempt a divorce. I know persons in the Cabinet who will never consent to such a measure. Then, was he to attempt it, his conduct would be exposed to such recrimination as to make him unpopular, beyond all measure, throughout the country. No: he never will attempt it. Besides, the crime of adultery on her part must be proved in an English court of justice, and if found guilty she must be executed for high treason. No: the Regent will never try for a divorce.

'As for the Duke of York, at his time of life and that of the Duchess, all issue, of course, is out of the question. The Duke of Clarence, I have no doubt, will marry if he can; but the terms he asks from the Ministers are such as they can never comply with. Besides a settlement such as is proper for a Prince who marries expressly for a succession to the Throne, the Duke of Clarence demands the payment of all his debts, which are very great, and a handsome provision for each of his ten natural children.

These are terms that no Ministers can accede to. Should the Duke of Clarence not marry, the next prince in succession is myself; and altho' I trust I shall be at all times ready to obey any call my country may make upon me, God only knows the sacrifice it will be to make, whenever I shall think it my duty to become a married man. It is now seven-and-twenty years that Madame St. Laurent and I have lived together: we are of the same age, and have been in all climates, and in all difficulties together; and you may well imagine, Mr. Creevey, the pang it will occasion me to part with her. I put it to your own feeling—in the event of any separation between you and Mrs. Creevey.... As for Madame St. Laurent herself, I protest I don't know what is to become of her if a marriage is to be forced upon me; her feelings are already so agitated upon the subject. You saw, no doubt, that unfortunate paragraph in the *Morning Chronicle*, which appeared within a day or two after the Princess Charlotte's death; and in which my marrying was alluded to. Upon receiving the paper containing that article at the same time with my private letters, I did as is my constant practice, I threw the newspaper across the table to Madame Saint Laurent, and began to open and read my letters. I had not done so but a very short time, when my attention was called to an extraordinary noise and a strong convulsive movement in Madame St. Laurent's throat. For a short time I entertained serious apprehensions for her safety; and when, upon her recovery, I enquired into the occasion of this attack, she pointed to the article in the *Morning Chronicle* relating to my marriage.

'From that day to this I am compelled to be in the practice of daily dissimulation with Madame St. Laurent, to keep this subject from her thoughts. I am fortunately acquainted with the gentlemen in Bruxelles who conduct the Liberal and Oracle newspapers; they have promised me to keep all articles upon the subject of my marriage out of their papers, and I hope my friends in England will be equally prudent. My brother the Duke of Clarence is the elder brother, and has certainly the right to marry if he chooses, and I would not interfere with him on any account. If he wishes to be King—to be married and have children, poor man—God help him! let him do so. For myself—I am a man of no ambition, and wish only to remain as I am.... Easter, you know, falls very early this year—the 22nd of March. If the Duke of Clarence does not take any step before that time, I must find some pretext to reconcile Madame St. Laurent to my going to England for a short time. St. George's day is the day now fixed for keeping the birthday, and my paying my respects to the Regent on that day will be a sufficient excuse for my appearing in England. When once there, it will be easy for me to consult with my friends as to the proper steps to be taken. Should the Duke of Clarence do nothing before that time as to marrying, it will become my duty, no doubt, to take some measures upon the subject myself.

'You have heard the names of the Princess of Baden and the Princess of Saxe-Cobourg mentioned. The latter connexion would perhaps be the better of the two, from the circumstances of Prince Leopold being so popular with the nation; but before anything is proceeded with in this matter, I shall hope and expect to see justice done by the Nation and the Ministers to Madame St. Laurent. She is of very good family and has never been an actress, and I am the first and only person who ever lived with her. Her disinterestedness, too, has been equal to her fidelity. When she first came to me it was upon £100 a year. That sum was afterwards raised to £400, and finally to £1000; but when my debts made it necessary for me to sacrifice a great part of my income, Madame St. Laurent insisted upon again returning to her income of £400 a year. If Mad. St. L. is to return to live amongst her friends, it must be in such a state of independence as to command their respect. I shall not require very much, but a certain number of servants and a carriage are essentials. Whatever the Ministers agree to give for such purposes must be put out of all doubt as to its continuance. I shall name Mr. Brougham, yourself and two other people on behalf of Madame St. Laurent for this object.

'As to my own settlement, as I shall marry (if I marry at all) for the succession, I shall expect the Duke of York's marriage to be considered the precedent. That was a marriage for the succession, and £25,000 for income was settled, in addition to all his other income, purely on that account. I shall be contented with the same arrangement, without making any demands grounded upon the difference of the value of money in 1792 and at present. As for the payment of my debts, I don't call them great. The nation, on the contrary, is greatly my debtor.'

Here a clock striking in the room where we were seemed to remind the Duke he was exceeding his time, and he came to a conclusion almost instantly, and I retired.

Creevey was a warm and intimate friend of Lord Kinnaird, who, like himself, had been a vehement opponent of the war with France. Lord Kinnaird was so indiscreet as to persist openly in his anti-national demonstrations long after the war was over. Being in Brussels in 1818, a certain French refugee named Marinet, then under sentence of death, offered to reveal to Kinnaird a plot for the assassination of the Duke of Wellington in Paris, on condition that Kinnaird would intercede for him with M. de Cazes. Kinnaird informed Sir George Murray, the Duke's Adjutant-General, by letter, who naturally asked the name of the informer. This Kinnaird refused to give, having passed his word that he should not do so; neither could he be induced to reveal it after the attempt upon the Duke's life had been made by Cantillon on February 10. Upon this the Belgian Government ordered his arrest. Kinnaird left Brussels secretly, taking Marinet with him. Both were arrested on arriving in Paris, but Kinnaird was released at the request of the Duke, who took him into his own house, to prevent him being 'lodged in the Conciergerie,' as the Duke explained to Lord Bathurst, 'which I certainly should not have liked.' On April 15, Kinnaird left Paris, for Brussels, as he informed the Duke, but really on his way to England, leaving behind him a letter addressed to the French *Chambre des Pairs*, accusing the Government, and, by implication, the Duke of Wellington, of breach of faith in the arrest of Marinet. Kinnaird's indiscretion brought him into very unfavourable notice at the time; he was even suspected of some degree of complicity in the crime, whereof the Duke freely acquitted him, though Lady Holland always afterwards spoke of him as 'Oliver' Kinnaird. There is nothing of interest in Kinnaird's letters at the time to Creevey, but one to his wife may serve to show him in the light of a wrong-headed busybody, without any useful field for his activity.

Lord Kinnaird to Lady Kinnaird

Paris, April, 1818

What shall I tell you of the proceedings here? My patience is exhausted. I have in vain claimed the interference of the Duke [of Wellington] and the justice of the Govt. in favor of a man unjustly imprisoned. I have suffered all sorts of calumnies to be spread agt. me for a long time. I will no longer submit to it, and have now given definite notice that I will leave Paris this week. . . . I would not trust our own courier, or Dukes, or Ambassadors. You have no notion of the mischievous attacks some ministerial papers have been making on me. You may believe I despise them, but I think I must say something in reply. . . .

In the summer of 1818 took place a general election, and Creevey received notice to quit Thetford, which he had represented since

1802. The reason for the new Duke of Norfolk making this change is not apparent; possibly he was dissatisfied with Creevey's absence from Parliament for more than three years; possibly, as Brougham had anticipated, the Duke's mother-in-law, Lady Stafford, may have induced him to choose one of her own friends. Anyhow, Creevey bitterly resented this treatment at the hands of his old friend Bernard Howard, and wrote him a very long letter of remonstrance. The correspondence is only worth referring to as illustrating a condition of affairs which ceased to exist in this country with the passing of the Reform Act of 1832. Creevey reminds the Duke that they have been acquainted for sixteen years.

The question I put to you, Duke, is this—Why have you not noticed me in your arrangements for the new Parliament, or why have you not given me your reasons for not doing so? Shall I begin with my claims upon you on publick grounds? I can only do this by comparing myself with the persons returned by you. I will take, for instance, the returns of Mr. Phillips and his son.... I have learnt, and am taught to believe, that Mr. Phillips's claims upon you are founded upon a large loan of money that he advanced to you two or three years ago.... I am certain that mature reflection will show you the fatal effects that such a precedent, if generally followed, would produce, as well upon your own body—the Aristocracy—as upon the Constitution itself of your country.... Need I point out to you, Duke, the certain and speedy result of such operations on the part of the Aristocracy? Would they not *then*, at least, be subject to the reproach, hitherto so unjustly and maliciously urged against them, of trafficking in seats in Parliament? ... How long do you think the Constitution and liberties of the country would survive the loss of publick character in the Aristocracy?

To all this, and a great deal more, the Duke replied very briefly, expressing regret that 'dear Creevey' was not 'in any situation that he desired, and in which the exertion of his talents might be useful to the country,' but refusing to acknowledge 'the right he had thought proper to exercise of reproaching him [the Duke] with imaginary injustice.' He is willing to attribute Creevey's 'extraordinary and unmerited asperity to some temporary irritation proceeding from misconceptions.'

Having, then, lost the seat which he had held for sixteen years, during four Parliaments; having, also, lost his excellent wife, and, with her, the greater part of his income, he moved with his step-daughters, the Miss Ords, from Brussels to Cambray, where the Duke of Wellington had the headquarters of the army of occupation. While there he kept, or attempted to keep, a journal, which is not without some passages of interest.

Extracts from Creevey's Journal

Cambray, 16th July, 1818. I came from Brussells to Cambray with the Miss Ords on 14th July, and got there the 15th. To-day I rode to see a cricket match between the officers near the town, and presently the Duke of Wellington rode there likewise, accompanied by Mrs. Harvey and Miss Caton. As soon as he saw me, he rode up and shook hands with me, and asked me if I was returned in the new Parliament, to which I answered that the weather was too hot to be in Parliament, and that I should wait till it was cooler. He asked me to dine with him that day, but I was engaged to the officers who were playing the match, and he then asked me for the next day.

17th.—I dined with the Duke.... Mrs. Harvey and Miss Caton were the only ladies. We were about sixteen or eighteen, I suppose; no strangers but myself. One of the first things said at dinner by the Duke was:—'Did you see Kinnaird at Brussells, Creevey?' to which I said:—'Yes, I saw him on Monday, just on the point of starting for Milan, where he means to spend the next winter.' Upon which the Duke said:—'By God! the Austrian Government won't let him stay there.'—'Oh impossible,' I said, 'upon what pretence can they disturb him?'—and then he paused, and afterwards added:—'Kinnaird is not at all busy wherever he goes:' to which I made no answer. This was the year in which Lord Kinnaird took up the Marinet from Brussells to Paris, to give evidence about the person who had fired at the Duke in Paris—an affair in which Kinnaird, to my mind, acted quite right, and Wellington abominably to him in return.... In the evening I had a long walk and talk with the Duke in the garden, and he was very agreeable.... We talked over English politics, and upon my saying that never Government cut so contemptible a figure as ours did the last session—particularly in the repeated defeats they sustained on the proposals to augment the establishments of the Duke of Clarence, Kent and Cumberland upon their marriages, he said:—'By God! there is a great deal to be said about that. They [the Princes] are the damnedest millstone about the necks of any Government that can be imagined. They have insulted—*personally* insulted—two thirds of the gentlemen of England, and how can it be wondered at that they take their revenge upon them when they get them in the House of Commons? It is their only opportunity, and I think, by God! they are quite right to use it.'

23rd.—Dined at Sir Andrew Hamond's, with Alava,[4] Hervey, Lord Wm. Russell and the Lord knows who besides. Young Lord William was very good about politics, and civil enough to say he was sorry I was out of Parliament.

No date.—Dined at Lord Hill's with my young ladies and Hamilton and a monstrous party, all in a tent at his house four miles from Cambray. I should just as soon have supposed Miss Hill—Lord Hill's sister—who was there, to have been second-in-command of our army, as Lord Hill; his appearance is so unmilitary. He and his sister seem excellent people, and Barnes tells me that there cannot be a better second-in-command of an army than Lord Hill. Col. Percy[5] is by far the best hand at conversation of the Duke's young men.

No date.—Dined at the Duke of Wellington's. The ladies were Lady Charlotte Greville and Lady Frances Cole. The Duke began by asking:—'Well, Creevey, how many votes have the Opposition gained this election? Who is Wilson that is come in for the City, and what side is he of?' I thought Lady Frances looked rather astounded at such familiarity, and upon such a subject. At dinner he began again:—'Who is to be your leader in the House of Commons?' I said they talked of Tierney, but I was quite sure Romilly ought to be the man.—'Ah,' he said, 'Tierney is a sharp fellow, and I am sure will give the Government a good deal of trouble. As for Romilly, I know little of him, but the House of Commons never likes lawyers.' So I said that was true generally, and justly so, but that poor Horner had been an exception, and so was Romilly: that they were no ordinary, artificial skirmishing lawyers, speaking from briefs, but that they conveyed to the House, in addition to their talents, the impression of their being really sincere, honest men. I availed myself of this occasion to turn to my next neighbour Lord W. Russell, and to give him a good lecture upon the great merits of Romilly and the great folly of our party in making Tierney leader, whose life had been in such direct opposition to all Whig principles. I found the young lord quite what a Russell ought to be.

In the evening I had a walk with the Duke again in the garden, and upon my asking some question about the Regent, as the Duke had just

[4] *Note by Mr. Creevey.*—'The Representative of Spain at the Court of the Bourbons, and at Wellington's headquarters also—a most upright and incomparable man.'

[5] Fifth son of the 5th Duke of Northumberland; aide-de-camp, first to Sir John Moore, and then to the Duke of Wellington. Carried the Duke's despatches to London after Waterloo.

come in from England, he said:—'By God! you never saw such a figure in your life as he is. Then he speaks and swears so like old Falstaff, that damn me if I was not ashamed to walk into a room with him.'

Our conversation was interrupted by Mrs. Harvey and Miss Caton coming up to the Duke with a Yankee general in their hands—a relation of theirs, just arrived from America—General Harper, whom they presented to the Duke. It is not amiss to see these sisters, Mrs. Harvey and Miss Caton, not content with passing themselves off for tip-top Yankees, but playing much greater people than Lady C. Greville and Lady F. Cole—to *me* too, who remember their grandfather, old Caton, a captain of an Indiaman in Liverpool; their father an adventurer to America, and know their two aunts now at Liverpool—Mrs. Woodville and another, who move in about the *third-rate* society of that town.

No date.—Dined at Sir George Murray's[6] with Alava, General Harper and a very large party. I sat next to Harper, who quite came up to my notion of a regular Yankee. I touched him upon the late seizure of the Floridas by the United States, but he was as plausible, cunning and jesuitical as the very devil. He was singularly smug and spruce in his attire, and looked just as old Caton would have looked the first Sunday after a Guinea voyage—in new cloaths from top to bottom. From the Floridas he went to fashionable life, and asked me if he could not live *very genteelly* in London for £6000 per annum.

Sir George was all politeness and good manners, but he is *feeble*, tho' they say excellent in his department. He has not a particle of the talent of Barnes, nor do I see any one who has, except the Duke. He [Murray] and his staff—Sir Charles Brooke and Eckersley—are for all the world like three old maids.

The young ladies and I were at a ball at the Duke's, and he was very civil to us all, as he always is, and called out to us in going to supper to sup at his table.

Monday [*no other date*]. . . . Hope of Staff Corps is to go on Thursday with dispatches to the Duke, and wishes me to go with him as he travels in a cabriolet, which I most cordially consent to do.

Thursday. Hope and I left Cambray about 5 in the evening—went thro' St. Quintin, La Fère, &c. I was much interested by Laon and its vicinity, as well on account of its singular position, as of its having been the theatre of so much fighting between Blucher and Buonaparte in 1814. The vineyards, likewise, on the right hand side of the road and on the slope of the hills before and after Sillery were very pretty. We got to Chalons between four and five, having travelled all night of

[6] Wellington's trusted and excellent Quartermaster-General during the Peninsular War.

course, and before the Duke; so we got the postmaster to let us shave and clean ourselves in his house, and that being done, we sallied forth to a restaurateur to dine, leaving a special messenger on the spot to summon Hope the moment the Duke's courier arrived. Hope was sent for before we had finished, and was at the post house with his dispatches just as the Duke drove up. I followed in a few minutes. Hope had told him I was with him, and when I came he shook hands out of the window. On his expressing some surprise at seeing me there, I told him I was trying how I liked travelling at the expense of Government. The Duke then said:—'Come on and dine with me at Vitry, Creevey,' and off he drove.

We got to Vitry about ten. The Duke had driven much faster than us, so as to have time to answer his letters, and to have the return dispatches ready for Hope. The inn we found him in was the most miserable concern I have ever beheld—so small and so wretched that after we had entered the gate I could not believe that we were right, till the Duke, who had heard the carriage enter, came out of a little wretched parlour in the gateway, without his hat, and on seeing me said:—'Come in here, Creevey: dinner is quite ready.' Dinner accordingly was brought in by a couple of dirty maids, and it consisted of four dishes—2 partridges at the top, a fowl at the bottom, fricassee of chicken on one side and something equally substantial on the other. The company was the Duke, Count Brozam [?], aide-de-camp to the Emperor of Russia, Hervey, Sir Ulysses de Burgh, Hope and myself. Cathcart and Cradock were not come up, but were expected every moment.

The Duke had left Paris at 5 in the morning, and had come 130 miles, and a cold fowl was all that had been eaten by his party in the coach during the day. Altho' the fare was so scanty, the champagne the commonest of stuff, and the house so bad, it seemed to make no impression on the Duke. He seemed quite as pleased and as well satisfied as if he had been in a palace. He and I had a very agreeable conversation for an hour or an hour and a half, principally about improvements going on in France, which had been begun by Buonaparte—land, &c., &c.—and then we all went to bed.

In the morning we all breakfasted together at five o'clock punctually. Our fare was tea in a great coffee-pot about two feet high. We had cups to drink out of, it is true; but no saucers. The Duke, however, seemed quite as satisfied with everything as the night before; and when I observed, by way of a joke, that I thought the tea was not so very bad, considering it was made, I supposed, at Vitry:—'No,' said he, with that curious simplicity of his, 'it is not: I brought it with me from Paris.'

He gave Cathcart and Cradock a rub for not being up the night before, and then we all got into our carriages—the Duke and suite for Colmar, and Hope and I for Cambray....

Sunday.—Hope and I got back to Cambray at about two o'clock in the afternoon.... Lady Aldborough came to Cambray.... I am as much convinced as ever that she is the readiest, quickest person in conversation I have ever seen, but she is a little too much upon the full stretch. Was she quieter, she would be more agreeable. The truth is, however, she knows too well the imprudences of her past life, and she is fighting for her place in society by the perpetual exercise of her talents.

Septr. 8.—On the evening of this day between 5 and 6 I saw the Duke's coach and six going full speed on the Valenciennes road, and I found after he was running away from the Duke of Kent, who had sent to say he was coming; so the D. of W. dispatched Cathcart to stop him, and went off himself....

Wednesday, 9th.—Barnes and I came over to Valenciennes in his chaise, and got there about half an hour before dinner. I met the Duke in the street, and he asked me laughingly if I had been to call on my friend the Duke of Kent, and said I should meet him at dinner. I thought from this I ought to call, so Barnes, Sir W. W. Wynn (whom I had picked up in the street) and myself went and wrote our names at the Duke of Kent's. This made us latish for dinner, and when we got there everybody almost was arrived, about sixty in number, I should say. As I was so late, I kept in the background, but the Duke of Kent saw me immediately, and forced his way to me. After shaking hands with me in the most cordial manner, and saying all kinds of civil and *apparently* most friendly things to me about my own situation (Mrs. Creevey being recently dead and myself being out of Parliament), and the regret of my friends in England at my absence, he began about himself.—'You may probably be surprised, Mr. Creevey, at seeing me here, considering the illness of my poor mother; but the Queen is a person of the greatest possible firmness of mind, and tho' she knows perfectly well that her situation is a hopeless one, she would not listen to any offers of mine to remain with her, and indeed nothing but her pressing me to come abroad could have made me do so.'

The Dutchess of Kent had an old, ugly German female companion with her, and the Duke of Wellington was going about amongst his staff before dinner, saying—'Who the devil is to take out the maid of honor?' and at last said—'Damme, Fremantle, find out the Mayor and let him do it.' So the Mayor of Valenciennes was brought up for the purpose, and a capital figure he was. We had an excellent dinner in a kind of occasional building, and as I got next Arthur Hill it was a very agreeable one....

Thursday, 10th.—Barnes took me out in his chaise about six or seven miles on the road towards Bouchain, where we found the troops on their ground, and then we got on horseback. The Saxon contingent I thought most beautiful, and the Danes I thought the dirtiest dogs I ever in my life beheld.

The Duke of Kent's appearance was atrocious. He was dressed in the *jacket* and *cap* of his regiment (the Royals), and but for his blue ribbon and star, he might have passed for an orderly sergeant. The Duke of Wellington's appearance was, as it always is on such occasions, *quite perfect.* I have never seen any one to be compared to him.... After the review, we went back to Valenciennes, and dined again with the Duke of Wellington.... The party to-day was much less—about 40. Lord Darnley, I think, was the only additional stranger. Sir Lowry Cole handed out Mrs. Hamilton, Sir George Murray Miss Ord, and General Barnes Miss E. Ord, and I got next to old Watkin, and talked over the Westminster election with him. In the evening the Duke gave a ball, which was as crowded as the very devil.

Friday, 11.—This morning Barnes and I set off to see the Russian troops reviewed.... The Count Woronzow, Commander-in-chief of the Russians, had sent forty pair of horses with drivers, &c., &c., to bring over such English persons as were to be present.... A little short of Bovary we found a relay of 40 other pair of horses standing in the road, and these took us to the ground.... Here again Cossack saddle horses were provided by Count Woronzow for all the strangers.... We had been all invited beforehand to dine with Count Woronzow, and just as the review was finishing, he rode up to every English carriage to say he was to have a ball in the evening.... After dinner, the ball opened, when my delight was to see the Mizurko danced by Madame Suwarrow and her brother the Prince Nariskin, Commander-in-chief of the Cossacks. The Dutchess of Kent waltzed a little, and the Duke of Kent put his hand upon her cheek to feel if she was not too hot. I believe it was this display of tenderness on his part that made the Duke of Wellington turn suddenly to me and say:—'Well, Creevey, what has passed between you and *the Corporal* since you have met this time?' So I told him of our conversation on the Wednesday at his dinner, not omitting, of course, the *pathetic* part about the Queen; upon which he laid hold of my button and said:—'God damme! d'ye know what his sisters call him? By God! they call him *Joseph* Surface!' and then sent out one of his hearty laughs, that made every one turn about to the right and left to see what was the matter....

The Duke of Wellington's constant joking with me about the Duke of Kent was owing to the curious conversation I had with the latter at

Brussells in the autumn of 1817, the particulars of which had always amused the Duke of Wellington very much....

Saturday.—We were all invited to breakfast at the Count's [Woronzow] this morning, but we were to go first at 9 o'clock to see the Count's school, which we did, and saw 400 or 500 private soldiers at their lessons—reading, writing and arithmetic, upon Lancaster's plan. Nothing could be nicer than the room, or more perfect than the establishment. This education takes eight months, and the whole army goes through it in turn. Besides this, there was another school where shoemaking, tayloring and other things are taught. As the Duke of Kent was to the last degree tiresome in examining all the details of this establishment, and asked questions without end, I expressed some impatience to get to my breakfast, upon which the Duke of Wellington, who heard me, was much amused, and said:—'I recommend you, whenever you start with any of the Royal family in a morning, and particularly with *the Corporal*, always to breakfast first.' I found he and his staff had all done so, and his fun was to keep saying all the time we were kept there —'Voilà le monsieur qui n'a pas dejeuné!', pointing to me.

I got, however, to my breakfast at last, and found the Dutchess of Kent and other ladies there likewise.... I must say the Count Woronzow is one of the most captivating persons I have ever seen. He appears about 35 years of age: there is a polish and a simplicity at the same time in his manner that surpasses anything I have ever seen. He seems all work—all kindness—all good breeding—without a particle of pride, ostentation or affectation. I consider him as one of the greatest curiosities I have ever seen.

September [*no date*].—I dined at the Duke of Wellington's, and was much pleased to find the Duc de Richelieu there, whom I had never seen before. He was just arrived, on his way to the Congress at Aix-la-chapelle. The Duke of W. introduced me to him, and I never saw a Frenchman I took such a fancy to before. His excellent manners, his simplicity and his appearance, are most striking and agreeable. We had a small party and no ladies. From Sir George Murray being between the Duc de Richelieu and myself at dinner, and my deaf ear towards him into the bargain, I lost much of his conversation. The Duke of Wellington, however, after Richelieu was gone, told me in conversation what had passed between them, which was not amiss. The D. of R. asked the D. of W. if he had heard what had passed at the Hague the other day at the christening of the Prince of Orange's second son, to which Wellington replied no. The D. of R. then told him that on that occasion, there being a dinner and *fête*, the Prince of Orange had made a flaming patriotic oration, in which he had expressed his devotion to his Belgic, as well as his Dutch, compatriots, and concluded by declaring he would sacrifice his life in repelling any power who dared to invade their country. Upon which the Duke of Wellington said to Richelieu:—'Who the devil does he mean? I suppose *you*—the French.'—'No,' answered Richelieu, 'it is said he meant you—the English.' There had been some talk of an army of observation being formed of our troops, to be kept in the Netherlands, so maybe it was an allusion to this.

I said to the Duke what a pity it was that the Prince of Orange, after distinguishing himself as he had done at Waterloo, should make such a goose of himself: to which Wellington said with his comical simplicity:—'So it is, but I can't help it. I have done all I could for him.'

Barnes has told me more than once during my stay at Cambray a fact about the Prince of Orange which, incredible as I at first thought it, must be true: viz.—that the Prince was mad enough to listen to some proposals made to him by certain French exiles as to making him King of France and dethroning old Louis Dix-huit. Kinnaird had often told me there was something of this kind going on, which I quite scouted; and then he told me afterwards, when he was interrogated by the police on the subject of Wellington's affair, that many questions were put to him on the subject of this plot in favor of the Prince of Orange, and as to what Kinnaird knew about it; but Barnes told me that Fagel, the Minister from the Pays Bas at Paris, told him (Barnes) that all was perfectly true; and not only so, but that in consequence of it the Prince of Orange had been obliged to answer certain prepared interrogations which were put to him by the allied Sovereigns on this subject. So it must be true, and Wellington of course knew it to be so during this conversation with me.

We had after this a very long conversation, and quite alone. I apologised for a question I was about to ask him, and begged him if I was doing wrong to tell me so immediately. I said Mrs. Hamilton expected to be confined in eight or ten weeks, and he would do me a signal favor if he would tell me if the army was *really* to leave France, as in that case she would never run the risque of being confined at Cambray, and left after the army was gone. He answered without the slightest hesitation:—'Oh, you must remove her certainly. I shall begin to move the army next month, and I hope by the 20th of November to have got everybody away.[7] I shall keep a single battalion for myself, and shall be the last to leave this place... so remove Mrs. Hamilton to Bruxelles or to Mons, but certainly out of France.'

He then went to politics, and publick men and publick speaking. He

[7] The Duke's farewell to the army of occupation was issued as *ordre-du-jour* on October 30.

said much in favor of Lord Grey's and Lord Lansdowne's speaking. Of the former he said that, as *leader* of the House of Commons he thought his manner and speaking *quite perfect*; and of Lord Lansdowne he said that, had he remained in the House of Commons he *must* have been the first minister of the country long before this time. 'But,' said he, 'they are lost by being in the House of Lords. Nobody cares a damn for the House of Lords; the House of Commons is everything in England, and the House of Lords nothing.'

I then favored him with my notions of some on the other side. I said there was no fact I was more convinced of than that Castlereagh would have expired politically in the year 1809—that all the world by common consent had had enough of him, and were tired out—had it not been for the piece of perfidy by Canning to him at that time, and that this, and this alone, had raised him from the dead, and given him his present great position. I then followed up Canning on the score of his infinite meanness in taking his Lisbon job and filling his present inferior situation under Castlereagh, whose present situation *he* (Canning) held in 1809, and then, forsooth! was too great a man to act with Castlereagh as his inferior....

It is a very curious thing to have seen so much of this said Duke as I have done at different times, considering the impostors that most men in power are—the insufferable pretensions one meets with in every Jack--in-office—the uniform frankness and simplicity of Wellington in all the conversations I have heard him engaged in, coupled with the unparalleled situation he holds in the world for an English subject, make him to me the most interesting object I have ever seen in my life.

The following memorandum, suggested by the publication in 1822 of O'Meara's *Voice from St. Helena*, refers to the autumn of 1818, immediately before the withdrawal of the Army of Occupation and the Duke of Wellington's return to England:

Memorandum

Having met the Duke of Wellington accidentally in the Park at Brussels, and walked with him at his request to the French Minister's house, and having talked a good deal about France now that the Allies had just evacuated it, I said:—

'Well now, Duke, let me ask you, don't you think Lowe a very unnecessarily harsh gaoler of Buonaparte at St. Helena? It is surely very disreputable to us to put any restraint upon him not absolutely necessary for his detention.'

'By God!' he replied in his usual manner, 'I don't know. Buonaparte is so damned intractable a fellow there is no knowing how to deal with him. To be sure, as to the means employed to keep him there, never was anything so damned absurd. I know the island of St. Helena well. I looked at every part of it on my return from the East Indies'—and then he described three or four places as the only ones by which a prisoner could escape, and that they were capable of being made quite inaccessible by a mere handful of men. I then said, from what I had seen of Lowe at Brussels in 1814 and 1815, he seemed to me the last man in the world for the general officer, from his fidgetty nature and disposition; upon which the Duke said:—

'As for Lowe, he is a damned fool. When I came to Brussels from Vienna in 1815, I found him Quarter-Master-General of the army here, and I presently found the damned fellow would instruct me in the equipment of the army, always producing the Prussians to me as models; so I was obliged to tell him I had commanded a much larger army in the field than any Prussian general, and that I was not to learn from their service how to equip an army. I thought this would have stopped him, but shortly afterwards the damned fellow was at me again about the equipment, &c., of the Prussians; so I was obliged to write home and complain of him, and the Government were kind enough to take him away from me.'

During the autumn of 1818, being one night at Lady Charlotte Greville's, then living at the Hôtel d'Angleterre, the Duke of Wellington coming in asked me if I had any news from England, to which I replied 'none but newspaper news,' viz. that the Duke of Wellington was or was going to be Master of the Ordnance: to which he said 'Ho!' or 'Ha!' but quite gravely, and without any contradiction, so I was sure it was true. From that hour he was an altered man—quite *official* in everything he said, tho' still much more natural and accessible than any other official I ever saw, except Fox.

A day or two after this conversation I met Alava, and, knowing his devotion to the Duke, I asked him what he thought of his new situation. He said he never was more sorry for any event in his life—that the Duke of Wellington ought never to have had anything to do with politicks—that he ought to have remained, not only as the soldier of England, but of Europe, to be ready to appear again at its command whenever his talents and services might be wanted. I have seen a good deal of Alava at different times, and a more upright human being, to all appearance, I never beheld.

The Opposition, which had lost one of its candidates for leadership in 1815, in the person of Samuel Whitbread, now lost another in Sir Samuel Romilly, and in the same dreadful manner—suicide. In replying to Mr. Bennet's letter announcing this event, Creevey took occasion to reply also to an earlier one, informing him of Tierney's election as Opposition leader in the House of Commons, which was little to Creevey's liking, for he and the rest of 'the Mountain' had always derided 'Old Mrs. Cole' as too timid for the part.

Creevey to Hon. H. G. Bennet

Brussels, Dec. 30th, 1818

...I must advert to the great calamity we have all sustained in the death of poor Romilly. His loss is perfectly irreparable. By his courageous and consistent public conduct, united with his known private worth, he was rapidly acquiring an authority over men's minds that, had his life been spared a few years, would I think, have equalled, if not surpassed, even that of Mr. Fox. He indeed was a *leader*, that all true Whigs would have been proud to follow, however his modesty might induce him to decline being called so.

And now I am brought to the question you propose me—viz.: what I think of your having chosen Tierney for the leader of the Whigs in the House of Commons. In the first place, I think you deceive yourselves by supposing the leader of the Whigs of England to be an article that can be created by election, or merely by giving it that name. A man must make himself such leader by his talents, by his courage, and above all by the excellence and consistency of his publick principles. It was by such means that Fox was our leader without election and that Romilly was becoming so, and believe me, there is no other process by which a leader can be made.

With respect to the object of your choice—as a piece of *humour* I consider it quite inimitable, and I am sure no one can laugh more heartily than Tierney himself in his sleeve as *Leader of the Whigs*; indeed his commentary upon the proceeding is intelligibly, as well as funnily, displayed by his administering a kind of Luddite test to you, which having once signed, you are bound to your captain for better and for worse....

Follows a very long survey of Tierney's public career from 1793 onwards, and an expression of opinion that his opposition to Fox, his defence of the East India Company, etc., etc., had for ever disqualified him for the post to which he had been elected.

chapter ten

1819–1820

AT THE END of 1819 or beginning of 1820 Creevey returned to England, after an absence, apparently continuous, of six years. In the interval he had lost his seat for Thetford, and, by the death of his wife, his income had fallen from a very comfortable figure to extremely narrow dimensions. On January 29 the long reign of George III came to a close. The reign, indeed, had ended ten years before, when the Regency was proclaimed, and the old king had passed the rest of his days in hopeless, but harmless, insanity, and bereft of sight. When it became apparent that his end was at hand, the party of the Princess of Wales perceived the necessity for her immediate return to England, inasmuch as the life of the Regent seemed not much better than that of his father. The Princess had been wandering over Europe and the East, giving rise to flagrant scandal by her irregular mode of life. When her husband became King, his Government offered her £50,000 a year to renounce her title of Queen and live abroad; but, acting under the advice of Brougham, she declined this, returned to London, and the consequence was the trial for divorce which occupied so much of Creevey's time and correspondence during the year. Meanwhile he paid a visit under Brougham's auspices to Lady Jersey at Middleton. From this time forward, his second stepdaughter, Miss Elizabeth Ord—'Bessy' and 'Barry' of a thousand letters—became his constant correspondent.

Creevey to Miss Ord

Middleton [*Lord Jersey's*], *Jan. 21, 1820*

...We got to Cashiobury [Lord Essex's] at ½ past five on Wednesday, too late to see the outside of the house, and were shown into a most comfortable library—a beautiful room 50 feet in length, full of books and every comfort...We passed a most agreeable evening. I did not see the flower garden, which is the great lion of the place. Brougham and I had a most agreeable drive here, not the less so to me from the extraordinary friendliness of him. ... We arrived here yesterday at five. We found only Lord Foley and Berkeley Craven, and they are gone this morning, so we compose only a quartette. The house is immensely large, apparently, for I have not seen it all, and cannot get out for the immense fall of snow during the night. ...

23rd January

... Shall I tell you what Lady Jersey is like? She is like one of her numerous gold and silver musical dickey birds, that are in all the show rooms of this house. She begins to sing at eleven o'clock, and, with the interval of the hour she retires to her cage to rest, she sings till 12 at night without a moment's interruption. She changes her feathers for dinner, and her plumage both morng. and eveng. is the happiest and most beautiful I ever saw. Of the *merits* of her songs I say nothing till we meet. In the meantime I will say that I presume we are getting on, for this morning her ladyship condescended to give me two fingers to shake, and last night asked me twice to give her my verses on the Duke of Northumberland, as she had mislaid and could not find the copy Gertrude Bennet had given her. ...

Liverpool, Jan. 30

... What think you of the accounts of the King? He is, I apprehend, rapidly approaching to his death—and then for the Queen and Bruffam! I did not tell you the other day, he has now in his possession the proper instrument signed by herself, appointing him her Attorney-General. The moment she is Queen—that is, the moment the breath is out of the King's body—this gives Bruffam instant rank in his profession, such as silk gown, precedence, &c., &c., in defiance of King, Chancellor and all the world, besides its importance in the public eye.

Henry Brougham to Creevey

Hill St., 5th Feb.

DEAR C.,

Your advice has been followed by anticipation (to speak Irish); at this moment my courier is within a couple of days' journey of the Queen. He was despatched on Sunday, for I had early notice from the D. of Sussex[1] coming to my bedside at 2 in the morning. The courier (Sicard) was with me by 7, and after some delay for a passport from the P. Minister, he was off. He took my appointment and Den-

[1] About the King's danger.

man's as Atty. and Solr. General, as I did not like to use the blank one I have with me. He also took a letter from me, giving her no choice, but *commanding* her instantly to set out *by land*, and be at Brussells or Paris or Calais immediately. Then she will demand a yatch (*sic*). . . .

Meanwhile, the change of name which Mrs. P.[2] has undergone has had a wondrous effect on publick feeling. She is extremely popular. . . .

Yours,

H. B.

The demise of the Monarch rendered necessary, according to the constitutional law of those days, a dissolution of Parliament, and this was accordingly effected by Royal Proclamation on February 29. Creevey was returned for the borough of Appleby, by favour of his friend the Earl of Thanet. Mr. Wilbraham, writing to Lord Colchester, the former Speaker, observed: 'I see no material change in your old dominions, the House of Commons, which is constituted of much the same materials as the last, with the addition of Creevey, who has become a great orator in his old age.'

The profit which 'the Mountain' had been waiting so long and impatiently to derive from the return of Queen Caroline turned to ashes in their hands. Popular sympathy, indeed, was vehemently—dangerously—in her favour, and the name of George IV had only to be mentioned to create a hostile manifestation. So far so good, from the Mountain's point of view; but, on the other hand, the question thus revived only made more manifest the schism in the Opposition. Lord Grey and the Old Whigs shrank from espousing the cause of the Queen, which, however just it might be, was in truth exceedingly humiliating and even unsavoury. Holland House held aloof from the movement, and there appears in consequence a marked change in the references by Creevey and his friends to that great Whig rendezvous and its inmates.

Creevey, though once more in the House, and active and vehement enough in debate and pamphleteering when urged thereto by his party, now took on rather (especially during the long-drawn and sordid months of Queen Caroline's trial and its aftermath) the role of observer, gossip and elder Statesman. The Party-man became pre-eminently the House-party man during this period when his

[2] The Princess of Wales, who had become Queen Caroline.

material resources were certainly at their lowest. He lived on his rich friends and well repaid them as an entertainer. Moreover there now began the letters to Bessy Ord on which his revived fame almost wholly rests.

In the Creevey papers probably more words were poured out over the sorry business of Queen Caroline than over any other event in Creevey's lifetime, and most readers would probably agree (the necessity for severe pruning being accepted) that that dingy episode should be the first to be sacrificed. This has been done and we take up the story again in February, 1822.

chapter eleven

1822–1824

Creevey to Miss Ord

Brooks's, Feby. 8th, 1822

...I dine at Sefton's again to-day. Did I tell you that Albemarle is to be married on Monday to 'Charlotte' Hunlock? Such is the case. The lady is 45, which is all very well if he *must* be married.

12th Feb.

...I dined with my lord and my lady and the young ladies at ¼ before 4, and we all agreed it was much the best hour to dine at. We were in the house by 10 minutes after 5, just as Brougham got up, and of course I heard every word of his speech, and of Castlereagh's answer to him.[1] It is the fashion to praise Brougham's speech more than it deserves—at least in *my* opinion. It was free from faults, I admit, or very nearly so; and *that* I think was its principal merit. Castlereagh's was an impudent, empty answer, clearly showing the monstrous embarrassments the Ministers are under, as to managing both their pecuniary resources and their House of Commons. The division was a very great one—under all the circumstances a most extraordinary one. The effect of the motion, if carried, was to take off 6 or 7 millions of taxes at once.... Against this sweeping motion the Government could only produce 212 votes, and for it were found such men as Davenport M.P. for Cheshire, Walter Burrell and Curtis members for Sussex, John Fane for Oxfordshire, Lawley for Warwickshire, Sir John Boughey for Staffordshire, and a good many Tory members for boroughs. Tierney thought the motion too *strong*, and would not and did not vote, and we had 21 of our men shut out—Lambton with a dinner at his own house, Bennett, Cavendishes and others. Tom Dundas, Chaloner and Ramsden, who had all come up from Yorkshire *on purpose*, were in the same scrape; Lord John Russell and others the same.

[1] Brougham's motion was upon the distressed state of the country, and for a reduction of taxation.

London, 16th Feby.

...I dined at Sefton's with the ladies, Brougham and Ferguson before four, and was in the House some time before Castlereagh began; and when he did turn off, such *hash* was never delivered by man. The folly of him—his speech as a composition in its *attempt* at style and ornament and figures, and in its real vulgarity, bombast and folly, was such as, coming from a man of his order, with 30 years' parliamentary experience and with an audience quite at his devotion, was such as I say amounted to a perfect miracle. To be sure our Brougham as a rival artist with him in talent and composition, play'd the devil with him, and made a great display....I thought I should have died with laughing when Castlereagh spoke gravely and handsomely of the encreased *cleanliness* of the country from the encreased excise revenue of soap....

Brooks's, Feby. 28th

My *benefit* went off last night as well as possible.[2] The 'front row' of course could not attend, so I went down and occupied it with myself and my books, with Folkestone on one side of me and Bennet on the other. I disported myself for upwards of an hour with Bankes, Finance Committees and 'high and efficient' public men....Our lads were in ecstasies, and kept shouting and cheering me as I went on, with the greatest perseverance. Brougham and Sefton were amongst my bottle holders in the front row, and in common with all our people complimented me hugely....Here is Grey, publickly damning the newspapers for reporting my speech so badly, but he has 'seen enough to satisfy himself it must have been very good.'

March 15th

...I made a very good speech (altho' you will find little trace of it in the newspapers), and rolled the new Buckingham Board of Controul about to their heart's content, and to the universal satisfaction of the House. Tierney of course betrayed me by his hollow support, and then I had all the weight of Canning's jokes to sustain, evidently prepared and fired upon me in the successive, and of course successful, peals.... I must, or ought to, regret very much that I let Canning off so easily; because, to do the House justice, they gave me perfectly fair play, and when I fired into the 'Idle Ambassador' at Lisbon, I had him dead beat. He dropt his head into his chest, and evidently skulked from what he

[2] It was a motion to curtail the powers of the Government under the Civil Offices Pensions Act of 1817. Creevey's speech occupies nine pages of Hansard.

thought might come.... It was a great, and perhaps the only opportunity of shewing up the Joker's life and what it has all ended in—banishment to India from want of honesty.... I think I shall have full measure of these bridal visits. I dine at Ly. Anson's to-day, on Sunday at McDonald's, on Thursday with the *young* people at the Duke of Norfolk's, to-morrow with the *Whigs* at Ridley's.

Brooks's, 16th March

I can't get the better of my chagrin at not having done myself justice upon Canning the other night.... I dined at Ly. Anson's yesterday. We had Coke and Ly. Anne, Miss Coke, Lord and Ly. Rosebery, Digby and Lady Andover, Hinchcliffe (Ld. Crewe's nephew), Mr. Lloyd and myself. I sat next Lady Anson by her desire. I was introduced both by her and Coke to Lady Anne, who, to my mind, has neither beauty nor elegance nor manners to recommend her, but if ever I saw *a deep one*, it is her. She was perfectly at her ease. On the other hand, I never saw more perfect behaviour than that of all the ladies of the family. Miss Coke I thought was *low*. We had, however, a very merry dinner, and I went upstairs and staid till eleven. I kept up a kind of running fire upon Coke, and Ly. Anson kept her hand upon my arm all the time, pinching me and keeping me in check when she thought I was going too far.... I was at Whitehall last night—Ly. Ossulston, Miss Lemon, Ferguson, Sefton and Vaughan, and then I came here (Brooks's), and was fool enough to sit looking over a whist table till between 4 and 5 this morning. Sefton and I walked away together, he having won by the evening a thousand and twenty pounds.

April 26th

...Another event of yesterday was Denman being elected Common Serjeant by the Common Council of London. The Queen's counsel, who on that occasion compared her husband to Nero! ... This was homage to Denman's honesty. I don't think Brougham could have succeeded, superior as he is to the other in talent.

Brooks's, April 27th

I had a long conversation here to-day with Thanet; I must say, 'altho'' it might appear to anybody but you parasitical *in his member* to say so, that in agreeableness and honesty he surpasses all his order—easy. To-morrow I dine with Sefton. Here is little Derby sitting by my side—very, *very* old in looks, but as merry as ever. Here is Brougham, too, but in a most *disgruntled*, unsatisfactory state. His manners to me are barely civil, but I take no notice, presuming that time will bring him round, and if it don't—I can't help it.

Brooks's, 3rd May

...Your philosophy is well and solidly grounded. These are feeble grievances as long as you are all well: nay, I might add, what are grievances like these to those of Lord and Ly. Salisbury—the one, the descendant of old Cecil and aged 80 years—the other, the head and ornament and patroness of the *beau monde* of London for the last 40 years, and yet to have £2000 per ann. taken out of their pockets at last by a rude and *virtuous* House of Commons....If this distress will but pinch these dirty, shabby landed voters two sessions more, there's no saying at what degree of purity we shall arrive. Meantime, all your place and pension holders must shake in their shoes....Here is Grey in such roaring spirits, and so *affable* that I should not be surprised at the offer of a place from him when he comes in, which I am sure he *now* thinks must be very soon indeed. But Abercromby for *my* money: he told me last night *it was all over* with the present men.

7th May

...Brougham was sitting at Holland House on Sunday morning with my lady and various others, when a slight thunderstorm came on, and, acording to invariable custom, my lady *bolted*. Presently the page summoned Brougham and conducted him to my lady's bedchamber, where he found all the windows closed and the candles lighted. She said she did not like to be left alone, so she pressed him to stay and dine, but upon his saying he must keep his engagement at Ridley's—'Ah,' said she, 'you will meet Creevey there, I suppose. What *can* be the reason he never comes near me?'—We both of us laughed heartily at her conscience and fears thus smiting her when she thought herself in danger; so I must leave her to another storm or two before I go to her.

Denbies,[3] *28th May*

...Mrs. Taylor says Lady Glengall told her last night she had not a single ticket left for the Hibernian ball out of her 100....You know the original plan was to have had the affair at Willis's Rooms. The leading female managers being Lady Hertford and Dowr. Richmond, &c., &c. The blockheads, it seems, made up their list of patronesses without including Ly. Conyngham in the number, and she was not a lady to submit quietly to such an insult; so she started this opposition ball at the Opera House, with the King as patron, and all the same ladies as patronesses that were on the other list, except Lady Hertford and Dowr. Richmond. The former is incensed at this practical retort from her

[3] Seat of W. J. Denison, M.P.

successful rival[4] beyond all bounds.... If you wish for anything in the public line, let me tell you that on Thursday or Friday last, Castlereagh, being in Hyde Park on horseback, met Tavistock, and tho' he has very slight acquaintance with him, he turned his horse about, and lost no time in unbosoming himself upon the state of public affairs. He described the *torment* of carrying on the Government under the general circumstances of the country as beyond endurance, and said if he could once get out of it, no power on earth should get him into it again.[5]

18th June

... On Saturday I dined at John Williams's in Lincoln's Inn, being carried there by Lambton in his coach, protected by *two* footmen. Sunday I dined at Cowper's with Sefton, Jerseys, Ossulston, George Lambs, Carnarvon, Kensington and Wm. Lamb.... I am sorry to find that my friend Sir Charles Hy. Williams has some great objections to him on the score of delicacy.

Cantley, July 21

... Well, I wonder whether you will be anything like as much interested by O'Meara and Buonaparte as I have been and am still. I can think of nothing else.... I am perfectly satisfied Buonaparte said all that O'Meara puts into his mouth. Whether *that* is all true is another thing. ... There are parts of the conversations, too, which are quite confirmed, or capable of being so, by evidence. For instance—when O'Meara lent him the *Edinburgh Review*, just come out, with a sketch of his life in it, he expresses to O'Meara the greatest surprise at some facts there stated, as he says he is sure they are, or were, only known to his own family. It turns out the article in question was written by Allen, and the facts referred to were told to Lord Holland when at Rome by Cardinal Fesch. Again; the conversations which Nap states to have taken place between him and young de Staël, the latter says are perfectly correct as to the periods and the subject of them, tho' he denies some of Nap's statements in them to be true. It is very difficult to predict what is to cause any permanent impression or effect, but, judging from my own feelings, I shd. say these conversations of Nap's are calculated to produce a very strong and very universal one upon very many subjects, and upon most people in future times, as well as our own.[6]

[4] In the affections of the King.

[5] Within a few weeks Castlereagh died by his own hand.

[6] Lord Rosebery, in his sympathetic study: *Napoleon: the Last Phase*, says of O'Meara's book—'*A Voice from St. Helena*, by O'Meara is perhaps the most popular of all the Longwood narratives, and few publications ever excited so great a sensation as this worthless book.'

Lord Castlereagh, who succeeded his father as second Marquess of Londonderry on April 8, 1821, but who will always be best recognised under the title which he raised to distinction, perished by his own hand on August 13, 1822. The circumstances are too well known to require further reference, except to note that the different causes mentioned by Mr. Creevey to account for this great statesman's derangement are wide of the mark. Castlereagh had submitted to a peculiarly nefarious system of blackmail by some villains who had entrapped him, and the agony of apprehension resulting from this, acting upon a mind perhaps overstrained in the public service during a long and peculiarly agitated period, brought about the disaster.

Suicide was of painfully frequent occurrence among public men in the first half of the nineteenth century. Paull, the enemy of Marquess Wellesley, in 1808—Samuel Whitbread in 1815—Sir Samuel Romilly in 1818—and now Castlereagh in 1822, are among the figures who disappeared in this melancholy manner from the stage depicted in these papers. It may be idle to speculate upon the source of a tendency which prevails no longer among our legislators; but those who have had occasion to peruse the memoirs and study the social habits of the period under consideration, cannot have overlooked two agencies which must have sapped all but the most robust constitutions. One was the habit of hard drinking, encouraged by all who could afford to give hospitality, in emulation of the example furnished by those who set the fashions. The other was the constant recourse to drastic physic and excessive bleeding remedy the disorders induced by high living. If these were not contributing causes to suicide, their discontinuance at all events coincides with a marked reduction in its frequency.

It had been agreeable to trace in Creevey's correspondence some signs of large-hearted regret for the removal of one who had borne so great a part in the national history, and had so long led the House of Commons. The spirit of party seems to have been too acrid at the time to admit any infusion of gentler sentiment towards a fallen foe.

Creevey to Miss Ord

Cantley, 14 Aug., 1822

...And now for Castlereagh—what an extraordinary event! I take for granted his self-destruction has been one of the common cases of pressure upon the brain which produces irritability, ending in derangement. Taylor will have it, and Ferguson also believes in this nonsense, that Bonaparte's charge against him as told by O'Meara, of his having bagged part of Nap's money has had something to do with it. Do you remember my telling you of a conversation Castlereagh forced upon Tavistock in the Park in the spring—about his anxiety to quit office and politicks and Parliament? He did the same thing to Ferguson one of the last nights at Almack's, stating his great fatigue and exhaustion and anxiety to be done with the concern altogether—just as poor Whitbread did to me both by letter and conversation two years before his death. It is a curious thing to recollect that one night at Paris in 1815 when I was at a ball at the Beau's, Castlereagh came up to me and asked if I had not been greatly surprised at Whitbread's death, and the manner of it, and then we had a good deal of conversation on the subject.

Death settles a fellow's reputation in no time, and now that Castlereagh is dead, I defy any human being to discover a single feature of his character that can stand a moment's criticism. By experience, good manners and great courage, he managed a corrupt House of Commons pretty well, with some address. This is the whole of his intellectual merit. He had a limited understanding and no knowledge, and his whole life was spent in an avowed, cold-blooded contempt of every honest public principle. A worse, or, if he had had talent and ambition for it, a more dangerous, public man never existed. However, he was one of Nap's *imbéciles*, and as the said Nap over and over again observes, posterity will do them both justice....

Now, what will come next? Will the perfidious Canning forego his Indian prospects—stay with his wife and daughter to succeed Castlereagh. I *think* not. I think the former enmity between him and Eldon has been too publickly exposed and encreased, by their late sparring match upon the Marriage Act, to let them come together. Then I think the Beau will claim and have the Foreign Office, and Peel will claim to lead in the House of Commons. *Mais nous verrons*! I suppose the King will approve the step Lord Castlereagh has taken, as he was Lady Conyngham's abhorrence, and Lady Castlereagh would not speak to Lady Conyngham.

What a striking thing this death of Castlereagh is under all the circumstances! This time last year he was revelling with his Sovereign in the country he had betrayed and sold, over the corpse of the Queen whom he had so inhumanly exposed and murdered. Ah, Prinney, Prinney! your time will come, my boy; and then your fame and reputation will have fair play too.... Taylor had a letter from Denison yesterday with a good deal of London jaw in it, and some of it is curious enough considering the quarter it comes from.[7] Bloomfield is to go to Stockholm as our minister! and then Denison says, had he not been discharged, the Privy Purse was in such a state, Parliament must have been applied to. Bloomfield's defence is, the Privy Purse was exhausted by paying for diamonds for Lady Conyngham; and all these honors and emoluments showered on him by the Crown are given him to make him hold his tongue....

Henry Brougham to Creevey

Carlisle, 19th Aug.

... Well! this is really a considerable event in point of size. Put all their other men together in one scale, and poor Castlereagh in the other —single, he plainly weighed them down.... One can't help feeling a little for him, after being pitted against him for several years pretty regularly. It is like losing a connection suddenly. Also, he was a *gentleman*, and the only one amongst them. But there are material advantages; and among them I reckon not least that our excellent friends who are gone, and for whom we felt so bitterly, are, as it were, revenged. I mean Whitbread and Romilly. I cannot describe to you how this idea has filled my mind these last 24 hours. No mortal will now presume to whisper a word against these great and good men—I mean in our time; for there never was any chance of their doing so in after time. All we wanted was a *gag* for the present, and God knows here we have it in absolute perfection. Hitherto we were indulged with the enemy's silence, but it was by a sort of forbearance; *now* we have it of right.

As for the question of his successor—who cares one farthing about it? We know the enemy is incalculably damaged anyhow. Let that suffice! He has left behind him the choice between the Merry Andrew and the Spinning Jenny;[8] and the Court—the vile, stupid, absurd, superannuated Court—may make its election and welcome. The damaged Prig or the damaged Joker signifies very little. I rather agree with Taylor that they will take Wellington for the Secy. of State, and that Canning will still go to India.... I rather think I shd. prefer the very vulnerable Canning remaining at home. By the way, I hope to live to see medical men like Bankhead tried for manslaughter, at the least. What think you of removing things from poor C., and then leaving him alone, even for 5 minutes? ...

[7] Denison was Lady Conyngham's brother.
[8] Canning and Peel.

George IV made a royal progress to Edinburgh in August of this year. Thanks, in great measure, to the influence of Sir Walter Scott, his Majesty was received in the northern capital with far more respect and enthusiasm than he had been accustomed of late to experience in the south.

From—Stuart to Mr. Ferguson of Raith

Edinburgh, 17th Aug., 1822

...I send you a *Scotsman* [newspaper], the Account in which as to the King is pretty correct. He has been received by the people in the most respectful and orderly manner. All have turn'd out in their holiday cloaths, and in numbers which are hardly credible....I have been much disappointed to-day with the levee....There was nothing interesting or imposing about it. A vast crowd, with barely standing room for two hours: afterwards moved to the Presence Chamber, where no one was for a minute....The King did not seem to move a muscle, and we all asked each other, when we came away, what had made us take so much trouble. He was dressed in tartan. Sir Walter Scott has ridiculously made us appear to be a nation of Highlanders, and the bagpipe and the tartan are the order of the day.

Henry Brougham, M.P., to Creevey

Lancaster, 21st August

...I dined the day before yesterday at old Bolton's circuit dinner, and found Canning there. I had a good deal of talk with him about Castlereagh, and he spoke very properly. Neither of us canted about the matter; but he shewed the right degree of feeling. I don't think he is going to be sent for, and am pretty sure he will go to India. If they are kind enough to do so excellent a thing as try it with the low, miserable Spinning Jenny, thank God for it! Only lose no time in reminding Barnes, as from yourself, of the magazine of ammunition for attacking him the moment the arrangement is made—I mean, in the debates of 1819, when I laid it into him in a merciless manner. It is pretty correctly given, and is a fund of attack....

Yours ever,

H. B.

Brougham, 24th Aug.

Dear C.,

I long to know your speculations upon these times, as I have heard nothing from you since we were bereaved of our Castlereagh;

therefore I can't be sure that you have survived that event.... Don't believe in Canning's coming in. He may be unwise enough to desire it, and Jenky may try for him, and it may go so far as a kind of offer; but nothing short of the event will ever convince me of his being in the Cabinet with these men and with this King....

Creevey to Miss Ord

Cantley, Aug. 24, 1822

This Royalty is certainly the very devil.... Sussex arrived on Wednesday between 3 and 4, himself in a very low barouche and pair, and a thundering coach behind with four horses—his staff, Stephenson, a son of Albemarle's, a Gore, servants, groom of the chambers, a black *valet-de-chambre* and two footmen, clad *en militaires*.... It has been my good fortune during his stay here to be considered by all parties as his fittest companion. Accordingly, I had a *tête-à-tête* with him of nearly *four* hours together on Thursday, and of 2½ yesterday, and my health has really been greatly impaired by this calamity. He has every appearance of being a good-natured man, is very civil and obliging, never says anything that makes you think him foolish; but there is a *nothingness* in him that is to the last degree fatiguing.... Althorpe was here yesterday, and told me there had certainly been rejoicings in the neighbouring market towns upon Castlereagh's death....

Robert Ferguson[9] tells me that he has seen a great deal of Major Poppleton lately, the officer of the 53rd who was stationed about Bonaparte. Bob says Poppleton is quite as devoted to Nap, and as adverse to Lowe as O'Meara, and that all the officers of the 53rd were the same. .... Poppleton has a beautiful snuff-box poor Nap gave him. What would I give to have such a keepsake from him, and, above all, to have seen him. O'Meara has a *tooth* of his he drew, which he always carries about with him....

Cantley, Aug. 29

... Did I tell you that our Sussex is to come back to us for Doncaster races? ... Miss Poyntz has refused Lord Gower, as has Miss Bould of Bould Hall Lord Clare.... Miss Seymour (Minny) when she landed at Calais had O'Meara's book in her hand, which, when recognised, was instantly seized by the police.... Did I tell you that Sussex says none of his sisters will touch Ly. Conyngham, which gives mortal offence to Prinney; nor can their justification be very agreeable; for they say, after

[9] Son of General [Sir] Ronald Ferguson, M.P.

his insisting upon their not speaking to the late Queen, how can they do so to Ly. C.?

Cantley, Sept. 7, 1822

...Maria Copley has read me a letter from Lady Francis Leveson from her new and noble parents' Cock Robin Castle, at the other extremity of Scotland. It is really not amiss as an exhibition of the tip-top noble domestic. Lord Francis[10] had left Edinbro immediately upon Lord Stafford's[11] illness, and Lady Francis followed immediately to pass a month there [at Dunrobin]. She says—'Figure to yourself my introduction into a room about 12 feet square, the company being Lord and Lady Stafford, Lord and Lady Wilton, Lord and Lady Elizabeth Belgrave, Lord and Lady Surrey, and Lord Gower. A table in the midst of the room, highly polished, I admit, but not a book nor a piece of work to be seen: the company formed into a circle, and every man and his wife sitting next each other, after the manner of the Marquis of Newcastle's family in the picture in his book.'

Henry Brougham, M.P., to Creevey

Brougham, 14 Sept.

DEAR C.,

Many thanks for your letter. I had, however, yesterday heard (*viâ* Bowood where the Hollands are) that all was settled. Canning succeeds to Foreign Office, lead of the House, &c.—in short, all of Castlereagh except his good judgt., good manners and bad English....Now don't *still* call me obstinate if I withhold my belief till I see them fairly under weigh. I know the Chancellor's[12] tricks: he is 'the most subtle of all the beasts.'...The Beau is still very unwell, and was cupped again on Thursday night.

Creevey to Miss Ord

Cantley, Sept. 19

...What a victim of temper poor Lambton is! He has been complaining to me of his *unhappiness*. I observed in reply that he had a good many of the articles men in general considered as tolerable ingredients for promoting happiness; to which he replied:—'I don't know that; but I *do* know that it's damned hard that a man with £80,000 a year can't sleep!' He has not much merit but his looks, his property and his voice and power of publick speaking. He has not the slightest

[10] Afterwards created Earl of Ellesmere.
[11] Created Duke of Sutherland in 1833.
[12] Lord Eldon.

power or turn for conversation, and would like to live exclusively on the flattery of toadies; nevertheless, I am doomed to go to Lambton: he will hear of nothing less, and I have shirked him so often, I suppose I must go....

One is accustomed to associate the introduction of the battue with the reign of Queen Victoria, and especially with the Prince Consort, but here we have an early example of the practice, and not only the practice, but the very term 'battue' is applied to it. Holkham was long famed for shooting, but it is certainly surprising to find that bags on this scale could be made by men shooting with flint-lock muzzle-loaders.

Viscountess Anson to Creevey

Holkham, Nov. 5, 1822

...Though not much of a sportsman yourself, you may be living with those who are, and I suppose it would be incorrect to write a letter from hence the day after the first battue—without mentioning that 780 head of game were killed by 10 guns, and that 25 woodcocks formed a grand feature in the *chasse.*

Upon Castlereagh's death, Wellington went on the embassy to Verona in his place. It was Canning's policy, on succeeding Castlereagh at the Foreign Office, to make it appear that his predecessor had entered upon an aggressive line in regard to European complications, from which he—Canning—extricated the British Cabinet. But in truth Wellington carried with him and acted upon instructions drafted by Castlereagh himself, whereof the keynote was 'to observe a strict neutrality.' Especially was this so in regard to the French invasion of Spain, then imminent. 'There seems nothing to add to or to vary in the course of policy hitherto pursued. Solicitude for the safety of the royal family, observance of our obligations with Portugal, and a rigid abstinence from any interference in the internal affairs of that country'—these are Castlereagh's own words as drafted for his own guidance when he, and not Wellington, was to have been the British plenipotentiary at the Congress; and they disprove the claim made by the partisans of Canning that it was he, not Castlereagh, who first established the policy of non-intervention in the domestic affairs of foreign countries so far as consistent with treaty obligations. This was the more notable, because the Emperor of Russia, formerly distinguished for liberal views, had of late ranged himself in line with the other crowned heads of Europe in desiring to repress by force the revolutionary movement in Spain, which country, he told Wellington, 'he considered the headquarters of revolution and Jacobinism; that the King and royal family were in the utmost danger, and that so long as the revolution in that country should be allowed to continue, every country in Europe, and France in particular, was unsafe.'

Creevey, having had rather a heated correspondence with Mr. Lambton (afterwards Earl of Durham) on political subjects, chiefly connected with an election for York, and being about to meet him at Croxteth, felt uncertain as to the terms on which they stood together. He therefore wrote to Lambton, bluntly seeking for an understanding.

Lambton to Creevey

Howick, Nov. 15, 1822

DEAR CREEVEY,

You have already smote me on one cheek, and I now, in the true spirit of scriptural precept, offer you the other. In other and more profane words, you have used me shamefully. You promised to come to our races: I kept a room for you until the second day after they had begun, altho' beds were as scarce as honest men; yet you neither came nor sent me word that you had altered your mind. You —— but I had better stop, or I shall work myself up into that vindictive spirit which you deprecate.

Now for a proof of my forgiving disposition. I not only shall meet you at Croxteth in perfect amity, but shall be happy to take you there, if my time suits your convenience. I am to be at Croxteth on Friday next, and sleep at Skipton on Thursday night. Skipton, I fancy, is about 15 miles from Farnley, and if you will join me there on Friday morning, I will carry you and your luggage safely to Croxteth. You must, however, break your usual rule, and let me know whether this offer suits you or not.... Don't talk to me about politicks—I have done with them. If you can tell me anything respecting the Leger—if you have any dark horse who is not spavined—I shall listen to you with attention; but as to Verona, the Bourbons, Reform, Spain, the Pirates, &c., &c., throw them to the dogs: I'll have none on't!

Yours, in the true spirit of Christian feeling,

J. G. LAMBTON.

Thomas Creevey

From a sketch at Brooks's

Viscount Castlereagh

From a drawing by George Dance

Lord Brougham

From an engraving by T. Wright after A. Wivell

Creevey to Miss Ord

Croxteth, Nov. 26, 1822

Well! I found the King[13] at Skipton before nine on Friday, breakfasting on his own tea, his own sugar, his own bread and even his own butter—all brought from Lambton. However, the Monarch was very amiable, and barring one volcanic eruption against the postboys for losing their way within 5 miles of this house, our journey was very agreeable....

Dec. 3rd

...Lord Hertford owes his blue ribbon to his having purchased *four* seats in Parliament since his father's death, and to his avowed intention of dealing still more largely in the same commodity.... We continue to go on quite capitally in this house. I never saw Sefton in greater force. I wish you could see the manner of both father and son to the different tenants we see from time to time on our different shooting and coursing excursions. What a contrast to the acid and contemptuous Lambton! However, poor devil, he pays for it pretty dearly, and will probably be a victim to his temper.... Lady Georgiana [Molyneux] amused me yesterday by telling me of a conversation she had with Lady Holland, in which the latter had deplored my present hostility to her, and had requested Ly. Georgiana's assistance in discovering the cause, and producing a reconciliation....

Croxteth, Dec. 12

...The truth is that all the Whigs are either fools or rogues enough to believe that our Monarch is really very fond of them, and that (according to the angry Boy[14] who left us yesterday) if we, the Whigs, could but arrange our matters between ourselves, the Sovereign would be happy to send for us. This is all he is waiting for; and with reference to it, Lambton told Sefton in *the strictest confidence* that it is of vital importance to gain Brougham's consent to Scarlett being Chancellor, and for Brougham to take the office of Atty. Genl.... You may suppose the anxiety of the Earl's mind till he found me for the purpose of unburthening himself of this confidential communication; and having done so, we indulged ourselves in a duet that might have been heard in the remotest corner of the house. Is it not perfectly incredible? Lambton was in constant communication with Grey whilst here, and (very judiciously!) shewed Sefton some of his dispatches on this subject....

[13] Lambton.
[14] Lambton.

Croxteth, 15th

...We all dined at Knowsley last night. The new dining-room is opened: it is 53 feet by 37, and such a height that it destroys the effect of all the other apartments.... You enter it from a passage by two great Gothic church-like doors the whole height of the room. This entrance is in itself fatal to the effect. Ly. Derby (like herself), when I objected to the immensity of the doors, said: 'You've heard Genl. Grosvenor's remark upon them, have you not? He asked in his grave, pompous manner—"Pray are those great doors to be opened for every pat of butter that comes into the room?"' At the opposite end of the room is an immense Gothic window, and the rest of the light is given by a skylight mountains high. There are two fireplaces; and the day we dined there, there were 36 wax candles over the table, 14 on it, and ten great lamps on tall pedestals about the room; and yet those at the bottom of the table said it was quite petrifying in that neighbourhood, and the report here is that they have since been obliged to abandon it entirely from the cold.... My lord and my lady were all kindness to me, but only think of their neither knowing nor caring about Spain or France, nor whether war or peace between these two nations was at all in agitation!

...I must say I never saw man or woman live more happily with nine grown up children. It is my lord [Derby] who is the great moving principle.... What a contrast to that poor victim of temper who left us last week! [Mr. Lambton].

Croxteth, 23rd

...Brougham arrived here on Saturday, on his way—or rather *out* of his way—to his nearest and dearest.... Of domestic matters, I think his principal article is that Mrs. Taylor's niece, Ly. Londonderry,[15] has transfered her affections from her lord to other objects: in the first instance to young Bloomfield, Sir Benjamin's son; and since, to a person of somewhat higher rank, viz., the Emperor of Russia, and that she is now following the latter lover to Petersburgh. Lady Holland is the author of these statements, and vouches for the truth of them.

Apropos to Lady Holland, in addition to all her former insults upon the town, she has set up a huge *cat*, which is never permitted to be out of her sight, and to whose vagaries she demands unqualified submission from all her visitors. Rogers, it seems, has already sustained considerable injury in a personal affair with this animal. Brougham only keeps *him*

[15] Frances Anne, only daughter and heiress of Sir Harry Vane-Tempest of Wynyard, Bart.

or *her* at arm's length by snuff, and Luttrell has sent in a formal resignation of all further visits till this odious new favorite is dismissed from the Cabinet.... But think of my having so long forgot to mention that Brougham says *many of the best informed* people in London, such as Dog Dent and others, are perfectly convinced of the truth of the report that dear Prinney is really to marry Ly. Elizabeth Conyngham; on which event the Earl here humorously observes that the least the King can do for the Queen's family is to make Denison[16] 'Great Infant of England.'

Miss Maria Copley[17] to Creevey

Sprotbrough, January 12th

... We have had a great deal of very agreeable society, chiefly composed of the old ingredients of Grevilles, Levesons, Granvilles, Wortleys, Bentincks, &c.; but they are now all flown—the Grevilles to Welbeck, Ld. F. Leveson to Madrid, the Granvilles to other battues.... The King is quite delighted with his Secretary of State, and was seen the other day at the Pavilion walking about with his arm round Canning's neck.

Two of your friend Lady Oxford's daughters are going to be married—Ly. Charlotte to a Mr. Bacon and Lady Fanny to a Mr. Cuthbert. The last is not so certain as the first, as somebody is to be asked for a consent, which I think it probable that most fathers, mothers and guardians would refuse. It must be a bad speculation to take a wife out of that school. Mr. Warrender[18] is going to marry Lady Julia Maitland at last, and Sir George is to be very magnificent.... Your friend, Lady Glengall, is in London, giving *ecarté* parties every night to the great detriment of society in general, and annoyance of the young ladies in particular. If things should go on *en empirant* this spring, I prophesy a meeting among that much injured race.... The Beau[19] has been staying at the Pavilion: he is in the progress of telling charming stories of the Congress. I would give my ears to hear them. He is very much recovered, but looks older and thinner from his illness.... *Write*, and tell me you are not bored to death by such a letter from a young lady.

[16] Lord Albert Denis Conyngham, 3rd son of Elizabeth Denison, 1st Marchioness of Conyngham. He was born in 1805, and was supposed to be the son of the Prince of Wales (George IV). [The reference is to Lady Conyngham's *brother*, W. J. Denison. Albert was born many years before the liaison with George IV began, and did not assume the surname Denison until 1849.—J. G.]

[17] Married Lord Howick (afterwards 3rd Earl Grey) in 1832.

[18] Succeeded his brother as 5th baronet of Lochend.

[19] The Duke of Wellington, who, when Castlereagh committed suicide in 1822, had been appointed Plenipotentiary at the Congress of Verona.

Sprotbrough, Saturday, 1823

Dear Mr. Creevey,

. . . The Taylors are still with us and we are within an ace of a schism about politics at least three times a day. Though I cordially agree with you about the Three Gentlemen of Verona, I cannot think your friend Mr. Brougham's speech prudent. At this time, when one must sincerely wish peace to be preserved in Europe, it has a most inflammatory tendency. I will not, however, *dare* to say a syllable about politics to you: a safer line of conduct for me is to agree with Michael [Taylor]. . . . I am in horror at the thought of the King's dying. In the first place (though I am no respecter of his), I think he does as well for us, or better than the Duke of York: second—we should have a horrid radical Parliament chosen: terzo—*London wd. be spoilt this year.* There speaks the young lady!

Creevey to Miss Ord

Feby. 4, 1823

. . . Who should arrive at Brooks's last night fresh from Paris but Og King of Bashan?[20] You never saw a fellow in such a state of fury against Cochon.[21] He is for a declaration of war this very afternoon in his friend Canning's speech. He complains bitterly that we are none of us up to the true mark: that if we would but give Spain a lift now before the Russians and Prussians come to be quartered in France (which he is perfectly sure is part of the present plan), the Bourbons wd. not be on their throne 3 months. . . .

House of Commons, ½ past 3

Just heard the King's Speech, and upon my word the part about Spain is much better than I expected. I don't see what Brougham is to do with his amendment after it. The first sentence relating to Spain[22] is a regular spit on the face to the Villains of Verona, and the whole certainly more in favor of Spain than of France.

Feby. 5, Brooks's

. . . Well! I had no difficulty in making Brougham prefer the King's speech last night to his own projected amendment, and to change his

[20] The 2nd Lord Kensington.

[21] Louis XVIII.

[22] 'Faithful to the principles which his Majesty has promulgated to the world as constituting the rule of his conduct, his Majesty has declined being a party to any proceedings at Verona which could be deemed an interference in the internal concerns of Spain on the part of foreign powers.'

regrets into warm admiration. You will see, however, that he by no means abandoned his plan of castigation of the Royal and Imperial scoundrels of Verona.... So faithful a picture of villains—portrait after portrait—was never produced by any artist before. If anything could add to the gratification the Allied Sovereigns must have received had they been present, it would be from the way in which our otherwise discordant fellows lapped up this truly British cordial like mother's milk. Peel could scarcely make himself heard, yet he went further than the Speech, and gave an unequivocal opinion in favor of Spain against France; but Liverpool went still further, and shewed clearly that he is in earnest in trying to keep the peace—that he thinks there is some little, *little* chance of it; and further, he clearly thinks that if war is once begun, we shall not be able to keep out of it.

Brooks's, 14th Feb.

I dined here last night much more agreeably, tho' not so cheaply, with Thanet, Brougham, Kensington, &c., &c. Every day's experience impresses me more strongly with the great superiority of Thanet over *every* politician that I see. He is gone to Paris this morning to add, as every one expects, £10,000 more to his already great losses at play. And yet he seems perfectly convinced of his almost approaching beggary under all the overpowering difficulties in which land is now involved!

Yesterday morning Lord Sefton drove me to the Freemason's Tavern, the great room of which is fitted up as a court for the tribunal which sits in judgment upon Lord Portsmouth's sanity or insanity. Certainly, never was a more disgraceful thing than the Chancellor's conduct on this occasion—to put the property of the family to the expense of £40,000, which it is said it will undoubtedly cost, rather than decide this point himself, which every one who has seen Lord Portsmouth has long since decided.[23] ...

The publick functionaries in Ireland are coming to close quarters. Wellesley has dismissed at a moment's warning Sir Charles Vernon, the Chamberlain, and two others—men who had held their situations about the Court for years. Their offence was dining at a Beefsteak Club last week, where Lord Chancellor Manners was likewise, and drinking as a toast:—'Success to the export trade of Ireland, and may Lord Wellesley be the first article exported!'[24] ...

I never saw a fellow look more uncomfortable than Canning. Independent of the difficulty of the times, he is surrounded by perfidy quite

[23] The 3rd Earl of Portsmouth. The enquiry lasted 17 days, and the jury pronounced him to be insane.

[24] Wellesley was Lord-Lieutenant of Ireland at the time.

equal to his own. People in office are in loud and undisguised hostility to him: it may be heard at all corners of the streets. I never saw such a contrast as between the manners of ministerial men even to him, and what it used to be to Castlereagh. Business begins in earnest on Monday, and I must launch my 'supply' on that or some early day, if my nerves are equal to it; but I find them fail me more and more every day.

Brooks's, 21st Feby.

...Well! we got into a fine mess the night before last upon our Joe's motion,[25] but Canning did what he could for us by his ill-timed and unnecessary vehemence and violence. His own people already pronounce that his irritability must prove injurious to him, and the loss of Castlereagh's composure and good manners is deplored in a manner not very flattering to his successor.

25th

...Yesterday I spent a very amusing hour with Sefton at the Opera House, seeing the *maitre de ballet* manœuvre about 50 *figurantes* for the approaching new ballet of *Alfred*....This done, we went to our *own* playhouse, where we saw 1st a *pas de trois* between Wilson, Hobhouse and Canning, and then a *pas de deux* between Brougham and Canning. ...After the House I dined at Sefton's *en famille*, and to-day I would have you know I dine with the Hereditary Earl Marshal of England, Premier Duke, &c., *alias* Barney, *alias* Scroope!

Miss Maria Copley to Creevey

Sprotbrough, March 6th, 1823

Our friend the Beau does not think Ferdinand's life worth a long purchase after the French army enter Spain. He says that they—the French—will meet with no more resistance in marching to Madrid than he does in going to the Ordnance Office. Two inches of cold steel will do his business very shortly....Lord Francis Leveson (at Madrid) is of the same opinion as to Ferdinand's prospect of a long reign....I hope *we* shall not interfere, as it must increase both our debt and our difficulties....

A still more difficult riddle for me to solve is your friend Mr. Brougham. Why does he make such love to Canning?—Why is he in none of your divisions?—Why is he in astonishment at the small demand of Ministers?—Is it catalepsy? All your good humour and civility make the debates very flat....

[25] Joseph Hume.

Creevey to Miss Ord

March 11th

I send you herewith Brougham's dispatch which I received yesterday. I had charity enough for him not to shew it to any one but Sefton, and he quite agrees with me that he is *mad*. His lunacy, you may plainly see, is to be in power. He cannot endure for a moment anything or any man he thinks can by possibility obstruct his march. He has himself entirely spiked his guns in the House of Commons; he has put it at Canning's feet, and then he is raving in the country that Hume should presume to open his mouth without his (Brougham's) permission.

There is little apparent madness in Brougham's letter referred to above. On the contrary, it seems brimful of common sense, chiefly referring to a projected attack on the Church of England by Joseph Hume, but it was not militant enough for Creevey.

Henry Brougham, M.P., to Creevey [enclosed in above]

Durham, Saturday

...As to Joseph, I hope it may do good. I know that things may with safety be brought on by him, which in any other man's hands wd. do harm. Therefore I always thought the attack on the Church was safer in his hands than in any others. But I fear he may throw away a great case, and (*except your testimony*) I see nothing in the other night's debate to change this opinion. Don't let us deceive ourselves. There are millions—and among them very powerful and very respectable people—who will go a certain way with us, but will be quite staggered by our going *pell-mell* at it. The people of this country are not prepared to give up the Church. For one—I am certainly not; and my reason is this. There is a vast mass of religion in the country, shaped in various forms and burning with various degrees of heat—from regular lukewarmness to Methodism. Some Church establishment this feeling *must have*; and I am quite clear that a much-reformed Ch. of Engd. is the safest form in which such an establishment can exist. It is a quiet and somewhat lazy Church: certainly not a persecuting one. Clip its wings of temporal power (which it unceasingly uses in behalf of a political slavery)[26] and purify its more glaring abuses, and you are far better off than with a fanatical Church and Dominion of *Saints*, like that of the 17th century; or no Church at all and a Dominion of Sects, like that of America....

[26] *i.e.* against Reform.

The Irish case is a great and an extreme one, and by keeping it *strictly on its own grounds* and abstaining from any topics common to both Churches, a body blow may be given. But if any means are afforded to the Ch. and its friends here of making common cause with the Irish fellows, I fear you convert a most powerful case into an ordinary one, which must fall.... I write this in court, and in some haste. Let me hear whether I am still in the wrong.

Creevey to Miss Ord

11 March

I never told you that I caught the Beau one day last week just mounting his horse, so I went up and stopt him, and had a very hearty handshaking.... I never saw a man's looks so altered. He is a perfect shadow, and as old looking as the ark.... There must have been an amusing scene between him and Slice[27] this day week in Ly. Salisbury's box at the Opera. Slice made a long oration to him against French aggression upon Spain, and ended with requiring to know Wellington's sentiments upon the probable result. The Beau contented himself by replying—'It won't succeed.' Slice would not be put off this way, and made a second harangue, ending with the same demand for an official opinion; but our Beau again wd. not advance further than—'It won't succeed.'

17th

... Thanet has won £40,000 in one night at Paris. He broke the bank at the Salon *twice*: the question is—will he bring any of this money home with him? I take it for granted *not*.

April 18th

You never saw such confusion and consternation as was produced in the Ministerial row by Burdett's speech [on Catholic emancipation].... In the midst of the debate arose that alarming episode between Brougham and Canning.... Brougham was laying about him upon Canning's 'truckling' to Eldon for his late admission into the Cabinet,[28] when the latter sprung up in the greatest fury saying—'THAT IS FALSE!' Upon this we had the devil to pay for near an hour, and Wilson had at last the credit of settling it by a speech of very great merit, and to the satisfaction of all parties. Brougham, I think, was wrong to begin with; he was

[27] H.R.H. the Duke of Gloucester.

[28] Implying that Canning, who had always advocated emancipation of the Catholics, had consented, as the price of his admission, not to press the question.

speaking under the impression produced upon him by Canning's blackguard observation to Folkestone the night before, viz. that 'if he had *truckled* to the Bourbons, as stated by Folkestone, at all events he would never truckle to *him*.' Brougham was going on like a madman, but Canning was much worse in his rage, and in his violation of the rules of the House.... The House generally was *decidedly* against Canning, as it had been the night before upon his passion and low-lived tirade against Folkestone, saying 'he spoke with all the contortions of the Sibyl without her inspiration.'... In short, Canning's temper is playing the devil with him, as I always felt sure it would.

28th

...Sefton and I were walking in the streets two days ago, when we saw my Lady Holland's carriage standing at a shop door; so Sefton said—'Now's your time! go and get it over.' So I did: I put my head into the carriage as if nothing had happened—shook hands and cracked my jokes as usual.... So when I left her she squeezed Sefton's hand with the greatest tenderness and said—'*Nothing* could be better done!'...

Og told me a story of the Duke of Buckingham which Canning had told him in confidence, and which ought to be preserved to perpetuate the base, intriguing spirit of this genuine noble Grenville.... Upon Castlereagh's death this said Duke, altho' Canning and he had never been on very good terms, wrote the most nauseous complimentary letter to Canning, taking for granted the Government would never let so distinguished a statesman leave the country, and urging him by all he owed to his country to accept the offer when made to him. Canning shewed this letter to Kensington at the time, convulsed with laughter at its style and mean contents. Not content with this, the Duke wrote another letter to Lord Morley, still more extravagant in Canning's praises, well knowing the latter was sure to see the letter, hoping Canning would not run any risque of serving his country by claims made for any of his friends, for that, when once Minister, all would be at his feet.

Well—upon Canning's first interview with Lord Liverpool after his acceptance of office, the latter said—'What is to become of India?' to which Canning replied it was an appointment to which he was quite indifferent, the only object he had at heart being an arrangement for putting Huskisson in a high and responsible official situation. Upon which Liverpool said he knew the Speaker[29] was desirous of going to India, and if Canning would see and sound the Directors—if they were agreeable to appoint him Governor General, then Wynne[30] might be

[29] Charles Manners Sutton.
[30] The Right Hon. C. W. Williams Wynn.

placed in the chair and Huskisson have the Board of Controul. Canning accordingly saw the Directors, but tho' they were very desirous of Wynne being removed from the Board of Control, as being perfectly inefficient, still they had the greatest possible objections to the Speaker as Governor General. However, Huskisson's appointment was so very agreeable to them, that at a second conference they struck. Wynne, who hitherto had shown no reluctance to this arrangement, being now called upon for its execution, declared his fixed determination not to give up the Board of Controul unless the Duke of Buckingham had that office, or was one of the Secretaries of State, and of course in the Cabinet. This claim being universally scouted, all was at an end.

May 3, 1823

...I dined at Hughes' on Thursday—17 or 18 people—crowded and dull as be damned. But then the footmen had such cloaths—such rich laced waist-coats—such beautiful new *silk* stockings and silver buckles! ...My Lord Lansdowne was *affable* beyond measure yesterday. He has had a special messenger from Marshal Soult, offering him in the first instance, and before any one else, his Murillos, taken by him when in Spain, and only asking as the price of them *one hundred thousand pounds*! My lord said Soult had shown them to him when he was last in Paris, and certainly they were the finest things ever seen—great altar-pieces, &c....I have been to look at the Queen's trial by Hayter, and never was I more disappointed—a regular daub—and yet I find myself singular in this opinion so far.

6th

I really had a most agreeable dinner at Sam Whitbread's brewery on Saturday. We sat down 22....The entertainment of the day to me was going over the brewery after dinner by gaslight. A stable brilliantly illuminated, containing ninety horses worth 50 or 60 guineas apiece upon an average, is a sight to be seen nowhere but in this 'tight little island.' The beauty and amiability of the horses was quite affecting; such as were lying down we favored with sitting upon—four or five of us upon a horse....

May 9th

...Yesterday I dined at Og's—his first great state dinner and new French cook, just imported; our company being Jockey of Norfolk, Althorpe, Bennet, Lambton, Ferguson, Titchfield, my lady [Kensington], two daughters and two sons, and I assure you we had a most jolly day of it....At night, Bennet and I went to Lady Derby's, and certainly an uglier set of old harridans I never beheld in all my life....Humbug

Leopold and Bore Slice were there. Lady Sefton and I sat together to quiz the whole set, of which none were ever more worthy. To-day I dined at Lord King's, and there is the devil to do about Lady Jersey wanting to get Brougham not to dine there, but to dine with her to meet Prince d'Arenberg, who wants particularly to meet Brougham. The latter tells Lady Jersey that as *Mrs.* Brougham dines at Ld. King's, he can't let her go there alone; so 'Sister Sally' writes to Mrs. Brougham to beg as a particular favor that she will dine at Lady King's without Brougham. Mrs. B. replies upon Sally, in a dispatch of four sides of paper, that she can't presume to do so—that she knows full well she never is asked anywhere but on account of Mr. Brougham, and that she can't think of incurring the odium of going anywhere without him....

10th May

...As I walked up to Lord King's door yesterday, up drove Brougham's carriage, and in it was Mrs. Brougham *alone*. So I handed her out, dressed like an interesting villager, all in white, with a wreath of roses round her temples, and she made Brougham's apologies to Lady King for *unavoidable absence on account of business*; so it was all very well, and I complimented her upon her powers of face. I sat next to her at dinner, and her languishing was really beyond all bearing.

June 3rd

...My visit to Stoke Farm has been *perfect*....As a place, it has no other merit than that of having Windsor Castle full in front of it, distant 3 miles. It is on a dead flat, if not in a hollow. It was Sefton's first residence 30 years ago, during which period he told me he had spent £40,000 on it, and he adds it may now be worth from £6,000 to £10,000....

24th

...On Monday, after dining at Sefton's, I went to Lady Jersey's. Her parties are not nearly so numerous as they used to be, and of course they are so much the worse, because they were never too crowded.... While I was talking to Ly. Jersey, Humbug Leopold interrupted us, so she sent me a message by her 'brother Brougham' to come to her next Monday, and stay and be one of the supper click, which always terminates these evenings....I suppose you know Ly. Elizabeth Conyngham's marriage with Lord Burford[31] is off. He became so unmannerly and cross that the lady sent him a letter of dismissal last Saturday.... Here is the town in a mutiny at the King giving Lord Salisbury's blue

[31] Afterwards 9th Duke of St. Albans.

ribbon to Lord Bath, quite unknown to any of the Ministers. *I* am delighted, because Lord Bath is the man who said that if he had seen Bergami and the late Queen in bed together it would not alter his vote *against* the Bill that was to crush her.

July 18, 1823

...I had really a charming day at Roehampton[32] yesterday. It is quite a superb villa or house, with 500 acres of beautiful ground about it, and all Richmond Park appearing to belong to it. What a contrast between Lady Duncannon and her sister Lady Jersey! The quietness and retiredness of the former. She seems, however, very merry and very happy with her nine white-haired children, some of them very pretty....

Stoke Farm [Lord Sefton's], 25th July

...My life here is a most agreeable one. I am much the earliest riser in the House, and have above two hours to dispose of before breakfast, which is at eleven o'clock or even later. Then I live with myself again till about 3, when the ladies and I ride for 3 hours or so....We dine at ¼ past seven, and the critics would say not badly. We drink in great moderation—walk out, all of us, before tea, and then crack jokes and *fiddle* till about ½ past 12 or 1....

March 1, 1824

...On Saturday I dined at Hume's, where I had the good fortune to sit between Mina and one of the Greek deputies....Mina[33] is my delight. Hobhouse wanted to flatter him at the expense of Morillo, Abisbal and Ballisteros, but Mina would not touch him. He spoke in high terms of the talents and courage of Morillo, and of the infinite difficulties all Spaniards were surrounded with. If ever I saw an honest man, he is one; and then he is so hearty and likeable....Yesterday I made my long owing visit at Holland House, and found my lord and my lady alone—she with a bad cold, and he, of course, nursing her. My visit seemed to answer, and I am to dine and stay all night there on Sunday. Would you believe it? Lady H. wd. not let Holland dine with Lord Lansdowne last week—a dinner made purposely for Mina, merely because she thought it might not please the King if he heard of it! Nor will she let Mina or any Spaniard approach Holland House for the same reason. Was there ever such a ——?

[32] [Lord Bessborough's Manresa House. J. G.]

[33] General Espoz y Mina, a distinguished Spanish soldier, commanded a corps under Wellington in the Peninsular war.

April 2

...In talking with Lady Derby about young Gill Heathcote's duel, she put me in mind that young Gill and Mrs. Johnson are cousins—their two grandmothers, Ly. Louisa Manners and Lady Jane Hallyday, having been sisters. So, as the Countess justly observed, after Gill had received Lord Brudenel's shot for maltreating his sister, he ought to have said—'Now, my lord, I must beg you to receive my shot for your conduct to my cousin!' Damned fair, I think....At night I am sorry to say I went with Lord Sefton into that famous, or rather infamous, salon in St. James's Street, where all the world at present assembles. It far surpasses the salon at Paris in splendor, tho' nothing like so large nor so agreeable. To me it appears inevitable that all the young ones must be ruined there. I found Sir Colin Campbell at the hazard table, young Lord William Lennox, Lord Bury and various others whom I knew—all in the face of day—no concealment, but in the great and principal apartment of the house....On Sunday, Sefton and I go to hear Irving,[34] and I am engaged to dine with him, altho' Sussex has since asked me to dine with him to meet Mina.

June 18, Stoke Farm

...Our course for the last three days has been to breakfast punctually at 10, to start for Ascot about 11, not to be home again before 6, and after dinner to be engaged in gambles of one kind or another with cards till one or later....Our old acquaintance Prinney was at the races each day, and tho' in health he appeared perfect, he has all the appearance of a slang leg—a plain brown hat, black cravat, scratch wig, and his hat cocked over one eye. There he sat, in one corner of his stand, Lady Conyngham rather behind him, hardly visible but by her feathers. He had the same limited set of *jips* about him each day, and arrived and departed in private. I must say he cut the lowest figure; and the real noblesse—Whig and Tory—were with his brother York.

June 22nd

...We are all full of a battle that is to take place in the H. of Lords between the Duke of York and our Scroop. Lord Holland has brought in a bill to enable Scroop, tho' a Catholic, to officiate in future as Earl Marshal. It was read a 2nd time on Saturday, tho' the Duke of York and old Eldon were in the minority; but since then the D. of York has become perfectly furious, and has written to every peer he knows, calling upon him to come and protect the Crown against the insidious Scroop.

[34] Edward Irving, the famous Scottish preacher.

We had a jolly day enough at Whitehall on Saturday, altho' I never see Sydney Smith without thinking him too much of a buffoon.

25th June

I dined last night at Lord Carnarvon's, where by comparison for amusement Bedlam[35] decidedly kept the lead, altho' our company were no other than the Dukes of Sussex and Leinster, Marquis Downshire, Earls Grey, Jersey, Darnley, Cowper and Rosslyn, Lords King, Ellenborough and John Russell, and last and least Messrs. Brougham and Creevey. Carnarvon never uttered, and little Sussex very justly whispered to me as we came away that 'it had been a *ma*lancholy day.'... Grey, Rosslyn, Cowper and Jersey went full fig from Carnarvon's to the Beau's, to meet the King who dined there, and Grey says to-day *cut* him most clearly and decidedly....

15 July

...We had beautiful weather at Newmarket... Sefton has a capital house, and, according to custom, his dinners were admirably arranged. Tavistock, Lord Jersey, Punch Greville[36] and Shelley dined there each day, and on Tuesday the Duke of Grafton and the Duke of York. I had never seen the latter in this sort of way before, and was extreamly entertained. He is the very image of the late Lord Petre; perhaps not quite so clever, and certainly not so polite—in short, a very civil and apparently most good-tempered idiot, without any manners at all. Shelley played the fool in patronising him and shewing him off, and Punch Greville disgraced himself by hunching him; but he took both in the same good humour, and we all drank freely in compliment to the royal guest....

Cantley, nr. Doncaster [Michael Taylor, M.P.'s], Sept. 7th

...I had a most prosperous journey down here. There never was such perfection of travelling. I left London at ½ past 8 on Friday morning, and, without an effort, and in a coach loaded with luggage, I was at Doncaster by 5 the following morning—a distance of 160 miles!... Lady Anson goes to town next week to be present at the wedding of her niece, the pretty 'Aurora'—'Light of Day'—Miss Digby... who is going to be married to Lord Ellenborough.... It was Miss Russell who refused Ld. Ellenborough, as many others besides are said to have done.

[35] He had paid a visit that morning to the new Bedlam, south of Westminster Bridge.

[36] Charles Greville [1794–1865], Clerk of the Council and political diarist.

Lady Anson will have it that he was a very good husband to his first wife, but all impressions are that he is a damned fellow.[37]

Cantley [*Doncaster Races*], *24th Sept.*

...George Payne's loss (in bets) turns out to be £21,000 and not £25,000 as I had been told when I wrote to you on Monday. The £4000 saved is better than nothing, but the whole thing is damnable....If one could suppose such a knockdown blow wd. cure him, it might turn out to be money well laid out; but I fear that is hopeless. He says he shall keep to hunting in future and cut the turf....Lady Londonderry is the great show of the balls here in her jewels, which are out of all question the finest I ever beheld—such immense amethysts and emeralds, &c. Poor Mrs. Carnac, who had a regular *haystack* of diamonds last night, was really nothing by the side of the other, tho' in beauty the two ladies are very fairly matched. Such a dumpy, rum-shaped and rum-faced article as Lady Londonderry one can rarely see....

Lambton, Oct. 20

...I got here on Monday night, the company being at dinner, and in the second course. However King Jog, hearing I was arrived, left his throne, and came out, and took me in with him. I found nearer 30 than 20 people there, in a very long and lofty apartment—the roof highly *collegiate* from which hung the massive chandeliers—the curtain drapery of dark-coloured velvet, profusely fringed with gold, and much resembling palls. The company, sitting at a long and narrowish table, never uttered a single, solitary sound for long and long after I was there; so that it really might have been the family vault of the Lambtons, and the company the male and female Lambtons who had been buried in their best cloaths and in a sitting position. Grey and Ly. Elizabeth and Lord Howick are here, the Milbanks, the Wiltons and Bob Grosvenor, the Cavendishes and Henry and his wife, the Dundas's, the Normanbys, Mr. Hobhouse, Sir Hedworth Williamson, young Liddel, Mat Ridley, Capt. Berkley and other captains and majors who ride at our races, not omitting John Milnes. To-day, too, my Lord and Lady Londonderry, with Sir Something and Lady Something Gresley, come. The place is really a fine one, considering how confined it is by coal-pits and smoke, and part of the house quite unrivalled....The capricious young tyrant and devil [Lambton] is all graciosity to myself....Mrs. Taylor had caught fresh cold before I left Cantley, so that she was bled on Sunday

[37] This marriage turned out badly, and was dissolved by Act of Parliament in 1830. 'Aurora' consoled herself by *three* subsequent marriages, and died at Damascus in 1881.

morning and fainted away.... We'll go to our races of to-day. Grey had over and over again expressed to me his nervousness about 14 or 15 of these young men starting for the Cup; the course being very slippery and not wide enough for such a number. You may judge, then, what cause there was for his apprehension when three horses out of the number came in without their riders.... Lady Wilton was standing up as white as a sheet, whilst Lady Augusta Milbank fell to the bottom of the coach as if she had been shot. Just then, however, the good-natured Mat Ridley came galloping up with all his might and main to announce that all was safe.... Milbank is the only one hurt... he had been bled, and is somewhat bruised.... Well—all being over, we came home and dined pretty punctually at seven—and such a dinner I defy any human being to fancy for such an occasion.... I handed Mrs. Dundas out (Miss Williamson that was) and a pretty good laugh I had out of her at our fare. A round of beef at a side table was run at with as much keenness as a banker's shop before a stoppage.... Was there ever such an instance of derangement, with all this expense in other subjects and all his means? I have just been saying to Milnes that it is a low Crockford's, and he admits it is so; but he adds that it is certainly better than last year, for then there was no beef at the side table, but only a sucking-pig! Oh dear, oh dear! it is a neat concern: and yet the comfort of these rooms is *beyond*. I have got my book I was in search of, and his civility about it makes me almost ashamed of thinking him such a stingy, swindling, tyrannical kip as he certainly is.

Well, as to *kips*, I think this Lord Wilton[38] must certainly be a decided one. He has the worst countenance, I think, I ever saw, and he appears a sulky, selfish chap: but she seems very happy... and there is a great charm in all she does....

Lambton, 23rd Sept.

... A very large division of us have got to quiz the whole concern of dinner, so that we really have a very jolly time. King Jog himself still sits silent and involved in thought.... We are really very much indebted to these grandees for the damned fools they make of themselves. Let me present you with a few particulars.... The night before last, between 12 and 1, I being in the library where the same cold fowl always is with wine and water, Lambton came in out of the hazard room, and, finding no water, begun belabouring the bell in a way that I thought must inevitably have brought the whole concern down. No effect was produced,

[38] The 3rd Earl of Wilton, a renowned character in the chase and on the turf.

The Earl of Sefton

From a contemporary portrait by an unknown artist

Earl Grey

From the portrait by Sir Thomas Lawrence

George Canning

From the portrait by Sir Thomas Lawrence and Richard Evans

The Earl of Liverpool

From the portrait by Sir Thomas Lawrence

so he sallied forth, evidently boiling, and when he returned he said:—'I don't think I shall have to ring so long another time.' This is all I know of my own knowledge; but, says Lady Augusta Milbank to me yesterday—'Do you know what happened last night?'—'Du tout,' says I.—'Why,' says she, 'Mr. Lambton rung the bell for water so long, that he went and rung the house bell, when his own man came; and upon saying something in his own justification which displeased the Monarch, he laid hold of a stick and struck him twice; upon which his man told him he could not stand that, and that if he did it again he should be obliged to knock him down. So the master held his hand and the man gave him notice he had done with him....

Lady Londonderry has two maids here—one French and the other Italian, the latter of which presides over the bonnet department. [Follows a story about the Italian.] ... So much for the Italian maid, and now for the French one. Mrs. William Lambton was going along a passage near her ladyship's room between 12 and 1 this morning, when she found *la petite* on the floor crying bitterly, and upon enquiring the cause, she said my lady had beat her so: upon which Mrs. W. Lambton sent her maid to her with some sal volatile, and just as she was administering it, my lord L. came out and would not let her have it, saying she did not deserve it and that she was shamming. Now I should be glad to know if there was *ever*! You never saw any one enjoy these things more than Grey, except indeed Lady Wilton. What a good thing she will make of it all for little Derby and the Countess!

Lambton, Oct. 24th

... I think I never saw Grey to greater advantage, nor Lady Louisa to so much. As for Lady Elizabeth, you never saw a creature so thin or altered in looks.... The other night Ly. Wilton, she, Hobhouse, Milnes and I had a jaw about life, youth and age. Ly. Elizth. was all for childhood—that she shd. never be so happy again, and that if it was not for her friends, she would as soon die as live. This may be Grey gloom, but I am afraid it must be the behaviour of Lord Lothian.

Croxteth, Nov. 10, 1824

... I left FitzClarence at Gosforth and continue to like him as well as ever. Ly. Sefton says he is out and out the best of the family.... Tho' shy, he is not without the *ingenuousness* of the family. He said the King was getting very old and cross—that the Duchess of Clarence was the best and most charming woman in the world—that Prince Leopold was a damned humbug, and that he [FitzClarence] disliked the Duchess of Kent.

chapter twelve

1825–1826

THE LETTERS OF 1825 require no explanatory introduction.

Creevey to Miss Ord

Newcastle, Jan. 3rd, 1825

... As I have taken liberties occasionally with my Sister's conduct, allow me on this occasion to do her justice. The night before I left her, she held forth upon a very favorite subject of hers, her *will*, how she had left me what she had for my life, and then divided it into various ducks and drakes to our cousins, so I let her have the sole possession of the subject without uttering a word myself. I thought, however, afterwards that I ought to put her in possession of my feelings and intentions on this subject, and accordingly I took some pains with a note which I wrote to her from Kinmel, and which I requested her to preserve as a record of my views. I stated to her the precise nature of my situation; I told her that some time or other about £400 would be to be raised out of my moiety of Uncle Eaton's property, to pay debt to that amount principally to Vizard, but that I should never be called upon myself to sell for that purpose, and that I hoped to be able to avoid selling altogether.

That in such case my intention was that she should have it subject to this debt for her life, and afterwards that it should go to you three, and I added as to this last disposition, that I did not feel called upon for any justification to my own relations in paying this piece of attention to those to whom all my obligations were due.[1] ... I ... received a most excellent answer from her, approving most cordially of my opinions....

Earl of Sefton to Creevey

Paris, Jan. 24th

Thanet[2] died this morning of a complication of disorders—mortification in the leg, erisipelas, cholera morbus, fever and gout. His own

[1] His will, made in 1835, was in very different terms.

[2] Creevey's patron, Sackville, 9th Earl. He died at Châlons. By his death, Creevey lost his seat at Appleby.

imprudence had been extreme. To see such a person die at a wretched Hotel without connexion or comfort about him, was really a most deplorable sight....

Creevey to Miss Ord

Feb. 1/2nd

I need not add that having been Thanet's Member, under all the circumstances of the case, will be a very agreeable reminiscence to me as long as I live, and I can't discover at this time that my happiness is affected to the amount of a pin's head at the loss of my seat; my belief is that such will continue to be the case....

Raby Castle, Feby. 16th

I can't go to bed, tho' in my room for that purpose, without having a word with you. First of all because I *hunt* to-morrow, and shall have no opportunity. Don't be alarmed at my talking of hunting, for Lady Darlington[3] insists on my riding her own horse 'Raby,' the safest and quietest horse possible, and her own groom is to accompany me.... Was there ever? ...

We dined about 20. I took out Ly. Augusta[4] leaving the Cyprian Countess to Taylor, but she called to me to come and sit next her. From her conversation I could find that little Sussex had given her a very favorable impression of me; however, be that as it may, nothing can exceed the civility of both her and My Lord ever since I entered the house....

Raby, Feby. 17th

We continue all sunshine. I was next Mylady at breakfast, and very pretty company we were, and she would have me take a crust of bread properly done up in paper in my pocket. Then the Ladies being present in the great hall when we mounted, I complained of having no *professional whip*, so Mylady sent for her own, and presented it to me. Well, then Mylord and I had a very agreeable ride of about 5 miles to cover, where I found 'Raby,' and such a horse, and such a chaperon of a groom or whipper-in to take care of me, and such a day, and such a scene for beauty and animation I never beheld. Our ground was on the high

[3] Elizabeth Russell, second wife of 3rd Earl of Darlington, afterwards Duke of Cleveland. At the time of their marriage, July 27, 1813, Lady Holland described her as Lord Darlington's 'bonne amie, Mrs. Russell, alias Funnereau.'

[4] Lord Darlington's daughter. Wife of Mark Milbank.

banks of the Tees where we found, and after a run of about an hour and a half or more killed, I going over every leap that any one else did, and being in at the death, but then these leaps are no great things, and such a horse, and guide made them really nothing. We afterwards went to another cover where we found again, but then I parted convoy having had a pretty good supply of exercise. My Whipper-in conducted me home. I then joined the Ladies in the garden, and damned agreeable we are, but as *Duets* are always the most agreeable, Mylady and I soon separated from the rest.... Then she would take me and shew me the stables, and she petted the horses, and had the cloaths taken off one or two to shew me their beautiful shapes, and she was *Myladied* up and down through every stable, and with faces as grave, and *hearts as devoted* as if she had been an hereditary Countess of Darlington every bit.... Yet from any thing that has passed her lips, as yet, I defy any one who did not know her, to discover her former vocation, or even her birth, parentage, and education. She puts me perpetually in mind of Ly. Dacre both in looks and voice, particularly the latter, tho' not in age, for she is as fresh as a four year old, and made for 'de laugh.' I never saw two females laugh more heartily than she and Mrs. Shaftoe at the story of Mrs. *Borch* and the potato.

The concern altogether is a very agreeable one. *He*, you know, is a very clever man, and his civility and attention to me are unbounded. He is now waiting to shew me the Baron's Hall.

Cantley, Feb. 21st

Don't you think we are very pretty Travellers? We left Raby at a ¼ past 10 this morning, we have come 90 miles; we ate mutton chops at Boroughbridge, we broke our axeltree, and by some miracle escaped an overturn at the entrance of Doncaster. Michael, Mrs. Taylor and I came on in a hack chaise, and we were all at dinner here by 8 o'clock. Every thing ended at Raby as well as it had begun.

It is quite clear to me that Mrs. Taylor and Michael without saying a word to *me* are at work for a seat for me....

London, March 7th

...Old Dow: Richmond upon the marriage that is about to take place between Mrs. Tighe's eldest Son, and a young Ly. Lennox: The Dow: had fixed...upon...Lord Hervey...The Duke took Tighe to his Mother's, and leaving him belowstairs, went up to announce the fact to her himself. She began with saying, 'Can't see Mr. Tighe—Lord Hervey—to be sure Ld. Bristol wrote an uncommonly handsome letter in favor of Mr. Tighe, but can't possibly see him—Lord Hervey.' So the Duke said it was quite impossible to resist the thing any longer, and he would step down and bring Mr. Tighe up, to which she kept going on, 'Can't possibly see Mr. Tighe, Lord Hervey,' and when the two Gentlemen came in they found her in the middle of the room *with her eyes shut*, and after some pause she said, 'Duke of Richmond, leave the room,' and then I suppose it was settled, but she goes on still: 'Never can go to Ireland after this connection with Mr. Tighe,'[5] and some one having asked her how the first family dinner had gone off, which consisted of the Bedfords, *Bathursts* &c. &c. to meet Mr. Tighe, she said, 'Quite shocking. Mr. Tighe talked such horrid politicks, Lord Bathurst very near leaving the room.'

March 16th

... There are all kinds of reports about the state of the King's health. From the *Apothecary* department it is said there is a general regular declining in strength and flesh, the symptoms in short of a general breaking up. From Halford's shop it is said he is better than he has been these two years *but* that his present extreme inactivity is very unfavourable to the continuance of his health. In the mean time Our *York* is all alive O! He dined at Sefton's this day week as gay as a lark, and gave them a description of a new house he (York) is going to build upon the site of his present one, which is to be pulled down forthwith, and he has taken Ly. Ellenbro's (Queen Caroline's that was) in South Audley Street for two years whilst his own is building. You may suppose the scale of his operations when I tell you that his principal apartment is to be 82 feet long. This I think for a gentleman in his 62nd. year without a sou in the world, and owing it is said at least a million of money, is pretty well, but it shews clearly that those who raise the money for him are confident he will get the Throne....

Stoke Farm, June 3rd

Well, we had a most prosperous day yesterday, got to Ascot quite in time for everything, and saw the finest Race that according to all the critics ever was seen between 'Bizarre' and 'Longwaist' for the Cup. We saw your old acquaintance *Prinney* looking quite as well, and nearly as merry as we have seen him in his best days. Contrary to his former practice, he drove up the Course to his stand, in the presence of everybody—himself in the first coach and four, the Duke of Wellington sit-

[5] Lady Louisa married Mr. W. F. Tighe, of Woodstock, Co. Kilkenny, in April. After the marriage the Duchess on one occasion stayed some time there but never spoke to her son-in-law.

ting by his side. There were three other carriages and four, and a phaeton after him, and I sh'd. think 20 servants in scarlet on horseback, and as all his horses are of the greatest beauty, the whole thing looked very splendid; in short, quite as it should be. Ly. Conyngham and Ly. Eliz'th., Ly. Mountcharles, Ly. Bathurst, . . . Ly. Cowper &c. &c. were the Ladies about him, but the *beauty* of the day out and out was Mrs. Hughes Ball ci-devant Mercandotti; she was in the D. of York's stand, and surrounded by all the dandys.

. . . This is one of the finest days possible, so Mylord drives the Ladies to Ascot, and Francis and I ride. What strength the women of this family have! Mylady and two of her Daughters were at Almack's till late yesterday morning, and Ly. Maria was with the Greys at Ld. Hertford's *Opera* till 3, and the same Lady Maria was off by 8 this morning with her Brother on horseback to Taplow, 6 miles off, to see her little Nephew Grenfell, and she was back again to breakfast. . . .

June 9th

. . . I have a card as large as life from the Earl and Countess of Darlington to dine with them on the 22nd, to meet the Duke of Sussex, so I take it for granted I must go, whatever may come of it, but, as you say, I w'd. much rather belong to this dry Earl of Thanet[6] than this bowing and scraping Earl of Darlington. Apropos to the former, Lord Robt. Spencer who is related to him, waited upon him in due form, and requested him to name his own day for dining, but which the Earl declined doing upon his accustomed allegation that he did not like dining out. . . .

June 23rd

. . . When I returned to my lodging I found Mrs. Taylor had been there and left word she w'd. call for me at ½ past 6, which she did, and we were the first[7]; little Sussex came about ten minutes after, but we did not sit down to dinner till ½ past 7, which was said to be the fault of a new cook. We were two or three and twenty I believe altogether. The Earl and Countess, Ly. Arabella, Miss Taylor, Sussex, his son D'Este, and Stephenson, Mr. and Mrs. Taylor, Jack Vane and Creevey, Mr. and Mrs. Brougham, and a Brother of Brougham's, Dr. and Mrs. Lushington, Mr. and Lady Louisa Lambton, Milbank and Ly. Augusta, Earls Grey and Roslyn, and Ld. Duncannon. The *humour* of the day was Mrs. Brougham. She came in more languishing than ever. I

[6] The late peer's brother, Charles.

[7] At the Darlingtons'.

announced to my different female friends my conviction that at length she would accomplish her favorite project of fainting, before she left the house. I handed Ly. Arabella down stairs and sat between her and Lambton. We had Mrs. Brougham nearly opposite. She was going her lengths the whole of dinner, so that I made Ly. Arabella nearly die with laughing at her. At last, however, her colour did really desert her face, and she actually bolted. Ld. Darlington left his seat and handed her out, but not a single Lady of the family either went with her or followed her. When Mylord returned, we told him we thought he ought to tell Brougham of it, who sat about 8 or 9 from her on the same side of the table, and so mylord did, but all the return he got for it was a twitch or two of the nose, and he kept his place as steadily as everybody else, and what became of Dear Mrs. Brougham I know not, for I neither heard nor saw anything more of her afterwards. The Raby Cook beat the new one easy. I wish you had seen the servants. I called them to Ly. Arabella the New and Old Imperial Guard. They were one and all in bags and bouquets, the four servants out of livery had brown coats with gold embroidery, and *frogs* exactly the same as the King's dress uniform, the six or seven Livery servants were in bright yellow dress coats. One end of the table was very very merry, which is more than I suspect the other was. *King Jog* was as amiable as be damned, and nothing will serve him but I must come and occupy my *own* room again at Lambton. Poor Ld. Grey looked terribly ill I thought, but it is said he is greatly improved....

I am much amused with Ly. Holland having set up a hue and cry after me. Duncannon said yesterday that in her different notes to people to come to her, she always ends, 'And pray if you have any influence with Mr. Creevey, do bring him.'...

Stoke Farm, August 24th

I found here our Aunt, the Duchess of Newcastle, the Frazers, and Billy Churchill (who was a great croney of Ld. Craven's); Dow: Salisbury had left that morning, which I was sorry for, as Ly. Louisa says it was very good fun to hear her and the Duchess of Newcastle together. The latter of these young people considers herself as entirely out of the World, so she asked the other for information upon all subjects which was very graciously supplied by her. I was very sorry the Duchess herself went away yesterday, for I took to her much, and to her *dress* still more. She came from Frogmore where she had been staying a week with Princess Augusta....

Cantley, Septr. 16th

... The Countess of Tankerville[8] and Ly. Emma came here yesterday to dinner, and are to be off this morning for Chillingham. This alteration in her Ladyship's plans she accounts for, from her fear of Ld. Tankerville's anger if she stays, as he has written to her that he shall be returned home from Scotland this week, and fully expects her to be so too.

This Mrs. Taylor and I consider as *fudge*, that her object in proposing her visit here was the D. of Devonshire, and he being off, she is so too. You know he gave a fête this year upon Ly. Emma's coming out; the fireworks and lamps having the word 'Emma' in every shape and colour. I cannot say much of the beauty of the young lady, she is very like the old Lady Tankerville, only 20 times more near sighted. As for the Mother, she is really beyond everything for *fun*. She has been making me laugh for hours, and I have made her tell her stories over and over again. I think she shines most about Mrs. Coutts,[9] with whom she has lately become acquainted at Worthing. It is impossible by letter to do justice to her *acting*, and her broken English. 'A Play being to be acted at Worthing... Mrs. Coutts... left her own box, and came to ours, and sat herself upon an empty bench, just behind us, and almost directly she began, "I am sure, Ly. Tankerville, you must find this a very wicked and illnatured world, I know I find it so to myself. I dare say you have heard all the stories they tell of me going to be married to Lord Burford.[10] Good God how can you think I wd. marry a boy. He is quite a child as compared with me; then when I think of my dear Mr. Coutts, how is it possible? To be sure Ld. Burford is quite charming; it is impossible to live with him, and not quite to love him; then his Sisters are so charming. It is so delightful to me after spending a morning with those vulgar people at my Bank to enjoy the society of these enlightened girls. ... I have not... a friend in the world, every body cheats me; I pay three times as much as any body else for every thing; then I can't manage my accounts, and tho' dear Mr. Coutts left me so much, I am very often short of money. Illnatured people say I married Mr. Coutts for money, how can that be when I give his Daughter £35,000 a year...." So I said, "My dear Mrs. Coutts, surely you might get somebody who is poor to take care of your concerns for £200 or £300 per year—for instance Poodle Byng."...'

[8] Corise de Grammont, brought up at Devonshire House.
[9] Harriet Mellon, widow of the banker.
[10] 9th Duke of St. Albans. She married him in 1827.

Septr. 24th

...I am just out of the Dining room at 10, and up to the chin (not in wine) but in *Ecarté* engagements for the rest of the evening.

Well, NO *dissolution*, we have it from official quarters in all directions, and with details. In short, it is settled, and *I am good* for July, or I shd. say October 1826. So 'its all mighty well, my Dears,' and I can say with great truth, that my principal gratification at this result is, that I think it is agreeable to you all, and that we can go on defrauding the public by not paying for any letter we write....

We have had a capital week; the Seftons old and young have been delighted and the *poor sufferer* Lambton has conducted himself with a philosophy, and even an amiability that his warmest admirers could never have expected. Only think, poor Fellow, of his giving 2,500 Guas. for dear 'Cedric,' who never lost a Race (having run 12) when he was Shelley's Horse, and travels down to Doncaster for the honor of being 4th.... The mob actually convulsed with joy at the Wentworth triumph over him. To conclude, he that very night buys a horse of Ld. Sligo, 'Canteen,' for 1,000 Guas. for the purpose of next day repairing his misfortune, when lo and behold *one George Payne* with an unknown horse 'Barytes,' which he likewise had just purchased, beats the great 'Canteen' in the cleverest way possible....

(In my bedroom, two o'clock in the morning) Mrs. Taylor and I having done Mylord and Mylady out of £3. apiece at Ecarté, so it's all mighty well, and nobody can afford it better.

...There were *two* dancing rooms, so...Ly. Londonderry[11] comes to Mrs. Taylor, in my hearing,... 'Don't you think, Mrs. Taylor, it w'd. be a good thing to have a Country Dance, and for me to begin it?' 'Oh! *my dear Child* it is exactly what I could wish you to do,' and so of course, being done by the Marchioness of Londonderry, all the Grandees, Duke of Devonshire (who was here after all), the Princes[12] of Brunswick, Ditto of Wowsk (Russian) were all at right hand and left in no time; the Molyneux Ladies had partners without end, Princes and Nobles, British and Foreign, and they have been quite delighted with their week, not omitting what they have done their Father out of at Hepper's.

Sept. 29th

...Monday I went with all the Ladies to the Ball. Tuesday we staid at home. Wednesday, Ball again. Thursday, the Ladies went to the Ball,

[11] Frances Vane-Tempest, second wife of 3rd Marquis of Londonderry. Mrs. Taylor's niece.

[12] Sons of the Duke of Brunswick, who was killed at Quatre Bras.

and I staid at home and won a pound or two of Little Sussex at Ecarté.

What think you of the impertinence of the Copley Girls that night? Altho' Lady Londonderry had told them that she meant to get up a Ball, with which they professed to be 'highly delighted' and said of course they would be there, and altho' the Duke of Devonshire had engaged Ly. Londonderry to dance with him, the said Copleys got up a musick party at Sprotbro' of the Mansfields, Vernons &c. &c., and not one of them came to the Ball, not even the D. of Devonshire. The latter, I believe, sent the *next morning* some kind of apology to Ly. Londonderry, saying his carriage was actually at the door, but that he was too unwell to venture out, and he returned that day to Chatsworth. Our Niece mentioned all this to her Aunt as a piece of great incivility, but without any anger, not so however her fiery little Marquis who talked about '*a* Sir *John*[13] Copley that lives in this neighbourhood' in a manner that it was thought w'd. find its way to Sprotbro.'...

I am somehow much convinced of the sincerity of Ly. Darlington. She said, 'I have asked it of Ld. Darlington as a personal favor to myself, and as the greatest he can do me. I feel, Mrs. Taylor, that I owe it to you, and I am sure it will be accomplished.' Then she again talked of there being one seat that might still be vacant, but she w'd. not dwell upon it without a greater certainty....

It is a curious thing, but it is not less true on that account, that altho' I really think I sh'd. not have minded being turned out of Parliament at present the least bit, *yet* I am really very much pleased to remain in, and to have the probability of another year to turn ourselves in. It is a funny thing, if after all, my conduct about the Catholics, which according to Brougham played the devil with my Parliamentary prospects, is in some measure connected with my stealing another year out of poor dear old Appleby....

Dear Dow Bland has just been going over Devonshire House with me, as we drank our Coffee together. She was a friend of the first Duchess, and says she was a real good one if she had not been spoilt. She adds that Ly. Melbourne was the real original devil of all that click, and that she extended her amours so late in life as to entrap Ld. Byron. The last fact I never heard before, but true or not I doat upon old Bland....

October 4th

...I still delight in our Blands. My only regret is that their *two* maids are not of the party. One of them is quite as much *rouged* as her Mis-

[13] His name was Joseph.

tress, she has only lived with them 23 years.... Old Bland is very great upon maid servants. She says, manufacturers and *education* have destroyed the race. The time was when she could have respectable young women—farmer's daughters—to be either dairymaids, housemaids, or even kitchen maids, but that now she can't pick up an article worth a farthing for love or money.... The only *weakness* I have as yet discovered in my friend's character is a propensity to claim an odd trick or an honor without the slightest pretensions to either....

...I am sorry to say her fraudulent activity at cards last night was redoubled, probably because it was her last go—for in addition to claims upon honors and tricks without foundation, she took to scoring up points that had never been gained, and this so palpably that her partner, Capt. Bouverie of the Blues, Lady Robert's grandson, and a capital player, and most gentlemanlike little fellow, was obliged to show her up in every one of her depredations....

Oct. 6th

The most interesting to me since I wrote last has been reading our Jaffa's[14] Memoir of the Russian Campaign....

Jaffa told Mrs. Taylor and myself a curious thing yesterday, whilst we were riding. 'There,' says he, 'it was just about the length of that village that I rode after Murat, with my pistol cocked, quite within reach of him, but I could not find it in my heart to fire at him, and no reflection has gratified me more since than my not doing so.' This was in Russia in 1812, and in 1814 Jaff was sent on some mission to Murat's Army or Head Quarters or Court, when he was presented to Murat who instantly put out his hand to him, and said he had always wished to see him, and thank him for his noble conduct, for that he fully expected his death from him. Now I must believe this to be *true*, and *if it is* I think you must admit it is a very curious historical *pint*.

Well, Mrs. Taylor has an answer from the Countess, and it's all mighty well as to my not going to Raby now. She then writes, 'Mr. Creevey's amusing and kind letter I received with infinite pleasure, and indeed whatever he either writes or says must always be entertaining.' Upon your soul!!!...

I saw Copley to-day in Doncaster and heard from him that Lord Charles Fitzroy is going to be married to Miss Cavendish. They are but a dry couple. Ld. George gives his Daughter £40,000. I asked Copley how he managed with his deaf Duke during the Race Week, and he said he was perfectly sure the said Duke never heard one word he said

[14] Gen. Sir Robert Wilson.

during the whole time. He mentions one trait of his friend that was not amiss. There is a Mrs. Lumley in this neighbourhood, a little, pretty, flirting, Irish woman, that all the men make up to, so the Duke to be in the fashion desired to be introduced to her, and the next time she saw him she presumed to *nod* at him, a liberty which he instantly resented by declaiming her to be a very vulgar woman, and that he never sh'd. take any further notice of her....

October 16th

...After Lambton Races we go to Newton House, where we shall stay about a week, and then we go on to Thorp (Milbank's) where we are to remain ten days or a fortnight, so it will be the latter end of November before *this* set of engagements end....

...I have just finished the 1st. of my 'Letters to Lord John Russell upon his notice of a motion for Parliamentary Reform.' I am extremely pleased with my work, and if an author is allowed to be a Judge of his own offspring, I think it will have great success, and produce no small effect. *Brougham* comes on Tuesday on his way to Town, whom of course I must consult as *Reviewer*, and if he approves, I shall give it him to take to Town, and let it go to press out of hand. I don't put my name to it at present....I hit damned hard in my work, and yet am as mild as milk.

Moore's Life of Sheridan, what I have seen of it, is damnable.

Lambton, Oct. 23rd

Just arrived, and if there is time before this Bell rings, I may as well open the campaign by giving a list, as far as I can see, of the Company—the Normanbys, Sir James and Lady Graham, Lady Tankerville and Lady Emma, Mr. and Mrs. Wm. Lambton. Mr. and Mrs. Taylor, Mr. and Mrs. Wyrvill, Lord Wilton, Bob Grosvenor, Frank Russell, Mr. Russell of this County, Sir Robt. Wilson and his Daughter, Milbank, General and Mrs. Grey, Lord Howick, Sir Alex'r. Don, Geo. Payne, Mr. Holyoak, Sir Hedworth Williamson, John Milnes, Cap'n. Berkeley, Hedworth Lambton, 'Dear Eddard,' Captn. Wyrvill, Major Healey, Captn. White, Mr. Creevey, Tom Duncombe, and others I must have omitted, but I know we are to be 37 at dinner, and Milnes tells me there is a great improvement in the concern. A new cook and a very good one, and the victuals much more plentiful.

Our Jog was graciosity to me to the outside, and nothing could be better than Lady Louisa—so it's all mighty well.

Lambton, Oct. 25th

Let me see. Events of yesterday.... The party at night at its different avocations, i.e., a noisy hazard table at one side of the hall, a match at Billiards at the other, Lady Tankerville, Mrs. Taylor, Lord Howick and myself at an animated rubber of whist in one part of the Drawing Room, Lady Normanby enchanting her ravished audience with her vocal and instrumental musick in another; when lo and behold out went the *gas* from the top of the house to the bottom. No, nothing can do justice to the scene, and the confusion it produced, for you must know the house is literally lighted by gas, there is not a candle to be had for love or money....

Our Milbank, having looked in vain for a candle stick last night, took a little Ormolu one from the Library table, and when it had served its purpose in lighting his candle in his bed room, he flung it out of his window that it might be not be found in his room.

The last full year of Lord Liverpool's long administration was a gloomy one. It was a time of grave industrial depression and acute distress which the Government endeavoured to relieve by a measure permitting a limited importation of corn. Liverpool's own health was breaking up under the strain of these anxieties and the ever-present Catholic question, and he was conscious that the life of his government and his own alike hung by a thread.

By contrast with the two preceding years of carnival, the first half of 1826 was, for Creevey also, tinged with disappointment and sadness.

Mrs. Creevey's brother, Charles Brandling, died in January. At the end of May Creevey was led to believe, through a mistake of Mrs. Taylor's, that Lord Darlington had offered him a safe seat at Winchelsea, a borough of eleven electors. It turned out, however, that Lord Darlington wanted Creevey to represent his chosen candidate, Lord Howick, at the election, and Creevey found himself committed to this exercise in altruism—and he carried it off, despite his bitter disappointment, with dignity and good humour. Then, at the end of June, Sefton's daughter Georgiana, the wife of Charles Pascoe Grenfell, died suddenly, leaving a family of young children. Sefton was for a time inconsolable, and Creevey, who was fast becoming almost a member of the family, shared its sorrow and proved a very present help in trouble. From this year the close intimacy between him and Sefton began, and (if indeed they were sons of the same father and Sefton had been aware of the fact all along) it must have been about this time that Creevey was informed of the truth about his parentage. For if certain allusions which occur in the correspondence from this time onwards bear a construction which may be put on them, the legend clearly became henceforth a secret acknowledged in the family. At the end of the year, Creevey went to live with his friends, the Taylors, at their house in Whitehall.

Creevey to Miss Ord

Feb. 4th, 1826

...I thank you for your letter of last night as being most agreeable and satisfactory to a feverish Author, because I may say without *muggery* I have the most perfect reliance on your combined judgements, and then in return you have some reason to be satisfied in seeing *your own* view of the case compleatly adopted by the 'Times' newspaper, which I am happy to say is not only the best written paper at present in the press, and the most sold, but its principles are notorious for *following* rather than leading public opinion, so I ought to conclude my case with the public is good. I say nothing now of those contingent sacrifices you allude to of being out of Parliament. I shall be 58 next month, poor Charles Brandling would only have been 57 to-day, and who would have supposed I should have outlived him? It is very cheap being honest at such an age. I don't care a farthing for anything in the world but you three and Anne's two children....

Lord John Russell to Creevey

Feby. 20th

I should have thanked you before for your pamphlet, had I not been at Paris when your letter arrived. I think it excellent, and calculated to do good when money ceases to be uppermost in every one's thoughts. I fear, however, there are *very few* cases in which Election Committees restore the right of voting to householders.

We have not yet done with bank and bullion. When you come to Town we will see what I can do about Reform this session.

Creevey to Miss Ord

Stoke, August 11th

...I am sure you'll be glad to know that we are looking *better* here. The young Ladies are getting round to their old manners with me, to let me try to amuse them, and in truth to be amused. *He* too has had some better nights, and by Lady Sefton's assistance in telling me when and where I am to fling myself in this way, we go thro' the day very well. These two little boys of Lady Georgiana's are quite charming, one turned 3 and the other 2. The eldest the image of its Mother—the same pale complexion, the same gentle and composed manner. The other is a more riotous chap, but both as *good* and tractable as ever they can be, and most companionable. They are on the lawn here with their Aunts and Grandmama for several hours every day, during some part of which Sefton has always some play with them, but it never fails to nearly overpower him when it is over, and it is one of the occasions when I am always upon the watch for him.... He and she and Lady Maria and I went in the carriage yesterday to see all that is going on at Windsor, and Mr. Wyatt-*Ville* himself did us the honor of conducting us thro' all the new apartments and showing us all the projected improvements. All the New Living Rooms make a very good Gentleman's or Nobleman's house, nothing more. Indeed I dare say Woburn is a better house, but then the situation you know is such a thing, and there is one part of the house newly created, which, with my propensities, is above all price, and that is a corridor 16 feet wide and 560 in length—a gallery connected with every living room, and which is to be filled with pictures. My eye, what a spot for a *'walky, walky.'* ...

Sefton is gone to Town to-day, and I flatter myself he is going to bring me a compliment of a new pair of spectacles, ones that will stick faster on one's head than my present ones. I only guess this from his *manner* last night in making me try *his*, and how the glasses suited. At all events he is pledged to bring me back some *Rhubarb Pills*.

Lady Sefton is gone to Taplow (Old Grenfell's) 7 miles off to see Lady Georgiana's baby, and another little girl between 1 and 2 years, for she has left 5 children....

Stoke, August 20th

... Sir John Lade[15] has undertaken to my Lord to place us all some day next week in a position from which we can see unobserved our beloved Sovereign enjoying the innocent recreation of fishing in the Virginia Water, and if this is once accomplished, it must afford matter for writing about.... Old Salisbury arrived yesterday.... *In* the phaeton were a spaniel and a pug dog as her ladyship's only companions....

[15] Famous Whip and Corinthian and crony of the Regent. *Vide* Doyle's *Rodney Stone*. Died in comparative poverty on a pension continued by Queen Victoria.

We play cards together each night, but before that Sefton had put us afloat at our tea table out of doors, and we are doing extremely well, I thank you. It is true she speaks if possible more slowly and more awfully than Lady Sefton, but she has evidently a very quick ear for a joke, however guarded her merriment may be.

I have only heard her as yet mention one of her Court Nannygoats. Before dinner was announced[16] she perceived a Royal whisper from the Monarch to Lady Conyngham, but God forbid she should even have guessed what it was about, but upon going out to dinner, altho' the Duchess of Gloucester was present, and it is unalterable law that one Royalty always takes out another, to the great horror of our old Sally, the King said, 'Come, my dear Salisbury, you must come with me. Mary (meaning the Duchess of Gloucester), the Duke of Dorset will take you out,' and the said Duchess knowing full well what this meant, took up a position *opposite* her Brother, thus leaving the young man to enjoy his device of sitting between the dear Marchioness of Salisbury, and *Conyngham*. Now was there ever? Only 64 years old yesterday week and can't be separated a couple of yards from his large Angel even at dinner. In the evening he plays at *shilling* whist, and likes it so much....

Stoke, Tuesday, August 22nd

...We have just lost our *Sally*, and I only wish you could have seen her four long tails with white reins, and huge tassels on each horse, and herself driving her dogs 20 miles to London.

Saturday and Sunday were so hot that none of us were able to ride, but yesterday my Lady with her four Daughters, and two Sons, and old *Sally* and I took the field to Bulstrode, and its environs—*Sall*[17] being the only one who mounted her horse like an arrow from the hand of her groom, the horse too being an uncommonly high one, milk white, dressed in a net, and a present (as she informed me) from her Son Salisbury who had given 200 Guineas for it. It seems the old girl has a jointure of £5,000 a year, and the house in Arlington Street, but Sefton says, runs out infernally....I had a good deal of jaw with her yesterday in our ride, and tho' I did not discover any of the talent Sefton gives her credit for, her *opinions* upon different matters were very amusing. By way of an outing for her, we have driven out the last two nights after coffee, about ten o'clock in two open carriages, taking the road to Salt Hill, and so seeing *the London Mails to the West of England arrive*

[16] At the royal cottage.
[17] She was now 76 years old.

and change horses &c., and *poor* as such amusement may appear to be for persons of our rank and age, I assure you it gave very great and general satisfaction, and so after a cool drive of ten miles about, we returned to our tea, and as near 12 as might be each night we have made up a rubber for *Sally* at crown points, and about ½ past one and after finishing 3 or 4 rubbers, she has retired to her *couché*....

August 25th

...Only think of our going yesterday in pursuit of Virginia Water, and absolutely springing the King Fisher himself, not fishing however, but in a little phaeton with Lady Conyngham, and what think you of his *hiding* himself, and our waiting to see him fairly unkennelled again. It is all true, upon my soul....

Croxteth, October 9th

I left London on Friday, and to my great delight had the coach all to myself. After travelling all night arrived at Prescot a little after five on Saturday evening, and as I was just going to order a chaise *two* ostlers came running up to say, 'My Lord's carriage is waiting for you, Sir,' and so in the family coach, and with My Lady's footman to take care of me, I came here. I found Sefton better than I expected....

November 1st

When Lady Sefton and I were left alone yesterday, I said, 'Well, really, Lady Sefton, I think I may now congratulate you upon Lord Sefton having at length got the better of his misery,' and she answered, 'Oh yes, Mr. Creevey, it is so, and it is all your own doing, and you are the only person who knows how and when to amuse him. Everybody else has failed. Poor Victor de L'Aigle who is the kindest and most attached creature in the world, came from France on purpose to see us, but instead of amusing Lord Sefton, his own eyes were always filling with tears when he looked at him. Then Mrs. —— used to amuse Lord Sefton extremely, but her manner is so daring that he took quite a horror at her. In short, you are the only person who understands him, and cleverness and jokes are the only things he will attend to.' Curious enough, is it not, and very satisfactory? ...

Novr. 18th

I am sure you would not wish me to miss Lady Foley.[18] It is very nearly the direct road to London. Then to see a Noble Novel Writer

[18] Daughter of 2nd Duke of Leinster and wife of 3rd Lord Foley.

who has never been known in the midst of all their ruin to degrade herself by putting on either a pair of gloves or a ribbon a *second time*, and who has always 4 *Ponies* ready saddled and bridled for any enterprise or excursion that may come into her head, is surely worth seeing, to say nothing of Foley, who without a halfp'orth of income keeps the best house,[19] has planted more oak trees than any man in England, and by the influence of his name and personal popularity returns two members for Droitwich and one for the County. Then he would get his next neighbour, Ld. Dudley, to meet me, so we should have 'Jean qui pluert et Jean qui ris,'[20] Ward being in a state of lingering existence under the frightful pressure of £120,000 a year....

The Duke of York's case seems a marvellous one. Sefton hears constantly of him from Head Quarters, and his first favorable report was from a curious quarter. *Ude*, the cook of all cooks in the great world, who lived for years with Sefton, and who now lives with the Duke, both as cook and friend, writes to Sefton begging him not to mind what the Papers say, for that his appetite is returned, and that he will do. This is confirmed by letters from Greville and Armstrong, both in the household....

Whitehall, London, Decr. 21st

Well, I must say that no man ever had a better *hotel* than I have, and I am equally certain that Mrs. Taylor is perfectly sincere when she expresses her hope that I will always use it as my own in future... and here our Taylor has just put his head into the room saying, 'My dear creature I beg you will ask whoever you like to dine here,' in which, too, I am sure he is likewise quite sincere, so that really in *my* circle I know of no such shop or such people....

[19] At Witley Court, Worcestershire.
[20] Creevey was not strong at French.

chapter thirteen

1827–1829

A BRIEF SUMMARY of the changes in the administration during the years 1827–8 will serve to explain some of the allusions in the letters which follow. Without it, the undercurrent of excitement which runs through them would be inexplicable to a generation to whom changes of governments, of dynasties, of constitutions, of national policies, are everyday affairs which evoke no unusual interest.

In February, 1827, Liverpool made way for Canning, who had long been preparing for that day. Though the King distrusted his Catholic policy, Canning had secured the favour of the Court. But he, like Brougham, was suspect to politicians of all parties, an adventurer and opportunist for all his brilliant gifts. He failed to form a Tory Government, among others Wellington, Eldon, and Peel refusing to co-operate with him. He was thrown back on a coalition, and his negotiations with Lord Lansdowne (Henry Petty) kept excitement at fever heat for many weeks.

His Government was formed in April and included Lyndhurst, Goderich, Huskisson, and Palmerston. But Canning died in August and all was to do again. Both parties were split up into factions, and Creevey's 'Mountain' was rent in twain. Lansdowne was a traitor confessed; Brougham, too shifty to be nailed down, was credited with every kind of infamy.

Canning was succeeded by Goderich (with Palmerston, Lansdowne, and Huskisson in his cabinet). Goderich gave place in January, 1828, to the Duke of Wellington, and the Duke saw George IV out.

Creevey enjoyed these historical events rather as an observer and student of politics than as a participator. He still found in the wilderness Paradise enow, and he poured out his wit and malice on all and sundry in public life with less earnestness and more vivacity than of old. The Man-of-fashion still dominated the Party-man.

Creevey to Miss Ord

Brooks's, Feby. 6th, 1827

. . . I went to Arlington Street, and found Lady Sefton as good as good, and quite merry; the young ones too quite alive, and all most anxious for my coming to tell of Papa having invited *Lady Holland* to dine there Sunday week after all his abuse of her, and all his vows that he never would again go near her. . . .

Sefton made me come into his own room after I had had my coze with the Ladies. I promised to dine there to-morrow to meet Sir Charles Stuart. As Little Sussex was prevented from dining with the Hollands from illness, I went from Arlington Street to Kensington, and wrote my name there. It seems he (Sussex) has been one of the many victims of the Duke of York's funeral, by catching cold in the Chapel. The Duke of Montrose has been at death's door from it, Roslyn is still confined, Wellington was very severely hit, and Canning's illness is from the same cause. By all the accounts Mrs. Taylor has from Stephenson about *Billy Clarence's* conduct at the funeral, it must have been perfect. What think you to begin with of these Princes being kept waiting in the cold Chapel an hour and a half before every thing was ready, during which period various peers made the most marked homage to *Billy*, and as Stephenson was the Duke of Sussex's train bearer, he was privy to all that passed. . . Whenever there was an interval he turned to Sussex with the same observation, 'We shall be treated *now*, Brother Augustus, very differently from what we have been.' . . . I quite long to hear our Sussex about it, and they say *Mrs. Kent* quite belongs to this click, so there ought to be some fun. The Duke of York's debts don't exceed £150,000, the new house included. He owes about £50,000 of it to his Sister Sophia.

It is said Prinney fell over head and ears in love with *Miss Chester*, the actress, the two nights he was at the play, and that Lady Conyngham has been made very uneasy, which of course is all my eye. . . .

Feby. 20th

. . . The Duke of Cumberland cannot be dead, as Lord Sefton has just left the Duke of Sussex who 'had not *hard* of it.'

Every one in the dark as to Liverpool's successor, tho' the general feeling is in favor of Canning being the man. . . .

. . . I have been called out by Barnes of the 'Times' who told me he had had a direct application if not *from* at least *on behalf* of the King to give no more account of his private life at Brighton. . . .

Feby. 22nd

...Tankerville keeps to his text that Peel went to Brighton to propose himself as Liverpool's successor, and he adds to it now, that the King's answer was, he was too ill to attend to business, but that he would think of it....Kensington, on the other hand, says that not a word has been said to the King about a successor to Liverpool....From all I hear my belief is that Liverpool is not going to die, and it seems to follow of course in the present state of the Cabinet that they will do nothing till he is sufficiently recovered to be consulted upon this subject. In the meantime by Kensington's account Huskisson must be infernally ill, so how these victims of the funeral will go on with their Corn Laws and Free Trade and Catholics one can't make out....

March 15th

...Well, now for Sally's benefit yesterday, or rather mine at Sally's House, and I assure you it was *perfect*. Being told by Lord Arthur to be very punctual to a quarter past seven, I was so, and found in addition to Sally, My Lord and Lady Sefton, Ladies Maria and Caroline Molyneux, their Brothers Henry and Francis, Lord Arthur and Lord Marcus Hill and Montgomery, and afterwards arrived Jack Fremantle....

...Our dinner was of the very best order in quantity and quality, and our establishment was three gentlemen out of livery, three sky blue footmen, and a page. Upon beginning my fish, a gentleman, without my asking for it, presented me with a large bottle of *ketchup*, and upon looking with some suspicion towards Sefton, the old girl who was next to him, had her eye glass fixed upon me, and in her solemn low toned voice said, 'You are very fond, Mr. Creevey, of ketchup, I understand, and so am I,' so this of course had been got up by Sefton and Atty, and we went on in the same playful way the whole time. To conclude, when we left the Dining Room for the Drawing Room (one opening into the other), in their all combining against me to push me first into the Drawing Room, which they accomplished by sheer force, the operation being so noisy that Lady Salisbury observed to Lady Sefton, 'What a row they are making, I wish I was there.'...We left at eleven, and in the passage passed her two cock'd-hat chairmen waiting to take her a-visiting to Emily, Marchioness of Londonderry, and Sefton said that upon her return, she would have, as she always had, a little hot supper of chicken or something else for her own private eating....

March 26th

Let me see, where did I leave off, and where am I to begin? Saturday was a considerable field day in Arlington Street, the Duncannons and the Jerseys, Geo. and Mrs. Lamb, Lord Foley, Punch Greville, and Genl. McDonald, and a very merry jolly dinner and evening we had. What remarkably fresh, clean looking creatures the sisters—Ladies Jersey and Duncannon are....

...What a handsome, spanking creature Lady Erroll[1] is, and how like her Mother, particularly when she used to be acting *Nell*. She looks as if she was quite uncomfortable in her fine cloaths and wanted to have them off....I shall of course dine at the Hollands' on Sunday week; the Jerseys I know dine there as well as the Seftons. I think I can't be reckoned amongst the *Slaves* of Holland House in accepting this invitation. You know what a sensitive, fanciful devil I am. 'Oh! thoughtless mortals, &c. &c.' I have now taken it into my head, right or wrong I know not, that there is rather a particular civility shown me on all hands, and then again I fancy it has something to do with my *work*, tho' I never *hard* of it till yesterday....

Brooks's, April 10th

Rum enough this, to be weather-bound at Brooks's so early in the day as 12 o'clock, but the fact My Dear you see is this. Our Young Ladies in Arlington Street asked me yesterday to come and breakfast with them today at ten, and so to walk with them at ½ before eleven down to St. James' Palace, to see the guard changed, and I kept my appointment accordingly, and a very good breakfast we young people had in the absence of Papa and Mama, but when the time for walking came, down came the rain, and it has poured ever since....

No Premier yet. It is now universally considered as true that the hitch is entirely between Canning and *Prinney*, and not between the former and his colleagues. The Sovereign is a true Protestant, and demands securities from Canning before he gives him supreme power that he will not use this new power in favor of the Pope....

My Lord and My Lady Sefton, Lady Katherine and myself in the carriage, and the other three young Ladies and Francis on horseback made a charming tour after I finished yesterday's letter. Thro' Dulwich, Herne Hill &c. &c....

Brooks's again

You see I thought it best to step out and take my place in the *Fakenham* Coach for Thursday, which I have done, price £2, and Fakenham is 9 miles from Holkham, and 110 from London, so I presume I will have to lodge there that night....

[1] Elizabeth FitzClarence, daughter of William IV and Mrs. Jordan, married 18th Earl of Erroll.

Holkham, April 14th

...I got to Fakenham (10 miles off) on Thursday about 9, the coach coming no further, so I dined very comfortably, went to bed, and came over yesterday morning in a CHAY before Church to which I went. My journey down was delightful, independent of the finish of the day. No tract of 100 miles is so full of associations to the Humble Individual who has now the honor to address you. I begin with my first entrance into life at Hackney, and then thro' my academical residence amongst all the Royal Male and Female Founders of Colleges at Cambridge to whom I am passionately attached with all their sins, and in defiance of Bruffam and the enlightened moderns who are now founding Stinkomiles College at the end of Gower Street in London.[2] Newmarket too was not without its reminiscences, and then I entered upon the County, one of whose towns I represented in Parliament sixteen years of my life, and on one side of me I had that house of Lord Bradford's where we once were at a Ball, and on the other side old Buckenham, and then again, for political reminiscences, I had Rainham before me, and Houghton, hard by, the Townshends and the Walpoles, and to sum up the whole, I was coming to the birthplace and the property of much the best politician that England has ever known, Old Chief Justice Coke. Such, My Dears, were the thoughts which accompanied me in my stage coach, and however feeble they may appear to others, I assure you I found them very agreeable companions....

Earl of Sefton to Creevey

April 13th

...The D. of Wellington...says, nothing shall induce him to connect himself with *that man*.[3] That he sh'ld. be liable to such impertinence, he could not put up with it....

Granville is Secy. for Foreign; Warde, Privy Seal; Robinson, Colonies. It is reported that Huskisson is to be Home Secy. The Great Seal to be in commission....

Creevey to Miss Ord

Holkham, April 17th

...The more one thinks of the whole smash, the more astonishing it is. How right poor Alava was when he told me at Brussels the morn-

[2] Brougham was largely responsible for the founding of London University. *Stinkomalee* was a contemporary jibe by Theodore Hook.

[3] *i.e.* Canning.

ing after we knew Wellington was Master of the Ordnance, that he (Alava) was horrified. That Wellington ought never to have become a *politician*, but to remain the soldier of England, aye the soldier of Europe, in case he should ever again be wanted. Such were Alava's precise and honest sentiments, and wise and much happier would the *Beau* have been had he acted upon these, instead of which, here he is, having extinguished Bonaparte and all the world in battle, at last floor'd himself by the very man he prevailed upon not to go to India but to stay and go halves with him in the Government at home. By God, it is too much....

...Our only accessor to-day has been Lord John.

April 21st

Well, so Lansdowne won't touch office. Canning and he met by appointment yesterday when the latter refused coming into the New Administration, but the meeting and termination of it were highly amicable....

Lord Dudley has refused the offer of the Privy Seal. In short, I think Canning in the greatest danger of failing in his project, and if he does so he falls ten thousand fathoms....

Whitehall, June 18th

...I was an hour at least in Berkeley Square [Lord Grey's], about half the time with her, and then came in My Lord. You never saw two poor creatures more sore than they are at all the abuse he meets with from the *Whigs*....Lady Grey said to me, 'Now, Mr. Creevey, having been here a week, is your opinion of Lord Grey's conduct as favorable as when you came?' Only think of their being driven to this, and only from his having acted an honest part, whilst the rest of his party have been mean knaves. He was much more instructive than any one I have met yet about the formation of Canning's Government, and his facts are all from the parties concerned. When the King had given Canning his commands, he *sent* for the Archbishop of Canterbury, and Bishop of London, and had them with him *five hours*; during which time he told them again and again, that Canning was to form a Cabinet upon precisely the same model as the last, that is to say, with a preponderance of one *against* the Catholics. It was known soon after this interview that Canning had been in the Palace, all the time of it, and as the King left the room once for about 20 minutes, the Bishops concluded it was to state to Canning what the King was communicating to them. And when Canning wrote a letter to the Speaker,[4] which he did, pressing

[4] Charles Manners-Sutton, son of the Archbishop.

him most strongly to become Peel's successor in the Home Department, he begged him not to return an answer *till he had seen his Father, the Archbishop.* This insinuation, however, that the Cabinet was still to be Anti-catholic would not do, and the Speaker returned an unqualified refusal. Canning then made the same offer, first to Wallace, and then to Lord Colchester, both thorough-stitch *Anti*-Catholics, but they were alike—inaccessible, and then it was that Canning stated his difficulties to the King, and produced Brougham's letter to Wilson when it was agreed between the King and Canning to take Brougham at his word, and Lord Lansdowne was sounded upon what terms he would join the Government. A meeting of *friends* at Lansdowne House drew up *the terms*, which were—that the Lord Lieutenancy, Lord Chancellor, and Secretary for Ireland should be friends to the Catholics, and Lansdowne to be Secretary of State for the Home Department, and to lead the House of Lords. This proposal, however, was immediately rejected by Canning, and the whole thing was off, and then came the meeting in the rump of the Whigs headed by Brougham which led to the surrender of Lansdowne and his followers into the hands of Canning upon any terms he might be pleased to grant them.... To continue my narrative of our beloved Sovereign, I went from Lord Grey's yesterday to Lord Darlington's, when Lady Darlington told me the following story. As I observed in a former letter, the King has taken to coming upon the course at Ascot before the Races to see the horses take their gallops and trials, so the day when Lord Darlington's horse, 'Memnon,' was to run, and one of the King's was in the same race, upon coming on the course in his phaeton with Lord Conyngham by his side, he met or passed Lord Darlington's top Jockey, Chiffney, upon one of Lord Darlington's horses, so the Monarch pulling up said, 'Well, Sam, so you are going to beat me today,' 'I don't know that, please your Majesty,' says Sam, 'but My Lord's is a good horse.' 'Aye, aye,' says Prinney, 'I know that, and I know that he'll beat me, but I don't care. I was always fond of racing, you know, Sam, and it makes me quite happy to take to it again.' And just at this time one of the King's race horses passed, and he observed to Chiffney 'There, Sam, now that's an Irish horse and this is an Irish*man* sitting by my side, and one can run about as well as the other. They have both been brought up, you see, Sam, upon potatoes, and can make no play at all.' Now was there ever? ...

June 19th

...Let me correct an error in our Biography of George 4th. It was *Bill* Chiffney, Ld. Darlington's *trainer*, and not *Sam* Chiffney the *jockey*, that the Monarch honor'd with his conversation, always calling him Bill.

The King seeing the Duke of Dorset on the course at the races sent for him into the stand. The Duke, you know, *struck* as Master of the Horse, avowing to the King his decided hostility to Canning, and accordingly was one of the majority with Wellington. As soon as he appeared, the King put out both his hands to him saying, 'My Dear Little *Sack*, how are you, and why did not you come to me before?' You know he was Lord Sackville before he was Duke. Very gratifying to Canning to see Opposition Peers treated in this manner,...

Barningham (M. Milbank's), August 19th

...You must have been struck I think with the long article from the 'Moniteur' upon Canning's death. I was, so much so that I could not resist flying a kite to Lord Grey by that post,... in exposing that universal Humbug, now so fashionable,... that Canning was the author of any *new* National Policy for the country. Never since I was born have I witnessed such delusions or such barefaced villainy. Nevertheless, as I have observed to Grey, I think France was *'cowed'* by the swaggering of Canning, and that she is going to be damned impertinent with the feeble devils who are to be Canning's successors....

Earl Grey to Creevey

August 21st

...I... missed the article in the 'Moniteur,'... I saw an allusion to it, however,... and from what you say I form the same opinion of it that you do. The Apostolical Party in France and throughout Europe, I have no doubt, detested Canning, and rejoiced in his death, and this is perhaps the best thing that can be said in his favour. But I am far from believing that his policy w'd. ultimately have been found so prejudicial to their interests as they may have apprehended, and what I think most to be regretted in his death, is that it took place before his character and conduct were fully developed....

I can tell you little more of the changes that Canning's death has made necessary, than you will see in the papers. I have heard, and I believe, that the King declared, almost immediately, that he w'd. have no more Whigs; and every thing that we have hitherto seen is entirely in the spirit of such a determination. Huskisson... has been offered the Colonial Office, and the head of the House of Commons. I suppose the appointment of Herries is deferred till Huskisson's answer can be received, which seems probable from his having been at Windsor and sworn as a Member of the Privy Council. By others it is said that he hesitates about accepting in any case, and again that strong remonstrances against his appointment have been made by our old friends. If his appointment does not take place, it is said Palmerston is to be Chan'r. of the Ex., but who in that case is to be Sec'y. at War? I have not heard; probably not a Whig.

The Duke of Wellington was offered the Army in such a way, that he could not refuse it, and his acceptance, together with the other changes, will necessarily give strength to the Govt. The Tory Opposition will be divided, if not annihilated then. Peel will probably look to a return to power by conciliatory rather than fertile measures, and it seems to me most likely that the administration will, at no distant period, be re-established on its old principles, and almost its old form, by the ecstacies of our old friends, who after submitting to indignities which will have rendered them helpless, will at last find themselves compelled to retire....

Creevey to Miss Ord

Lowther Castle, August 27th

...I think I am settled here for life. I don't know where to begin, and before I do begin I shall have to end, as Lady Caroline, Mrs. Taylor and I are going an airing, and at present I am rather *bosky* after luncheon.... There is nothing like an *impression*. At five o'clock yesterday evening, I thought I was entering the most formal house in England, and at half past six dear Lady Lonsdale and I were going out arm in arm to dinner, three boys of Colonel Lowther's pulling with all their might and main at my coat flaps to make me stay and play with them, and in the evening, as we could have no cards from its being Sunday, Lord Pollington was kind enough to entertain us with his excellent imitations of squeaking pigs, Guinea Fowls, dialogues between crying children, and the devil knows what besides....

Lowther, August 28th

A line merely to say how very cosy and comfortable we continue to be, tho' now reduced to a family party....

I ought to mention that our last day at Barningham went off to admiration, we being all alone, and Milbank toiled all morning in the Greta to catch me a dish of trout for dinner which he accomplished, and our evening concluded with a very severe batch at whist, which was enlivened by the following circumstances:

The day before, the Clergyman of the Parish dined with us, and his

Wife, the latter being a fortune from *seeds*, good for £15,000; such a devil for ugliness and dress as you never beheld—a regular strolling player in a barn, a cap bolt upright of a yard's length, her hair behind nearly pulled up to the roots to be got into the cap, and in the front an amethyst star half mast high; so I did nothing but rave about her, and at our Whist, Lady Augusta entertained, 'Well, I believe after all that Mrs. Callings is a very good kind of woman at bottom,' so, says I, 'I know nothing of her bottom, but she is a deuced comical one at top,' which soon made for our Mark, and Gusty blushed and roared, and laid down her cards, ever and anon bawling out 'L-o-r-d, Mr. Creevey, what a droll man you are. Nobody but you could have said such a thing.' But I must leave you, my dears, being called away for a laking excursion.

Doncaster, Sept. 20th

...Charles Greville and Lord Warncliffe (Stuart Wortley) *and I* were very merry together last night upon the subject of a leading article in yesterday's *'Times' newspaper*—a puff of Brougham by himself, claiming the Solicitor Generalship for him as the one remaining man of talent in the country, and treating his competitor, *Shadwell*, as so low a concern 'that no parish would elect him as their vestry clerk.'...

Mrs. William[5] asked me to chaperon her and young Mary to the Ball, (Billy being disabled) which I did, and walked by her about the room a good deal, and you can't imagine what enquiries were made by the *quality* from me, who my pretty friend was....

All your race was at the Ball to-night, young Mrs. James Ord keeping up her improved looks....Sir *Tho. Lawrence* came up to Mrs. Willm. ...as a patroness no doubt of himself and his art, and he condescended to express his admiration of young Mary's countenance....

Wentworth, September 24th

...On our arrival here on Saturday we found Milton and his eldest Son without their coats playing at cricket with the servants just in front of the house. The party was then purely domestic. The dear amiable old man, his Sister, Ly. Frances Fitzwilliam, Milton and Ly. Milton, their two grown up Daughters and Son, Fred Ponsonby, a young Mr. Spears and a Mr. Duberly; afterwards came the Cowpers, and tho' last, not least, Princess Lieven. I have always heard a great deal of the talents of Madame Lieven, and I think I have heard she is considerably afflicted with *ennui*....I used to have some hold on Ly. Milton for a

[5] Brandling.

laugh, and with Cowper for an ally we did great things, so much so that Mad'e. Lieven more than once stretched her *snipe* face towards my corner with something like an expression of a wish in it to be of our party, and so when we went to Coffee, and I was standing by the table, she got up from her chair, came up to me and began talking immediately, and our intercourse was from that moment so prosperous, that at parting just now she was pleased to express her regret that I was not going to Chatsworth (where they are going), but to hope, at all events, it would not be long before we met in London, and if you come to that, Prince Lieven, who arrived here to dinner yesterday from London, was pleased likewise to say when he squeezed my hand at parting, that he was very happy to have the pleasure of making my acquaintance. Was there ever? The Snipe considered me all the time as being in Parliament, and I thought it quite unnecessary to undeceive her, so it was 'all mighty well.' ... I had a great deal of conversation with her, and very agreeable she was. Afterwards at the request of Ly. Cowper's Daughter, she sat down with great good humour to the pianoforte, and played most beautifully, and I am sure most skilfully, and I was the only man who attended. She asked, *'Monsieur Creevey aimez de musique?'*[6] and when she had finished she came to me and said in the French language, how very few men in England were fond of musick, and when we were going thro' the Stables this morning, and poor Old Billy was shewing her all his horses, which are beautiful and most numerous, she slipt from under his arm to come and say to me, 'I have just as much pleasure in looking at these horses as you Englishmen have in hearing musick.' ...

Raby, Oct. 6th

... The *Pop* was not forthcoming at dinner yesterday. ... Mrs. Taylor says there is a rumour in the family that there has been the devil of a blow up between her and her *maid*. ... The Marquis[7] seems absorbed in thought. ... The King ... has given him permission to quarter the Royal Arms with his own, in compliment to his descent in the female line from Charles the 2nd. and Miss Villiers, in the person of the first Duke of Cleveland. This accession of dignity gives him *two crests*, the Royal Lion and his own crest, and both are to find their way upon the servants' buttons, and the question is which is to have the place of honor. And here, I must say, I think the Marquis reasons with very logical accuracy—'*If*,' says he, 'I had the same rank with my Royal

[6] Creevey's French!
[7] Lord Darlington had just been created Marquis of Cleveland.

Ancestor, the *Duke* of Cleveland, spurious as that descent is, I should prefer it to my own, and place the Lion before my own crest, but as the *Marquis* of Cleveland is not a Royal title, and still is equally spurious, I shall prefer my own title, and place my crest before the Royal Lion.' *Upon your soul!* Now 'r-a-a-lly' was there ever? Is it not *too*? . . . I must go and tender my homage to the *Haradan* [Lady Cleveland]. . . . The first day after I came she walked me down to Staindrop with her, the neighbouring town about a mile off, and we paid visits to the Apothecary's family, the Steward's family, and shopped a little. In the course of our walk she abused *James* Brougham without reserve, and I thought was coming rather near the Brother, so I said, 'I wonder whether he will be Solicitor-General?' 'Impossible,' said she, 'he is pledged you know to support Government without taking office'; 'and yet,' says I, 'he complains of being excluded. I have seen it under his own hand.' 'That's very odd,' says she, 'I am sure Lord Darlington considers him as pledged not to take office from all he has said and written to him, and I should think would have a very different opinion of him if he did so. I am sure, at least, *I* should, but Lord Darlington has a letter from him this morning proposing to come here next Tuesday, but he never mentions the Solicitor Generalship, nor anything of the kind.' Was there ever such a double-faced villain?

Old Sussex comes here on Monday, and Cis Buggin[8] too. Was there ever such a low lived concern? and Brougham comes to meet them, so they will have it all their own way in politicks. . . .

Howick, October 13th

We were all Monday at Durham, and got here on Tuesday which you will be glad to hear was time enough to catch our old friends the *Bathursts* tho' it was only for a day. . . . Lady Bathurst was so entrenched in hat and feathers, and gave me so little encouragement (as I thought) to bring my bad ear into action, that for the first quarter of an hour I thought my prospects very gloomy indeed, but I presently broke the line with dear old Dow: Julia Lady Petre, *souverin* her happy *'Blind Man's Buff'* days with Lord Grey when she lost her gown and one shoe, and I never looked behind me afterwards. You may suppose how well I stood before the dinner was over, when Grey said, 'Let me send you a piece of this red herring, Creevey, I know you will like it,'

[8] Lady Cecilia's surnames are confusing. Born a Gore, daughter of 2nd Earl of Arran, she married first Sir George Buggin. Adopting her mother's maiden name of Underwood, she married secondly, as his second wife, H.R.H. the Duke of Sussex in 1832. Queen Victoria created her Duchess of Inverness in 1840. She died in 1873.

and Lady Bathurst added, 'And let me, Mr. Creevey, recommend you to eat some of the cream cheese with it, you can't imagine how well they eat together,' and so of course I did, and having done so I said, 'Bless me, what *a pretty coalition*,' and Grey blushed and laughed with his face downwards, and she laughed too. She is a palavering, perfidious, decayed flatterer with no talents to begin with, and very scanty remains of good looks to end with....

What think you of Lady Londonderry when she slept at the Bishop of Durham's, asking if there were *no cambric* sheets?...

Mrs. Taylor to Creevey

Whitehall, Nov. 12th

...I write to announce Mr. Brougham's first visit to me last night. He was visibly in very bad temper, and talked at and against every body I liked. Poor Ld. Grey came in for a large share of his abuse for having changed his opinions so far as to receive Ld. Bathurst into his house....

...I told him what an agreeable summer I had spent going about with you, and how well we had found *Ld. and Ly. Grey*, that he was grown twenty years younger since he left London, and what an agreeable party we had there....

The Government people are visibly sore and frightened to death of Ld. Grey, and really scarcely seem to think they can go on.

I hope you will be able to come to us as soon as Miss Ord is settled at Rivenhall. I shall be curious to hear how you got on at Croxteth....

Creevey to Miss Ord

Croxteth, Nov. 21st

...I arrived...yesterday....After My Lord had *insisted* upon my having a mutton chop dressed for me, I pottered about over my old haunts, and upon my returning found Mr. and Mrs. Hopwood, their son, the Captain, and Miss, arrived from Hopwood and Count Montrond[9] and Tommy Duncombe from London...One of the young ladies said, 'We have seen a good deal of Mr. Brougham lately, he went to the play with us 3 or 4 times, and you never saw such a figure as he is. He wears a black stock or collar round his neck, it is so wide that you can see a dirty coloured handkerchief under tied tight round his neck. You

[9] Count Montrond, roué and gambler, witty, sly and dangerous, escaped the guillotine to be distrusted and employed both by Bonaparte and Talleyrand.

never saw such an object, or anything half so dirty.' This is all that has passed hitherto respecting the 'Archfiend.' ... Mull[10] was pleased to express his great satisfaction at my restoration *to the bosom of my family*. So ... it's all mighty well. But I have scarcely time to tell you more, for Sefton made me go out with them to their shooting ground, and our post for Prescot goes at four, it being now very near that hour....

Nov. 22nd

... The *Pet* continues to be every thing I could wish, and I cannot help flattering myself is as near upon the *Rat* as possible from his new Allies. He said to me last night over our tea, 'You know, Brougham had the offer made him of being Chief Baron?' 'Yes,' said I, 'from Canning, and for the purpose of getting rid of him.' 'Yes,' said Sefton, 'just so;' but this morning after breakfast he has been as good as a play. He lays it down as a fact known to all that Lord Dudley and Lady Copley or Lyndhurst are *one*, and that he never thinks of the Foreign Office or anything else but her, whilst Copley himself never thinks of the Court of Chancery or any thing else but his parties at Roehampton, and his pleasure generally. 'So,' says Sefton, 'I took an occasion the other day at Brooks's to tell Abercromby at some length what a damned fool Copley was making of himself, and how sure he was of being deceived in all ways, and very soon too, and so,' added Sefton, 'Abercromby took to profound silence for some time, and at last said with his peculiar solemnity, "It is a subject that has given me great uneasiness for some time past and I have always been afraid of hearing the observations you have just made."' After this conversation, and a little more upon our new subject—our victory at Navarino, in which we are both so united in opinion—Sefton said, 'I think I'll write to Grey to-day and congratulate him upon his Boy being safe,' and of course I encouraged him so to do, and then we all went to the stables, and Joss was bid to strip Mr. Creevey's new horse, and to turn him round in the stall. I have been told more than once before of his beauty, and of his being quite made for me, and certainly to my mind I never saw a handsomer horse. Was there ever? ...

Permit me to mention an alteration *in* our breakfasts. I observed yesterday four silver covers, top, bottom and sides, and upon their being taken up they were all hot dishes—kidneys at top, mashed potatoes at

[10] Lord Molyneux. From now onwards it may be observed that Creevey makes frequent reference to the Molyneux as 'his own' or his *real* family. These references suggest but by no means prove the truth of the legend of his parentage.

bottom, 3 partridges at one side with bread sauce, crums &c. &c., Pattys at the other. To-day Mutton cutlets at top, mashed pots: at bottom, omlet at one side, and a pheasant the other. Now *r-a-ally* as Mrs. Taylor would say, 'I think that is *trop*, is it not?'...

Permit me to conclude with a piece of muggery I have just received, and which we old chaps are mighty fond of. Lady Louisa showed me a letter from Lady Georgina Grey in which she is pleased to say, of all their visitors at Howick this year, the one they were most sorry to part with was Mr. Creevey &c. &c. &c. Upon your soul! Old School Lane! and am for ever.

Croxteth, Nov. 25th

...Yesterday was beautiful, tho' the ground was covered with snow, so it was settled to shoot in Craven Wood, and as the ladies' cottage is there, they always give a kind of jollification upon such occasion, and much dissatisfaction was expressed, when it was reported that Mr. Creevey was going to Liverpool, but Lady Sefton said, 'Mr. Creevey is going to see his Sister, and he always does what is right. Would you have any game sent to your Sister, Mr. Creevey?' 'Not *yet*, thank you, Lady Sefton,' says I. 'You have had but one battue yet, and it is a bad pheasant year (which is the case), besides I am going to draw upon Lord Sefton for my Grand-daughter's birthday.' So off I walked to Liverpool, and as I was sitting cozing with my Sister, up drove my Lord's gig and groom in it, and so, thinks I, what is this for, when a card comes in, 2 pheasants and one hare with Lady Sefton's compliments to Miss Creevey, and a message from Lady Sefton to Mr. Creevey, that she has sent the gig for him, it must be uncomfortable walking. Now, r-a-ally was not all this pretty attention *too*? However, having no great coat, and being wet in the feet, I preferred trudging it back to an open carriage. I found my Sister in the most perfect preservation in all ways, and looking better than ever I saw her in my life. I got back here about half past five, and as the birds were all flown, I flew too to my own bedroom where having discarded all my cloaths but my shirt and banyan, my Lord came and made me a visit in his banyan and slippers, and a very agreeable half an hour jaw we had. When he talks politicks with me, I am always thinking whether he is withholding any thing from me, as he has been so much in Brougham's and the new Whig camp, but still I don't think that is his character; I mean concealment....

In the meantime what an age it is before one learns how the Turk takes this Navarino touch....

My new Horse is quite charming, was bought on purpose, and only cost 120 gns. Joss always calls him Mr. Creevey's horse.

... Croxteth, Saturday morning Dec. 15th, 10 o'clock and not a soul come down yet, and such a morning for rain, but my own great coat, and our Mary's umbrella were quite sufficient protection in the gig.

Miss Creevey's drum went off to admiration last night and my Lord's pheasant and hare with Hannah Rickman's cakes and Miss Creevey's Port and *Madeira* made the ladies as well as gentlemen very gay and merry. Before I left him for Liverpool my Lord had two letters, the first from De Ros, and the second from Punch Greville, both overflowing with matter and jokes against the Government, and which My Lord read aloud with great apparent satisfaction. De Ros says, 'Nothing can equal the consternation of the Ministers, that they have Cabinet Councils every other *hour*, that the Ambassadors are at one another's doors all day long, that Esterhazy runs about the Town like a wild cat, and that Dudley's *frame* is so diminished from the united impression made upon it by the *Turk*, and the *tender* passion, and with the fear of Earl Grey always before his eyes, that his face is scarcely visible to the naked eye. With a great deal more of very pretty fun....

Mrs. Taylor to Creevey

I have sent you a 'Times' of to-day, which I think shows by the abuse in it of Ld. Grey the fear the Government, or the Archfiend, have of him. The mess thickens, beautiful Ld. Goderich resigns, nominally on account of domestic illness, but in truth the Finance and every thing else is in such a state, and with the King quite beyond his power to controul (*wanting restraint* more than his Father did) that he cannot go on....

Lansdowne fails to make any communication as to his successor to Knighton. Nobody seems to have an idea what is to be done. Lambton and the others, it is supposed, will not get their peerages. It is really quite delightful to see the wretched supporters of this miserable Government, for they are at a loss what to say, having committed themselves as they have done....

What a situation Ld. Grey is placed in, everything turns up to support his opinions, and all they have to say of him—that he has had Ld. Bathurst at his house! ...

chapter thirteen (*continued*)

1828

ALTHOUGH CREEVEY SOMETIMES referred to Ireland as his native country, though born in Liverpool, he was turned sixty before he visited that land. Over the serene waters of Privilege his bark floated, little disturbed by political storms and changes of Government. When occasion demanded, he was political and sympathetically partisan, but his mind was fixed on writing social history, and in 1828 his Sussex fortnight and his autumn tour in Ireland documented domestic life of a century ago in a score of famous Whig country houses in West Sussex and Ireland.

One of the little girls at Bessborough whom Creevey praises in the letters which follow, more than once referred at the end of her long life to that visit and to the wit and charm and kindness of 'dear Mr. Creevey,' and the present editor, her grandson, has a clear recollection of her words which bridge 134 years.

For Creevey himself it was a memorable visit, marked in his records with a white chalk, and he who in an age of licence spared neither sex nor age in criticism, had nothing but reverence and admiration for Lady Jersey's sister, Lady Duncannon.

Creevey to Miss Ord

Feby. 11th

. . . As Taylor dined at the Speaker's yesterday, I had to do the honors to old Lord Robert Spencer, and really my tête-à-tête with old 'Comical' was both curious and entertaining. He, aged 81, was just returned from a visit to his Sister, Dowr. Pembroke, in Richmond Park, aged 94 and quite well. In our unreserved moments his criticisms upon men were quite delightful. He considers the wit Sydney Smith as a 'boisterous Mountebank.' He is intent upon my becoming better acquainted with a contemporary of mine and his—the Earl of Egremont by name—aged 77, who, Bob says, is made for me. . . .

My next messmate in the streets was Sir George Warrender, whom

I was for passing with a 'How are you, Warrender!' but no such thing could be submitted to, I assure you, so off he went with, 'Well, Creevey, wonders will never cease! I met Lord Bathurst at the Duke of Buccleuch's in Scotland, who said he had met Mr. Creevey at Lord Grey's, and that altho' he had always entertained the strongest prejudice against him, he had found him the most agreeable fellow possible.'...

Feby. 18th

We were 17 at dinner at Little Sussex's, the Clevelands, &c. Sussex you know is always very civil to me, but upon my soul! yesterday he was *beyond*. I never was so dosed in my life. 'You never come near me, Creevey.' 'I always come, Sir, when you do me the honor to invite me.' 'Yes, but why don't you come without inviting. You know I should always be delighted to see you, and the oftener the better. How is Mrs. Hamilton, and the Ladies, and young Hamilton?' All this *roaring* out during dinner; then again with the Clevelands on each side, 'Are you coming into Parliament again, Creevey?' 'No, Sir.' 'I wish you were, and yet I don't know why I should, for it's a damned state of things. For myself I've done with politicks, but I'm always with *you*....'

March 3rd

It is a pity I cannot accommodate the D. of Norfolk by dining with him, and eating some of his *six year old mutton*. I was rather sorry I could not accept this 2nd. invitation. When you read too the other *affectionate* invitation from Countess Grey, you must admit it was a proud day for *old School Lane*....

...After *such* an invitation, I could not be otherwise than well received by Mylady who was with her Lord and Roslyn and Rogers in one room, the young Ladies with others in the next. A visit there is always agreeable. In the midst of it Grey called me from the young ones, saying, 'Creevey, I want to shew you something,' and going to a retired table he put into my hand a letter he had received from Ld. Cleveland, enclosing one he, the Marquis, had received from Brougham. The object of both is peace and friendship between Grey and Brougham....

...Brougham's letter is the composition of the same tortuous villain as ever, and in folly and insanity by no means inferior to his former effusions. We both *roared* at it. He takes a merit to himself in never having denied the expressions imputed to him, but swears that no offensive meaning can be attached to them, and appeals to his known *devotion* to Lord Grey *now*, and for ever past, in support of this. In short, such a mean lyar never existed....

March 5th

Here is Wm. Ponsonby[1] asking me to do him and Ly. Barbara *the honour* of dining with them on Saturday, and George Ponsonby[2] with a letter from Lord Robert Spencer urging him to secure Creevey to meet Ld. Grey at Woolbeding for a few days, which I will if I can....

March 6th

...Dumaresque told me that the Beau made him get into his cabriolet that he might have some conversation with him, and upon the Colonel expressing some fear that he was working himself to death, the other replied, 'I am damnably worked it's true, but nothing will kill me.' Sir Colin whom I met in the street yesterday, said, 'We'll be hard put to it, Mr. Creevey, to carry the Duke through all his trouble and fatigue.' So also said Earl Dudley in St. James's Park to-day. Not such was his opinion of me, vowing he never saw me look so fresh and well. 'Pretty well,' says I, 'for a man who was 60 yesterday.' 'How do you manage it?' says he. 'By never thinking of Turks, Russians, or English Politicians,' said I....

Stoke, June 3rd

...I found Earl Grey and his Daughter, Montrond, &c., &c. I mention those two because I had a walk with each....

My walk with Montrond was at his own request, during which he was pleased to observe that it was very foolish for a clever man ever to read; that books only interfered with his understanding, and ought only to be read by foolish people to talk about, and to conceal their own poverty of matter. So much for old parlez-vous.

Our dinner went off to perfect admiration, tho' we were *only* 23—Anson, Duncombe, and Shelley being kept by the House of Commons. De Ros not arrived, nor yet Henry Molyneux.

I never saw My Lord in greater force, nor better trim, and all was perfect, and my Lady of course ditto, and she and I played at Ecarté for an hour and a half....

June 4th

...Nothing could exceed yesterday in all ways. It was a pleasure too to see our beloved Sovereign enjoy it as he seemed to do, and I never saw him look better in all my life. He drove up the course with little

[1] Third son of 3rd Earl of Bessborough. Married Barbara, daughter of 5th Earl of Shaftesbury. Created Lord de Mauley.

[2] Son of 1st Lord Ponsonby. His second wife Diana Bouverie, daughter of Lady Robert Spencer. They succeeded to Woolbeding.

George of Cumberland by his side, with 7 carriages and 31 outriders, besides footmen seated behind the carriages. Indeed if you come to that, I thought we were not amiss. My Lord turned out *four of his own* carriages, two with his own horses, and two with 4 posters in each. We passed George Payne driving his four in hand just before we reached Ascot, Lord Worcester by his side on the box, and Holyoak and others on the roof. It was a sincere pleasure to me to see George's horse 'Belzone' beat the King's *two* horses.... Jersey went into the King's stand after the Race and found the Sovereign in high good humour about it, observing he had always said Mr. Payne's horses would be too much for his mare, and he added *he was a little nervous about Thursday*; i.e. when his Mare 'Fleur de Lys' that he bought off our Mat Ridley, is to run for the Cup. Sefton had got a private stand prepared for his party, so all was charming. I belonged to the same carriage with Lord Grey, and he was as pleased as Punch all the time. In the evening, that is at dinner, we had 13 quarts of turtle from the London Tavern to console us, and there is to be a similar importation to-day. The dinner was sufficiently gay, and the night even *boisterous*, in as much as at our *Gallery* or low Whist Table, Mull, Jules and I sang a medley of French and English so loud and to tunes so charmingly popular that we broke up the *deep* whistle table, and the Clerk of the Council, Greville, was so sulky, he would never utter afterwards; Sefton, Grey, and all the Ladies being convulsed at our merits and success....

June 5th

...Old Dow: Salisbury was on the course yesterday, and went from thence with Downshire and Atty Hill to dine at the Christopher at Eton, and go down [up] with Downshire's Tom Hillsbro' in a boat to Surly Hall (4th of June), and Mull and Geo Anson who were there, saw her in the midst of the boats and boys.

Whitehall, June 17th

...Frances[3] and I took the field at last, and arrived at Holly Lodge[4] about 5. Somewhat late for a breakfast, you will say, that was fixed for *one*, but Lord Chesterfield, Mrs. Fox Lane and Lady Radnor were in the carriage before us, and Lord Bristol and family in the one behind us, so that we were not singular, you see. The day must have thinned the party considerably, but there were quite enough to make it very pretty, and very gay. The ground too being well suited to the occasion in its own gaiety in flowers, walks, and lawns, &c.... In a short time

[3] Mrs. Taylor.

[4] Duchess of St. Albans' (Mrs. Coutts).

we went into the house, every room of which was full of tables, and eatables, and having very soon fallen in with *Nell,* she would willingly have conducted us to the room where the Duchess was regaling the Dukes of Cumberland, Sussex, and Prince Leopold with *turtle,* but we preferred humble company and humbler food, so we took to the Chesterfield and Bristol party—*white* soup &c. When old Dow. Coutts made her round into the other room we fell in with her, and I was presented, and a more disgusting, frowsy, hairy old B. could not have been found in the Seven Dials....

You would have been pleased to see a group of our London young ladies shooting with bows and arrows at targets—the elegant attitudes they put themselves into were really *too.* We were there about 2 hours, and it answered extremely well....

Earl of Sefton to Creevey

August 1st

... We shall be delighted to see you Monday, and are determined to make you go with us to Chichester the 11th, for Goodwood Races. We go to the Inn, and you will be much amused....

August 2nd

I forgot to tell you in my letter yesterday that we shall only stay 2 or 3 days at Chichester, and then go to Ld. Robert's. I think the whole of this will suit you, as you will have quite enough of Michael in your Northern trip, and I have often heard you say you had a wish to go to Ld. R's.

Creevey to Miss Ord

Dolphin Inn, Chichester, August 11th

... The drive here of sixty miles,[5] is not, I think, to be surpassed for beauty in England for that extent. The men and maids were the advanced guard, and we followed in the shooting carriage....

Our Hotel here we found really perfection, and the dinner not less so when it came. During its continuance, a note came from the Duchess of Richmond to Lady Sefton, really an extremely pretty one, saying she could not bear to think of her being so near them and at an Inn, and saying also that owing to some excuses they had received, they could now take them in, and begging them to come. This being declined, the Duke has sent my Lord half a Buck lest we should starve here. Sefton

[5] From Stoke, Windsor.

says he would not have gone there upon any account. I have been always in error in thinking they were there before. They never were, they were *here* at this house upon a visit to Berkeley with his Regiment, but both Sefton and my Lady have been most intimate with the Duchess from her childhood, and her note expressed her obligation to both....

August 13th

Our 'Bobadilla' has won, and very easily too.

This makes it impossible that I should go into the North with the Taylors.

Well, and so what shall I do with myself? Shall I be off for France, or Ireland? Sefton swears I shall stay a fortnight at *least* at Stoke, to which place we shall get on Sunday. On Saturday we go early to Petworth, and stay all night. Ld. Egremont[6] was in the Stand today when this was settled.

Bedroom, Woolbeding, August

...This corner of Sussex is as desirable for a residence, if not more so, than any I know; and Goodwood is the choicest spot; *dry* soil and *down* are first rate ingredients with me; then the Park is very spacious, beautifully wooded, with every inequality and variety of ground, and commanding beautiful views of both *sea* and land. The house is a handsome one to look at tho' of an irregular shape, but the interior, which I went over yesterday, is perfection.... The Hall which you enter has very handsome pillars in it, but they don't crowd it and darken it as they do at Lowther, Thorndon, Wentworth, and Raby. They are not in one's way, and it is a charming room or place to walk about in, as the Duke and I did without hats on.... The Duke took me about the house in a most good humoured, natural way, and I should have liked to have spent two or three hours more there. The Dining Room, Libraries, &c. &c. are all as good as possible, and there are some beautiful pictures scattered up and down in different rooms and staircases, that one ought to see collected in the picture gallery which is to be. Everybody belonging to the founder of the family, Charles the 2nd., is to be found there, as you may suppose, in original pictures by different masters.... An original one by Vandyke of your Charles the 2nd. as a boy, and as like as two p's....

There were quantities of visitors in the house, many of whom, of course, one knows as *brother dandys* or Turf Men and many I did not.

[6] George O'Brien, 3rd Earl, died 1837 when Petworth and the Seymour and Percy inheritances passed to his natural son, George Wyndham, created Lord Leconfield in 1859. The 4th and last E. of Egremont died in 1845.

They were scattered about in the Libraries, Billiard Room, Hall, and Drawing Room... and the whole seemed as gay and cheerful a concern as one could see anywhere, and I came away mighty pleased with both the Master and his house. What a contrast, we all said, to Arundel. That horrid, dismal *benighted* castle, with a gallery in it 190 feet long of the most dingy oak, and a window at the *top* of each end to light it, and everything else in the place equally dismal. Lady Sefton said really a good thing upon the subject. There are about a dozen enormous owls in the keep... imported of late years from America, as large as eagles, and the same black brown colour, with enormous eyes set in large scarlet or orange coloured borders, the latter being parts of their eyes....

We found here[7] the Ponsonbys[8] of course, and *Fan*,[9] Sir Geo. Robinson, Rogers and Motteux. Poor Lord Robert is feeble in all ways I think except in *eating*. The place is very limited, the house likewise, the dining room excepted, which is excellent. The dinner inferior to no one's, and the wine aussi, but then all's told, for any thing more dull cannot possibly be conceived....

Woolbeding, August 16th

...The day is brilliant....I had not a notion of seeing trees of such magnitude and of such modern growth. There are Cedars, Planes, Spanish Chestnuts, &c. all really monstrous trees, one may say, and all of his planting....I walked over to Cowdray and about its ruins yesterday, and a great place it must have been of Queen Elizabeth's time of building. Poyntz has built another modern moderate house in another part of the Park. He came over here to make a morning call yesterday at *half past six* accompanied by Lady Clinton (another of his Daughters), Lord Clinton, Miss Poyntz, William Bathurst, Pierpoint &c., and we walked by the fountain,[10] which is always the subject of admiration, but Bob never mentioned where it came from of course in the presence of the Montagues.[11] We had a much more jolly day yesterday than the one before....

Stoke, August 18th

...We started about 3 for Petworth, which was only 7 miles off, Sefton's object being to see Lord Egremont's Racing Stud before dinner;

[7] At Woolbeding.

[8] George Ponsonbys.

[9] Frances, daughter of Lady Robert and the Hon. E. Bouverie.

[10] This famous fountain, ascribed to John of Bologna or to Benvenuto Cellini, stood at Cowdray until the fire.

[11] Mr. Poyntz married the last Lord Montagu's heiress. Creevey later corrects a 'canard' that Lord Robert 'appropriated' the fountain in the confusion of fire.

passed thro' Cowdray Park which tho' pretty enough is very inferior to all other parks and places in that district. It has one ornament, however, which I should fancy is not to be found through England besides, and that is a very considerable avenue of Spanish Chestnut Trees as large as the oldest oak trees one sees, and as fresh as the youngest. We were soon, as you may suppose, at Petworth, the outside of which was familiar to my recollection of 30 years past, when I rode from Chichester to look at it. A very long, modern white or grey building of two stories high without a wing or a portico or pillar or even a *door* except you call a window one; for it is more like the latter than the former. I think there are 21 or 22 great windows in a line in front, but the length is immense. ... I was much amused in going thro' one room, where I was lost in admiration of a portrait of Lord Strafford by Vandyke, and another of an Earl of Northumberland by the same, to hear Lord Egremont say as he was walking on, 'Lord Sefton, there is your Mother,' 'God, so there is,' said Sefton, 'and very like too,' and shortly afterwards walking by the side of one of the young Ladies he said, 'There's your Grandmother,' and true enough there was the Margravine. Now far be it from me to insinuate that these two ladies belonged to my Lord's Seraglio, but certain it is never persons were more worthy of it, and in truth I dare say they were so. What made this the more funny to my own private thoughts was our stopping shortly after in another room, at a modern showy picture in which Lord Egremont was a principal figure, when the Royal and Foreign Grandees were in England in 1814. They spent a day and night at Petworth, and as artists are always allowed to do what they like there, one of them was upon the spot to make a picture of this melting scene.... The figures are the Emperor of Russia with his Sister the Duchess of Oldenburgh upon his arm in the act of being introduced by the Prince Regent to Lord Egremont.... Lord Yarmouth behind the Prince, Lord Charles Bentinck behind the King of Prussia.... Lord Egremont, Lady Burrell, and all her Sisters in front, and her Brothers and others behind, and on looking at this side of the picture Lord Egremont said, 'Lady Sefton, don't you see anybody you know there?' and sure enough there is Berkeley Craven as like as life. It was comical, was it not, to see him in such company after what had just passed? and I should not at all wonder if he was one of old Egremont's very numerous Stud....

... We formed in a very excellent habitable library and drawing room united, our party being nearly domestic—us five, Ld. Egremont and Misses Wyndham, Mr. King and Mrs. who was one of the Misses Wyndham, and a Brother of his, the eldest male Wyndham, Lord Charles Somerset, and his Daughter, Mrs. Wyndham, Lady Emily

Marsham (sister to Lord Romney and niece of Lord *Egremont*, and who lives at Petworth) a Chaplain and another young Lady....

The dinner was of the first order, turtle, venison, moor game, &c. without stint. The servants, too, very numerous tho' most of them very advanced in years and tottered, and comical in their looks. The wax candles too were sufficiently numerous to light us all up well tho' we were at one end of a room sixty feet long, the waincoat of which was Gibbons' carving in wood.... However, all went off extremely well.... By half past ten the Ladies of the house were all gone to bed, leaving those of this house to follow their own inventions, nor was this the only proof of the early habits of the whole house, for observing a footman bring in a glass of wine and water to the Chaplain, Sefton said to me, 'You'd better take this opportunity of getting some too, or you'll be done,' so I went and asked him to bring me a glass likewise, and the self same footman returned in a very few minutes saying the Butler *was gone to bed*. I thought Sefton would have burst at this, as being much too good a thing to have ever happened.... Mr. King's account of the servants was, that there were more of them in that house of both sexes, and in all departments, than in any house in England, that they were all very good in their way, but that they could not stand being put out of it, and were never interfered with, that they were all bred upon the spot, and all related to each other....

...I was rather fidgetty in the morning to be about the house after the pictures, but my valet did not bring my cloaths till near nine, and then I started. In coming into the Hall, it is but justice to the servants to say, that if they like early hours to go to bed by, in the morning they are at their posts with the lark, for I found there two gentlemen out of livery, and *the* foot boy with coffee pots, tea pots, kettles, chafing dishes to keep rolls etc. hot, and everything in the eatable way, and I was directly asked whether I would breakfast *then*, and *where* I would have it. This, I was told afterwards, always lasts from 9 till 12. I declined their offer for the present, and I begged one of the gentlemen to conduct me.... As my guide never left me I could only run over these pictures hastily, and come away.... Fortunately in one of the rooms, old Egremont came *slouching* by me; so says I, 'Pray, Lord Egremont, what is that curious picture of the coach and six...?' 'Ah!' says he, 'it is a devilish clever picture, is it not? Let's go look at it,' and so we did, and it was a picture of Charles the 2nd. going an airing with *Ladies* just turning out of Whitehall. The present front of that building being part of the picture, and all in the calèche and out of it being portraits. Having observed upon the horses, and other things in it being so clever, he fixed his eyes upon a picture of a handsome woman, that was evidently being copied, and he said, 'Did you ever see a handsomer face than that?' 'Never,' says I, 'by whom was it done?' 'By Sir Joshua Reynolds,' says he. 'How long has it been painted?' '50 years,' said he, and as he still stood looking at it, I at length said, 'Whose picture is it, Lord Egremont?' 'Oh!' he said, 'it was a lady not much known in the world,' and he turned away....

Well, here is our old Duchess of Newcastle, and she and Lady Sefton and I had a real set to at Ecarté last night, and to-night I shall have old Sally Salisbury to play at whist with, and Greville and Giles and Lord and Lady Worcester. This day week, the Cowpers and Lievens come, and I am told I shall not stir till they are gone, ... and now prepare yourself for a resolution I have come to of taking a trip to *Ireland*, when I leave this place. My mind is quite made up....

Stoke, August 24th

...I am greatly indebted to you for all your information, and learning about *Cellini*, which I shall put by in a safe corner, as well as for your trouble in extracting Lord Egremont's pedigree from the peerage. Upon the first subject let me observe in justice to Lord Robert, that Sefton heard him say, Poyntz had given him the fountain....

...We have really had a very jolly week here, the two old girls, Newcastle and Salisbury, staying all the week, and being above even themselves, altho' the Duchess considers Old Salisbury as the arrantest old profligate the town can produce, and on the other hand Sally holds the Duchess in the uttermost contempt as an unenlightened provincial. The voices of these lovely females too are everything one could wish. Sally's is that of Lord Thurlow, whilst I know no pipe so slender as that of the Duchess,...

August 28th

...Madame Lieven goes to call on Mrs. Conyngham but she returns here. Nothing can equal her graciosity except her playing upon the pianoforte, which is real genius and inspiration. My Lord and his Daughters were lost last night in astonishment and admiration of her performance. Do you remember my ever having been mixed up at Brussels with the Prince—Pierre D'Aremberg? I had, and now have, some indistinct impression of it, but he, however, brought it to a *pint* yesterday at dinner by calling upon Monsieur Creevey to drink a verre de vin with him as an old ami de Bruxelles, and then I heard him telling all about him how I succoured the Blessés après la Bataille de Waterloo, and afterwards we had such handshaking and pawing that r-a-ally I was never more affraid of exposures in my life, and he has been at it again this morning. He says Brussels is increased by a third, and greatly beautified—the ramparts being converted into Boulevards, and very good houses built upon them....

August 29th

What a *natural* Wag Alvanley is; how different from these artificial conversation makers Luttrell, Rogers & Co. Never man was so improved as William Lamb, whether from gaining his title, or losing his Wife I know not.

...Montrond, too, is a natural and really a gay wag, always alive, and yet in the quietest way. We continue great cronies, and he is always a resource. Our Luttrell can't bear the sight of him, because he told him he could not for his life make out what was the advice he gave to Julia. Luttrell's poem, you know, of 'Advice to Julia,'...

Creevey to Miss Ord

Dublin, Septr. 11th

Well, to-night I am off for Duncannon per Mail to Waterford....

On Saturday...I dined...at Lord Francis Leveson's, and I must say once and for all, that greater civility I defy any one to receive than I have done from him, his rib, and from Lady Charlotte. Our company was the Jerseys, Lady Cloncurry, *Lady Morgan*,[12] Miss Latouche, and the Men I forget. The Morgan was of course the Lioness. She was dying for a display, but Lord Jersey who was on one side of her was so cursedly affraid of her, that he was nearer crying than trying to bring her out.... My fun was in making my playfellow Miss Latouche *burst* at Mother Morgan who was just opposite to us. In person she resembles a tetotum. Her face and neck were painted a bright red, her bonnet was of the same colour in silk, and circular in shape, turned up all round at the edge, with four red feathers at equal distance from each other, drooping, or rather flowing from the bonnet like water. Her attachment to the colour was shown in her gown, and descended even to her shoes. We had a very agreeable day altogether. Lord Francis took me aside before dinner to tell me who the Company was for fear of accidents, and it was well he did so, as Miss Latouche fell to my lot, and I might as well have talked to her of Wm. Lamb as of any body else whereas it turned out that dear Miss Latouche was own sister to Lady Brandon that Lamb is in the Crim: Con: with....

[12] Sydney, Lady Morgan, a very successful novelist of Irish life (1783–1859).

Bessborough, Sept. 13th

... This is a charming place; I ought to say *as to its position and surrounding scenery*—magnificent. The House itself is a handsome Grey stone House, in shape and size like Howick as *it was*. It was built in 1745, and the Lord Bessborough who built, showed his taste in his selection of the spot for doing it. Its South Front is on a slope in the Park, with a very handsome and very wide terrace....

Duncannon is all kindness and intelligence, and My Lady all amiability....

Sept. 14th

... There are from 14 to 20 children of the Duncannons[13] here, all most amiable and *white*. The eldest son, a young man grown, and a capital fellow with the best manners. Miss Ponsonby, the eldest of the race, seems too a most good, refined, amiable person, tho' in appearance a striking and yet unfavorable likeness to her Grandmother Bessborough, even in her advanced years. A Mr. Fane, brother to the Brussels Fane, is a visitor here at present, and a stupid, pompous, rum touch he is, and Mr. McDonald, son of the man at the Horse Guards, is another visitor, and then we have Mr. Gurney who has £800 a year as steward and for managing the property, and who turns out to have been in the same college with myself at Cambridge, and a man I knew a little of formerly....

... This climate is such that *myrtles* grow out of doors all the year round without protection of any kind, and are now in the highest beauty, as you would see if the *posy* I am now wearing was placed before your eyes. The little girls tap at my door twice a day with a bunch of this article. We are now all going to Church....

Sept. 19th

... My delight in this place remains unabated. Lady Duncannon is a charming person, her life here is devoted to looking after everybody, and in making them *clean*, and comfortable in their persons, cloaths, cottages, and everything, and her success is great indeed. *He too* in addition to his greater qualities is all after their cleanliness. I wish you had seen us walking up Pilltown last Saturday. Good old Irish usage in cottages and indeed houses is to place the dirt and filth of the house at the entrance instead of behind it, and this was reformed in every house but one as we walked thro', and Duncannon having called the old woman out of this one told her he *would not* have that filth remain in

[13] John William, afterwards 4th Earl of Bessborough, married Lady Maria Fane, daughter of 10th Earl of Westmorland. They had thirteen children.

that place, and she must remove it out of sight; to which she was pleased to reply, 'Well, my dear, if you do but walk by next Tuesday not a bit of the dirt shall you see remaining, and as for the matter of that, now in your Honor's presence will I lay the first stone of my new back yard,' and away she went with a huge stone in both hands....

Yesterday Duncannon presided in the same room at his Petty Sessions, and I was as much struck with his good sense as with the effect that his presence and impartial administration of justice must produce upon the great population of these parts.

The History of this family may be said to be the history of ill fated Ireland. Duncannon's great Grandfather began building this house in 1745, he finished it in 1755, and lived in it till 1757 (two years), when he died. His Son left Ireland when 18 years old, and having never seen it more, died in 1792. Upon that event his Son, the present Lord Bessborough, made his first visit to the place, and he is not certain whether it was *two* or *three* days he staid here, but it was one or the other. In 1808, he and Lady Bessborough came a tour to *the Lake of Killarney*, and having taken their own house in their way either going or coming, they were so pleased with it as to stay here a *week*, and once more in 1812 having come over to see the young Duke of Devonshire at Lismore, when his Father died, they were here a month. So that from 1757 to 1825, 68 years, the family was [here] 5 weeks and two days.... My dears, it is absenteeism on the part of Landlords, and the havoc that middle men make with their property that plays the very devil.... I think the 2nd. girl[14] here (a very tall one of 14 or 15) is likely to be as beautiful a woman as one shall see, and so very amiable too. They are all, both girls and boys, and Mother and Father; and all that is quite charming. I am happy, however, to say there are but 12 of them. I'll tell you a curious *pint*. Miss Ponsonby (upon whose judgment I have perfect reliance) has a school at Roehampton as well as here, and she says the difference in her scholars is perfectly astonishing, her Irish ones are not only so much quicker in learning, but so very much more desirious of doing so than her English ones. She says it is an absolute pleasure to teach the former. The Mother is divine....

Sept. 22nd

...My affection for Dear Bessborough remains to the last....

...We dined an hour earlier yesterday because our two eldest boys had to go 20 miles after dinner to catch the packet below Waterford, and

[14] Augusta, married, first, William, Earl of Kerry; secondly, Hon. Charles Gore. Bishop Charles Gore was her youngest son.

to go by her to Milford Haven. The eldest, Johnny,[15] aged 19, going to his private tutor, and Freddy,[16] aged 13, going to a school at Dulwich where there are 12 boys. They are charming creatures, as they are all....

I think I never had a *greater benefit* than in this house....

Creevey's tour next took him to Killarney Lakes, to Lord Donoughmore's at Knocklofty and later to Kilkenny.

Creevey to Miss Ord

Woodstock, Kilkenny [*Mr. Tighe's*], *Nov. 3rd*

...I really think a more worthy, amiable and obliging young person is not to be found than this Lady Louisa Tighe.[17] I had heard from every one before how much beloved she was by all around her, and I have no doubt it is so. She is quite in Lady Duncannon's line as to her devotion to her poorer *nibbers*.

...What think you of old Dowr. Richmond being here for 3 months, and never once during the time speaking to Tighe? Was there ever such impudence? He being, not only the most gentlemanlike, well-bred person possible, and evidently he and his wife the happiest [couple] with each other. All the *nibbers*, of which there are shoals, say his behaviour under this outrage was perfect. Do you know that this is the house from which those *chiennes* Lady Eleanor Butler and Miss Ponsonby, the heroines of Llangollen, escaped to that retreat they have occupied ever since. Lady Eleanor Butler,[18] aunt to the present Lord

[15] The 5th Earl.

[16] The 6th Earl. Well known as a cricketer at Harrow and a founder of I.Z.

[17] Fifth daughter of the 4th Duke of Richmond; married in 1825 the Right Hon. W. F. Tighe of Woodstock. It has often been told of this lady that she buckled the Duke of Wellington's sword-belt when he left her mother's ballroom on the morning of Quatre-Bras; but this she always emphatically denied. She died March 2, 1900.

[18] Youngest daughter of the 16th Earl of Ormonde [*de jure*]. Writing from Llangollen to his son on August 24, 1829, Mr. John Murray has the following:—

'We had a great treat yesterday in being invited to introduce ourselves to the celebrated Miss Ponsonby, of whom you must have heard as becoming early tired of fashionable life, and having withdrawn, accompanied by a kindred friend, Lady Eleanor Butler, to a delightful, and at that period unfrequented, spot a quarter of a mile from Llangollen, overhanging the rapid and beautiful river Dee. Lady Eleanor died there a few months ago at the age of 91, after having lived with Miss Ponsonby in the same cottage upwards of 50 years. It is very singular that the ladies intending to *retire* from the world, absolutely brought *all the world* to visit them; for, after a few years of seclusion, their strange story was the universal subject of conversation, and

Ormonde, got over their castle wall that I have seen in the town of Kilkenny, broke her arm and was caught. When she escaped the second time, she and Miss Ponsonby found their way here.

Dublin, Nov. 15th

. . . Yesterday, we had a nice domestic little snug party at the Erroll's', in the Castle, Lord and Lady Wm. Paget, Berkeley Paget, his Wife and Daughter, another dragoon Paget, Lyster and myself, and in the evening Lady Cecilia Latouche, and her Daughter, and a very jubby day we had, Lady Erroll playing and singing her Mother's kind of songs in the evening; the merits inferior I must admit to her divine original, and yet certainly like her; the whole to conclude with a game at fright. . . .

Don't you think Lady Duncannon's note to me a very pretty one? *Spencer*[19] is a young giant of a boy under 5 years old, and in petticoats. He and the other two boys would see me half way to Pilltown the day I left Bessborough, without their hats. It would do you good to hear Lady Duncannon express her terrors of the Seftons; that Lady Sefton is so *'awful.'* 'But the young Ladies,' said I? 'Oh,' said she, 'they are all awful, and tho' Lord Sefton is all politeness in his own house, one always feels certain he is quizzing one all the time, and I was never so terrified of anything as going to stay at Stoke.' To be sure there is some difference between Lady Sef-ton and Lady Duncannon. I should like to see the former selling cloaths to poor people without shoes and stockings for four or five hours every Saturday. . . .

Croxteth, Decr. 6th

. . . I intended, you know, to come here by last Tuesday's Chester Mail, but having learnt that it was the custom of that coach to be upset about twice a week, and having *by perfect accident* discovered that there was a daily coach that passed at ½ past nine in the morning by Kinmel to Liverpool, you won't be surprised that I availed myself of this discovery,

there has been no person of rank, talent and importance in any way who did not procure introduction to them. All that was passing in the world, they had it fresh as it arose, and in four hours' conversation with Miss Ponsonby one day, and three the next, I found that she knew everything and everybody, and was, at the age of 80, or nearly so, a most inexhaustible fund of entertaining instruction and lively communication. The cottage is remarkable for the taste of its appropriate fitting up with ancient oak, presented by different friends, from old castles and monasteries, &c., none of it of less antiquity than 1,200 years [!]. She declared to me that during the whole fifty years she never knew a moment that hung heavy upon her, and no sorrows, but from the loss of friends' [Smiles's *Memoirs of John Murray*, ii. 304].

[19] Sir Spencer Ponsonby-Fane.

and came by this coach last Wednesday. We stopt an hour and a half at Chester, then there was a little delay in crossing the Mersey in the steam boat, and the whole to conclude with a Liverpool hackney coach that was not very *lively*, as dear Pat would say, and ran me very fine for my dinner....

I was much struck on this occasion with the different manner of Earl Sefton, and Taffy Hughes. The day I got to Kinmel, I said before dinner to Taffy, 'Have I the same bedroom, Hughes, that I had the last time?' 'Indeed I cannot tell you, but we will soon know if you will ring the bell.' How like our Pat Duke of Leinster.

Well, I had written to Sefton saying I should be here by breakfast last Wednesday, so arriving as I did at seven, and every servant being then occupied in putting the dinner on the table, the Pet with his quick ears heard my crawling coach, and I saw him coming down the stairs, and he was out of the house with, 'It's you, old Fellow!' before my man could get down from his coach; then there was such a hollowing for my own footman Charles that brought him in no time; then, 'You have your own room that you had last time,' and my portmanteau being up in a jiffy, he (my Lord) would help me to unstrap it, and in short, tho' the dinner was on the table, I dressed and was quite in time for sufficient turtle, and all other good things. The party assembled I found to be My Lord and My Lady, the three young Ladies and Berkeley, Mr. and Mrs. Smythe-Owen, Mr. and Mrs. Strickland, (the latter a parlez-vous, and by far the handsomest, best dressed woman I ever saw,...), so it was all mighty well, and Lady Louisa in the course of the evening told me, she really believed Papa would not have come to Croxteth at all if I had not been coming. Was there ever?...

Knowsley, Dec. 13th

Knowsley without Lady Derby is like a house with all the fires and candles put out.

But *she* still shines tho' out of sight,
For she has carried off the light
And left us dark in blackest night.

2

And never more shall Countess reign
O'er Knowsley and its Stanley train
So bright as this from Drury Lane.

Sublime, is it not? but the poor player, I fear, can never show for good again....

Whitehall, Dec. 22nd

Well, after all, *home* is *home*, be it ever so homely. I left Croxteth about 2 o'clock on Saturday. Bad as the day was, my Lord *would* drive me and my portmanteau in the shooting carriage to the 'Saracen's Head Pot Ale House' on the Prescot road to catch the *Umpire*, and as we were a quarter of an hour before our time he *would* wait with me in that fashionable hotel till the coach came up, and so see me off. I mention the *pint* to show the terms on which we parted; then, the *Ladies* informed me that they were *all* making up a Xmas-basket for *my* Ladies, and the *young people*, and it was to start to-day.... *This pint* again will shew you, that it's all mighty well with *all* the worthy family. My journey was ... rather dawdling and time ... pressing, I laid hold of a *Jarvey* at Islington, and such an artist could not have been selected in the whole town, for he absolutely flew with me, and well it was so, for we dine at ½ past six now-a-days, and they had begun dinner, but Mrs. Taylor left hers and came out upon the steps to meet me, and to bring me in by force, dirty as of course I was, so it was all very well, and 'damned fair' in Mrs. Taylor after all our snubs; and Fergy was here, and also Harry Vane, and an Oxonian pedagogue of Michael's.

After dinner, I of course retired to my toilette, then returned, had two kisses of Lady Glengall, played at cards till one o'clock, won three pounds, and went to bed, and so ended my campaign from Croxteth.

I am off now to take my place in a coach to the *'Place Ladies,'*[20] as we are always full this Xmas time.

[20] His stepdaughters at Rivenhall Place.

chapter thirteen (*continued*)

1829

THE SUCCESSIVE STAGES in the conversion of the Tory Government to Roman Catholic Emancipation have been abundantly discussed without bringing home to the apprehension of most people that, in truth, there were no such stages. The appointment of the Duke of Northumberland in succession to Lord Anglesey was in accord with the spirit of a General Order which had never been suspended or revoked—No indulgence to Roman Catholics. It is the secrecy and suddenness of Wellington's movements which have perplexed historians, accustomed to the more tentative and tortuous ways of politicians.

Creevey to Miss Ord

Whitehall, Feby. 3, 1829

...Every one was up with the news of the day—that Wellington had decided to let the Catholics into Parliament....I have always, you know, been convinced that the Beau must and would do *something* upon this subject, and what it is to be we now must very shortly know....

5th

Our only visitor last night was Sefton, who arrived about 12, bringing with him the correspondence between the Duke of Wellington and Lord Anglesey, which the latter had lent to Sefton to be returned the next morning at 11. He read it to Mrs. Taylor and me, and it was ½ past one before he had done. The Beau, according to custom, writes atrociously, and his charges against Lord Anglesey are of the rummest kind, such as being too much addicted to popular courses, *going to Lord Cloncurry's*, being too civil to Catholic leaders, not turning Mr. O'Gorman Mahon out of the commission of the peace, &c., &c. There are letters full of such stuff, and Lord Anglesey in his answers beats him easy in all ways....The Whigs are quite as sore as the Brunswickers at this victory of the Beau over Prinney and his Catholic prejudices. They had arranged the most brilliant opposition for the approaching session, and this coup of the Duke's has blown up the whole concern.

At Brooks's last night the *deceased* poet Rogers came up to beg I would meet Brougham at dinner at his house on Wednesday.

6th

...It does Wellington infinite honor; the only drawback to his fame on this occasion is his silence to Anglesey as to his intentions; but he has been jealous of his brother soldier playing the popular in Ireland, and so has sacrificed the man, while adopting his opinions.

7th

Here is little Twitch, *alias* Scroop, *alias* Premier Duke, Hereditary Earl Marshal, who is sitting by my side and who reckons himself sure of franking a letter for you before the session closes.

11th

...'Ra-ally,' as Mrs. Taylor would say, Peel makes a great figure.[1] His physick for the [Catholic] Association is as mild as milk, and *for a year only*. It is such a new and important feature in this Tory Revolution to have no blackguarding or calling names of any one. There begins to be an alarm about the Lords, but I have no doubt without foundation. It is clear to me from the Duke of Rutland's speech that he will ultimately support the Beau, and I have my doubts whether the Bishop of London[2] won't do so likewise....Lord Sefton has broke the bank at Crockford's two nights following. He tells me he carried off £7000.

12th Feby., 1829

...Our party at the deceased poet's [Rogers] last night was his brother and living poet and wit—Luttrell, Sefton, Lord Durham, Burdett, Lord Robert [Spencer], Brougham and the Duke of Norfolk, and we had a merry day enough....

Sulby, March 18

Rather stiffish to-day, my dear; it can't, of course, be *age*! but going four and twenty miles on a hard road at a kind of hand gallop is rather shaking, you know, to those not used to it....The men we have had here are principally Pytchley, who, in dandyism, are very second-rate to the Quorn or Melton men....Osbaldeston himself, tho' only 5 feet

[1] As Home Secretary, Peel was responsible for the government of Ireland.
[2] C. J. Blomfield.

high, and in features like a cub fox, is a very funny little chap; clever in his way, very good-humored and gay, and with very good manners. ... I am very fond of all these lads being dressed in scarlet in the evening. It looks so gay.

Earl of Sefton to Creevey

Arlington St., ... March 25th

... The King was delighted with the duel[3] and said he should have done the same—that gentlemen must not stand upon their privileges....

Stoke, 11th April

... The King was very angry at the large majority [for the Catholic Relief Bill] and did not write the D. a line in answer to his express telling him of it. The Beau's troubles are not over yet. The distress in the country is frightful. Millions are starving, and I defy him to do anything to relieve them.

Creevey to Miss Ord

Whitehall, May 28th

... I went to the Park, but the review was over, so we only learnt that the Beau had had a fall from his horse, but was not hurt; and in coming home here a little later who shd. I meet riding in a little back street near Coventry Street but the said Duke. So he stopt and shook hands.... I said:—'Well, upon my soul, you are the first of mankind to have accomplished this Irish job as you have done, and I congratulate you upon it most sincerely.... You must have had tough work to get thro'.'—'Oh terrible, I assure you,' said he, and so we parted.

June 1st

... It is a well known fact that Lord Durham is doing all he possibly can to make Lord Grey act a part that shall force him into the Government, meaning in that event to go snacks himself in the acquisition of power and profit; which, considering that he got his peerage by deserting Grey and by helping Canning to defeat Wellington, is consistent and *modest* enough! So after dinner [at Lord William Powlett's] the levee being mentioned, Grey said in the most natural manner he would never go to another; upon which Lambton remonstrated with him most severely and pathetically, and George Lamb thought Grey was wrong; but Grey held out firm as a rock—said that it was quite against his own

[3] Between the Duke of Wellington and Lord Winchilsea.

opinion going the last time, but that he had been quite persecuted into it—that this last personal insult from the King in never noticing him was only one of a series of the same kind, and that for the future he should please himself by avoiding a repetition of them. You may easily fancy the amiability of Lambton's face at his avowal.... You see these impertinent and base renegade young Whigs have had their appetites for office if possible sharpened at present by Lord Rosslyn having just accepted the Privy Seal.... Rosslyn told me of it himself in the street on Saturday.... I know that he accepted with Lord Grey's concurrence, but I am equally sure, from Lord Grey's manner, that he thinks he ought not to have done so.

August 20th

... As you see only the *Morning Post*, I am afraid you are quite in the dark as to what is going on in France.... All are furious against the new Ministry, and with great reason. To think of making Bourmont the War Minister! He is the man who deserted from Bonaparte and came over to us the night before the battle of Waterloo.[4] General Gérard recommended him to Nap as a General of Division on that occasion, and said that he would pledge his life for his *honor*. The deserter is now to be Minister for War, and will have to face Gérard as a member of the Chamber of Deputies! ... Even the old Ultras think the experiment puts the throne of Charles Dix in danger.

The Liverpool and Manchester Railway, the promotion of which Creevey had so stoutly opposed in committee of the House of Commons, was nearly finished, and about to be opened for traffic.

Creevey to Miss Ord

Knowsley, Nov. 1st, 1829

... You have no doubt in your paper reports of Huskisson's return to office. Allow me to mention a passage which Lord Derby read to me out of a letter to himself from Lady Jane Houston, who lives very near Huskisson.... 'Houston saw Huskisson yesterday, who talked to him of his return to office as of a thing quite certain, and of Edward Stanley doing so too. Indeed he spoke of the latter as quite the Hope of the Nation!' As the Hope of the Nation was present when this was read, it would not have been decent to laugh; but the little Earl gave me a look that was quite enough.

[4] It was on the morning of June 15, three days before Waterloo, that Bourmont deserted; and he went to Blücher, not to Wellington.

Croxteth, 7th

...I left little Derby devouring Bourrienne with the greatest delight, and he is particularly pleased with the exposure of the ignorance of 'that damned fellow Sir Walter Scott.' The Stanley and Hornby party were rather shocked at the great bard and novelist being called such names, but the peer said he was a 'damned impertinent fellow' for presuming to write the life of Bonaparte.

Croxteth, Nov. 14th

... To-day we have had a *lark* of a very high order. Lady Wilton sent over yesterday from Knowsley to say that the Loco Motive machine was to be upon the railway at such a place at 12 o'clock for the Knowsley party to ride in if they liked, and inviting this house to be of the party. So of course we were at our post in 3 carriages and some horsemen at the hour appointed. I had the satisfaction, for I can't call it *pleasure*, of taking a trip of five miles in it, which we did in just a quarter of an hour—that is, 20 miles an hour. As accuracy upon this subject was my great object, I held my watch in my hand at starting, and all the time; and as it has a second hand, I knew I could not be deceived; and it so turned out there was not the difference of a second between the coachee or conductor and myself. But observe, during these five miles, the machine was occasionally made to put itself out or *go it*; and then we went at the rate of 23 miles an hour, and just with the same ease as to motion or absence of friction as the other reduced pace. But the quickest motion is to me *frightful*: it is really flying, and it is impossible to divest yourself of the notion of instant death to all upon the least accident happening. It gave me a headache which has not left me yet. Sefton is convinced that some damnable thing must come of it; but he and I seem more struck with such apprehension than others.... The smoke is very inconsiderable indeed, but sparks of fire are abroad in some quantity: one burnt Miss de Ros's cheek, another a hole in Lady Maria's silk pelisse, and a third a hole in some one else's gown. Altogether I am extremely glad indeed to have seen this miracle, and to have travelled in it. Had I thought worse of it than I do, I should have had the curiosity to try it; but, having done so, I am quite satisfied with my *first* achievement being my *last*.

chapter fourteen and last

1830–1838

THE LAST YEARS of Creevey's life were spent (as Greville put it) in 'a more settled way of life.'

When Grey took office in November, 1830, after the death of George IV and the downfall of the long Tory administration, the new Premier appointed his old friend and admirer to the office of Treasurer of the Ordnance, a sinecure worth £1,200 a year. True, that particular plum was not expected to last long and Creevey handsomely accepted its abolition at Althorp's hands in 1833. But Grey, who at the end of Creevey's life was as much his hero as Fox had been at the beginning of his political career, had still a last favour to bestow, and by 1834 Creevey was assured, as auditor of Greenwich Hospital, of a sheltered and carefree retirement. Indeed, the lines:

> 'I often wished that I had clear
> For life £600 a year,
> A handsome house to lodge a friend,
> A river at my garden's end'

might have been written for him.

Here, it was his intention to settle down, sort out his papers and write that *History of his Own Times* which he had long projected. Indeed to that end in 1835 he required his faithful copyist and archivist, Bessy Ord, to bring down the mass of letters, memoranda and pamphlets then in her hands. It was natural that, once assured of a settled way of life, Creevey's political vehemence moderated. He remained a shrewd observer of the political dog-fight but the sparkle of his social gossip showed no slightest sign of decline nor did his appetite for society. He was out of Parliament as Member for Appleby when his friend Thanet died, but in the middle of the Reform Bill dog-fight his old friend 'Folky' (now Lord Radnor) brought him back to the House to help 'kill the Rotten Boroughs.'

Radnor brought in Creevey and Brougham's brother, James, for Downton, inherited from the 2nd Earl's marriage to Miss Duncombe, and the handful of electors felt no surprise that neither of their representatives troubled to visit them!

The great drama of Reform (which has been exhaustively described by scores of historians) is, truth to tell, not the liveliest of Creevey's descriptive efforts, and no doubt that is accounted for by his new security. His lively pen was still at the disposal of his party in hard-hitting pamphlets, and as an elder statesman his counsel was valued, remarkably so by Grey and ostensibly by Brougham, now jockeyed out of obstruction on the Woolsack.

Creevey's country house visits and race meetings continued as strenuously and enjoyably as ever. He lived a great deal with the Seftons at Stoke Farm, 'his own, his *real*, family,' and indeed Sefton could not do without him. Lady Grey was clearly devoted to him and relied on his help in her own domestic worries.

When in London, where he kept a lodging, he still frequented Holland House, dined, whenever it suited him, with Lord Essex and very often with the Duke of Sussex.

In August, 1835, he travelled up to Edgehill, Liverpool, for his sister's funeral and amicably settled up her affairs with her humble relatives.

Her death assured him for the rest of his life an income (with the Greenwich salary) of about £1,100 a year. He lived into the reign of Victoria, and from Stoke Farm recorded his admiring observations on 'the little tit,' every inch a Queen, and he clearly appreciated the significance of the new reign. Some time before his sister's death he acquired what Greville called a mistress and the more charitable may call a maid. Emma Murray, whoever and whatever she was, certainly comforted his old age and it was to her and not to the Ords that he left the few hundreds he had to dispose. In January, 1838, he paid his last country house visit at Holkham, where he and his eighty-four-year-old host (who survived him by some years) vigorously footed it in a country dance. Then he returned to Jermyn Street. Of late years he had been a constant victim of influenza, gout and cupping and, following a day visit to Greenwich, where he dallied without his greatcoat gossiping with Sir Thomas Hardy's daughters, he returned with a chill to take to his bed, and he died on February 5, 1838.

It remains only to deal with three points of biographical interest: the provenance of his 'papers,' his standing as a politician in his day, and the riddle of his parentage. The last is treated in an appendix. First as to his papers. Greville has come to be judged as no gossip but as a diarist accurate and reasonably impartial in his commentaries. His remarks on Creevey's mistress were proved to be true when I unearthed Creevey's will. It may be accepted as broadly true also that Brougham and others confidently expected that Creevey, known all his life as an industrious and trenchant recorder of events, must have left behind him diaries and memoranda highly damaging to the reputations of some of his intimates.

And no doubt in Jermyn Street, and perhaps at Greenwich, the latest files of his papers still remained. It may be that the solicitor Vizard persuaded Emma Murray, the residuary legatee, to part with them for sealing up and perhaps burning. But that there was found anything in the nature of a continuous diary is most unlikely. Creevey's 'diaries' were first in the form of letters to Miss Ord—who understood her duties and was constantly at work arranging and copying them, of his correspondence with his political contemporaries, of memoranda and pamphlets, all preserved for his long-declared design to write a history of his time in retirement at Greenwich.

His 'orders' to Bessy Ord to bring the vast bulk of these papers to Greenwich were sent out on June 9, 1835. The orders were not obeyed. Whether or no it was due to the instalment of Emma Murray, the Misses Ord never again visited the house at Greenwich, and in any case the arrangement and transfer of the papers would have taken much time. Whether Brougham, Sefton or Vizard secured, sealed or burned some current papers, we shall probably never know. The treasure they never handled (several million words) was still in Bessy Ord's keeping and has come down to us, and from them was to be written the diary that never was. And the letters in that collection, even those in Brougham's autograph alone, are proof enough of the justice of the nicknames which Creevey applied to him. Vizard's call on Emma Murray was in effect the failure of a mission.

What is a just estimate of Creevey's status as a politician and party fighter among his contemporaries?

A satirist is not always a good historian, and Lytton Strachey, when in 1922 he published in *Books and Characters* his little squib on Creevey, left on the reading public a very partial and trivial idea of his worth. A toady, a place man, a gossip, a playboy. Strachey's verdict has for too long been accepted. The big guns of his own day in politics totally contradict such a portrait, and Strachey cannot have read very carefully the *Creevey Papers* of 1904. It is true that we have learned a great deal more about Creevey than was known in 1904 or for thirty years later, but the verdicts of such men as Fox, Grey, Wellington, Melbourne and Hobhouse were known then and Strachey could have read them. Creevey entered Parliament in 1802. He began to take an active part in the House in 1804, in which year he made his first important speech (war in Ceylon) which Fox praised very highly. The impression he made on the House and on his party grew very quickly, and when the time came to complete the Talents ministry, there was no question of leaving Creevey out. It was merely a question of what minor office would best suit his fighting qualities. When it is recognised that, at this period, eighty per cent of the chief portfolios were held by peers or political patrons, and that men of much higher quality, such as Sheridan, Canning, Brougham and even Tierney, had to struggle long and hard to overcome the prejudices against men of obscure origins, it is a signal proof of Creevey's abilities that, with origins even more humble and obscure than any of those named, he gained recognition after only two or three years of novitiate; and it is certain that but for the divisions among the Whigs which kept them in opposition during the twenty-three years of Creevey's prime, he would have risen much higher. Hobhouse, whose nature abhorred a boisterous practical joker at a country house party, was compelled to concede that there 'was no doubt at all of Creevey's superior abilities, [a man] with a quick and strong memory, who, when serious, showed sound and honest views and discovered qualities which might adorn a higher character than he had endeavoured [perhaps 'had the opportunities'] to acquire.'

Melbourne, who knew him better than several of his contemporaries, some years after Creevey's death confirmed that, though bitterly partisan, he was exceedingly shrewd.

His papers show that throughout his career, Wellington, a good judge of character, treated him, a political foe, with the respect due to a man of standing and ability. Whitbread, Romilly and the lesser band of sincere social reformers constantly relied on his counsels and co-operation, and the same papers clearly show that Brougham, whom he repeatedly lashed, constantly showed the same respect for his political shrewdness. Lady Holland, and Holland also, confirmed his status and towards the end of Creevey's life the Greys accepted him both as an elder statesman and as a family friend and counsellor.

He bulks large in Hansard, having made in his time 150 speeches which, read even today, confirm Fox's verdict on his first important intervention in debate. There is no doubt that Strachey's hasty verdict was totally unjust, partial and misleading, and deserves correction.

In the politics of his day, he was a man of some account. By the same token, Strachey's tailpiece ('The curtain had gone down and on the new stage that was preparing for very different characters, there would be no place for Mr. Creevey.') is singularly inept on the social side. For seventy years longer, society continued to welcome and enjoy such practitioners as they could find in Creevey's line of drawing-room entertainment; but it may be doubted if they ever found his equal. Two or three days after his death, Louisa Molyneux wrote these words to Bessie Ord: 'No time can ever efface from my mind the feelings of respect and attachment to his memory nor of gratitude for his constant kindness, which has added to all the pleasures and diminished all the sorrows of my life.'

Greater men than Creevey might be satisfied with such an epitaph.

APPENDIX I

The Riddle of Creevey's Parentage

PROBABLY ALL WHO have to do with biography will acknowledge the fact that the *truth* too often comes to light *after* and not *at* the publication of a definitive biography, even of one which is the result of years of patient research. The truth will out . . . but reluctantly. One cannot obtain a warrant to search the attics of every country house and the hidden places of men's memories, and so it is that vital facts often come to light immediately after interest is aroused by the publication of a biography. The puzzle of the origins of Thomas Creevey (which are of no great importance) was the despair and hobby of several years of my life, and the ups and downs of my efforts to get at the truth are perhaps of sufficient interest to set down.

In 1766 and 1767 a Captain William Creevey was a householder in School Lane, Liverpool, near the Blue Coat School. He was well known locally as captain of slave-carrying vessels trading out of Liverpool. His parents were also Liverpool residents, Thomas and Mary Creevey, and he had a younger brother, Hans, and two sisters, Margaret and Eleanor, the latter respectably married to a Liverpool man, John Eaton.

Captain William was not highly educated, and had not amassed a fortune by his profession. In 1764 he married Phoebe Prescott, and made his will which, in phonetic spelling but otherwise clearly, assured to her the enjoyment of his estate during widowhood, and the sum of £400 if she remarried.

Between 1765 and 1768 two children were born to Mrs. Phoebe Creevey, a daughter, Jane, and a son, Thomas, born on March 13, 1768. This Thomas is the writer of *The Creevey Papers*. Not many months after the boy's birth William Creevey died, for his will was proved at Chester Consistory Court on November 28, 1769. Further information reveals that Phoebe Creevey married again and died in 1812 as Mrs. Lowe.

There is no mystery here on the face. All seems plain sailing. But doubt had been thrown on Creevey's parentage in 1903, just after the publication of *The Creevey Papers*, when public interest in Creevey had awakened. Sir Herbert Maxwell, the editor, wrote the following letter in *Notes and Queries* (vol. 151, p. 330):—

When I was editing *The Creevey Papers* (John Murray, 1903), it often occurred to me as strange that Thomas Creevey, a person of somewhat obscure birth, should have been admitted on such familiar terms to the Whig circle—the most exclusive of all political parties. It was not until these volumes had been published that the puzzle was explained to me in 1903 by the 16th Earl of Derby (1841–1908), who told me that Creevey was a natural son of the 1st Earl of Sefton (1748–1795), and that his mother was conveniently married to William Creevey, a merchant of Liverpool. Creevey, therefore, was a half-brother of the 2nd Earl of Sefton (1772–1838) his junior by four years, though they both died in the same year. Lord Sefton's friendship provided Creevey with an easy passport into Whig society. The statement about his birth and parentage on pages V, VI and VII of the Papers (vol. I) stands to be altered accordingly.

Thirty years later, when I was editing Creevey's writings once more, Sir Herbert repeated the gist of this letter to me. In communicating it he had forgotten or perhaps had never seen facts given to *Notes and Queries* by Mr. R. Stewart-Brown. I was unaware of the letters in *Notes and Queries*, but acting on the hint given me by Sir Herbert, I searched Creevey's correspondence for proofs of the legend concerning his parentage.

Weight had clearly to be accorded to local tradition supplied by so high an authority as the 16th Earl of Derby (who was born only three years after Creevey's death); and supporting proofs came to hand. First, facial resemblance between the portraits of Creevey and of his reputed father, which stand as the frontispiece and opposite page 4, respectively, of *Creevey's Life and Times*. Experts in physiognomy have assured me that there are significant features of resemblance in the two portraits.

More important, I discovered passages in Creevey's letters to Miss Ord, in which in various but ambiguous terms he acknowledges the Molyneux as his *own* or his *real* family, and the 2nd Earl of Sefton as his 'brother,' statements which are difficult (though not impossible) to explain except on this assumption. See especially references on pp. 215, 252, 312, 331, 334–5, 352, 380, 396, 420 of my *Creevey's Life and Times*.

I therefore inclined to the view (and expressed it) that Creevey was the issue of an illicit amour between Lord Molyneux (1st Earl of Sefton) and a girl of humble origin, for whom before the child's birth a marriage of convenience was arranged with a Liverpool 'sea captain or merchant,' William Creevey, who therefore fathered the illicit child. Such indeed was the tradition within Lord Derby's memory. Putting the liaison as having taken place in 1767, young Charles William, son of the Hon. Thomas Molyneux, who had succeeded his uncle as 8th Viscount Molyneux at the age of eleven, would at that time have been just short of nineteen years old.

It was not until 1938 that the information which Mr. Stewart-Brown had given to *Notes and Queries* in 1926 was brought to my notice. Here was considerable fresh light on the identities both of Creevey's mother and of William Creevey, and the evidence of dates, which controverted the theory of a pre-marriage liaison between Molyneux and Creevey's mother, who was twenty-five years old at the relevant time.

John Gore's *Liverpool Directories* of 1766 and 1767 show Captain William Creevey as a householder in School Lane, Liverpool, during those years. The captain's will proves that he had been married to Creevey's mother at least as early as 1764 and that he died a few months after Creevey's birth, probably in the early part of 1769. The fair and reasonable course would be to reject the theory dishonourable to Mrs. Creevey and to accept out of hand the slaver captain as Creevey's father. But the supporting evidence of a more romantic origin remains strong, and, if it be accepted, Creevey's origin must be traced to a liaison *after* the marriage and perhaps during one of the captain's enforced absences beyond the seas. The tradition is not greatly weakened by that assumption, but he would be a bold man who would uphold it beyond peradventure.

One more argument indeed for the Molyneux tradition could be reasonably added to the chain of circumstantial evidence—the poverty of Mrs. Creevey. Without assistance from an outside source, she could hardly have paid for the education of young Thomas so far above his station. Her own relations were all in the humblest possible circumstances; and the Creeveys (other than Mrs. John Eaton who undoubtedly assisted in Thomas's upbringing) vanish from the scene of Thomas's youth. One other child, as stated, was born to the William Creeveys—the daughter. She never married, was a model of convention, very careful and precise, treated her brother as a naughty boy to the day of her death, and lived out her life in a round of 'drums' and tea-parties in a small house in Liverpool.

APPENDIX II

Creevey's School at Hackney

IN THE COURSE of my researches into the early years of Thomas Creevey, I became inquisitive to learn something more than Sir Herbert Maxwell had disclosed thirty years before of the name and nature of his private school at Hackney. All that Sir Herbert told us was that Creevey received instruction at a private school in Hackney—' "Old School Lane," he calls it'—and thence proceeded to Cambridge. (In point of fact, as we now know, 'School Lane' was Creevey's birthplace in Liverpool, and not, as Sir Herbert guessed, at Hackney.)

I came upon the name of 'Newcome's' by a happy chance when looking up in *D.N.B.* the career of Charles Callis Western (Lord Western of Rivenhall), who was an early friend and valuable patron of Creevey at a vital point in his career. I found that Western was educated at Newcome's School, Hackney, and I jumped to the conclusion (which proved to be correct) that they had been fellow pupils at Newcome's.

When *Creevey's Life and Times* was already set up in print I chanced on other and more illuminating references to Newcome's School (in Lane Poole's *Life of Stratford Canning*, and elsewhere). As far back as the reign of Richard I, the family of Newcome, or Newcomen, was established in Lincolnshire. A member of it, Stephen, became Rector of Caldecot, Hunts, in 1617, and founded a family which presented to the Church (often by exercising the family right of presentation) ten generations of beneficed clergymen in direct succession, producing no fewer than forty priests, including an archbishop and lesser dignitaries, between 1617 and 1850. Cambridge was their Alma Mater, and Queens' the college of their choice.

[1]In the eighteenth century, Hackney was little more than a rural village in the north-east of London, remarkable, as Daniel Defoe

[1] Extracts from *Newcome's Academy and its Plays* by E. Alfred Jones (London—The Bibliographical Society, 1933).

has said, as the retreat of wealthy citizens and for long the residence of noble families and illustrious men, including the author of *Robinson Crusoe* himself.

Here was a famous Academy for the education of young gentlemen and sons of noblemen in the eighteenth century, which enjoyed a reputation for scholarship not inferior to that of Westminster and St. Paul's, the two great Metropolitan schools of the time. The founder would seem to have been Benjamin Morland (1657–1733), of Jesus College, Cambridge, afterwards (1721–33) High Master of St. Paul's School, who was buried in Hackney. The second head master was the founder's son-in-law, the Rev. Henry Newcome, LL.D., of Emmanuel College, Cambridge, who continued the school, now known as Newcome's Academy, until his death in 1756. His successor was his son, the Rev. Peter Newcome, Fellow of Queens' College, Cambridge, and Fellow (1742) of the Royal Society, who died in 1779. He had, however, been succeeded in 1765 by his halfbrother, the Rev. Henry Newcome, also of Queens' College, who piqued himself upon his knowledge and correct delivery of the English language. The last of the line, apparently from 1789, was Richard Newcome, a grandson of the first Henry Newcome, and he in his turn was followed in 1803 by the Rev. Charles Thomas Heathcote, D.D., who retained the Academy until his death in 1820, after whose reign the old school house and grounds were acquired by the London Orphan Society.

Hackney seems to have been regarded as peculiarly suitable for private schools. In 1770, the Rev. James Pickthorne was running a school at Hackney, and in it Samuel Rogers received some education. It may be that the establishment of Pickthorne's school led to the substitution of the name of 'Newcome's' for the earlier name of Hackney School. Pickthorne appears to have retained longest the name of Hackney School.

From an unpublished manuscript of autobiographical notes written down by Charles Bosanquet (1769–1850) we get a picture of this curiously mixed, fashionable, semi-barbarous seminary for the sons of noblemen and gentlemen. Bosanquet was sent to Newcome's by his mother in 1776 when only seven years old. 'Except for Jack Pelham,' he was much the youngest boy in the school. He remained there until 1785 when at the age of sixteen he was sent abroad to be finished. Soon after, a change in the headmastership took place, Richard Newcome succeeding his father, of whom Bosanquet says:

'Newcome in my day was no scholar and a bad schoolmaster, gouty and violent,' though he admits that the school had attained in Newcome Senior's day a high character. 'His son Richard,' he goes on, 'less capable than himself to conduct the school, it passed out of their hands and in a few years came to an end, and the house was pulled down.' Nevertheless, Richard Newcome was still in charge of it in the year 1793 when Stratford Canning was, at the tender age of seven, confided to his charge by Mrs. Canning. Writing his impressions of the place years afterwards, Lord Stratford says:

'How the Muses ever came to settle at Hackney under the auspices of Mr. Richard Newcome I find it difficult to conceive. That somewhat priggish potentate had been preceded in the tuition of seventy or eighty boys by his father whose ability and conduct had given reputation to the school.' Henry Newcome had clearly been a character. When one of his boys, summoned for chastisement, threatened to kill himself, Newcome rang the bell for a carving knife and placed it in the boy's hand. The school was housed in a large antiquated brick building with gable ends and latticed windows, having the air of a respectable old manor house. Richard Newcome and his family lived in a bright new house near by, while a resident usher (in Canning's day 'one of the Coleridges') maintained order in the school-house. There was no lack of playground and ample time for recreation. There were great trees for climbing and for 'nests,' garden walls, which invited midnight evasions, and a pastrycook's shop which cried out for the treatment which it frequently received. In summer the boys were taken down to bathe in the River Lea, an excursion dreaded by the smaller boys for the reason adduced by 'girt Jan Ridd' in his recollections of Blundell's.

The curriculum, if haphazard and scrappy, was rooted in high tradition. The three R's were subordinated to classic drama. Annual recitations and the enactment of a play by the elder boys every third year were regarded as incentives to study, and doubtless were eyewash for parents and guardians. The acting obviously was a feature of the school. Bosanquet and Canning speak highly of Shakespeare productions. Military victories and political events of importance were exploited in the cause of education and celebrated with whole holidays. Creevey records that Newcome set him to learn by heart from the press-report Erskine's speech in defence of Dean Shipley in the famous libel action. But the rudiments of instruction were hard to come by—Creevey certainly was turned empty away—and 'awfully rough the manners of the boys themselves. The smaller ones were neither more nor less than slaves. Children of tender age were often sent on a cold November evening to pilfer turnips from a neighbouring field and many were the logs of firewood or kettles of boiling water I had to carry up the dark and winding staircase. Compared with one of us Caliban was a sybarite and our Prosperos ever ready with hand or stick....

'The Sabbath, though free from lessons, was a dismal day. The formal walk to church in a line of two abreast, headed by the master and closed by his usher; the droning organ, the long-drawn spiritless sermon....'

Perhaps the reality was not quite so black as Lord Stratford paints it. What man could ever resist exaggerating the rigours of his schooldays for the benefit of a 'rising generation of young sybarites'? But it was bad enough. The classic tradition distracted the eye from much that was rotten and of ill repute. 'The habit of swearing,' says Bosanquet, 'was so inveterate that I never got rid of it. It was a most profligate, abominable school. I was kept there seven [? nine] years, learned very little, and was most unhappy.' But the school's reputation clearly died slowly, and Richard Newcome had an eye for business. 'A large entablature of painted wood bore a list of distinguished names in gold letters on a blue ground and served at once to decorate the schoolroom and to stir a generous emulation in youthful breasts.' No doubt it served a third purpose when prospective parents visited the school. For the first name on that roll of honour was that of the Prime Minister, the Duke of Portland. Thanks to the industry of Charles Bosanquet, we have a list of many of those illustrious alumni. He says:

'The school was patronised by many families of distinction. During my time there [were] 2 of the Duke of Grafton's sons, Fitzroys, Lord Charles and Lord Henry, a Southampton Fitzroy, two Pelhams, one of Lord Chichester's sons; two Rushouts, the eldest now Lord Northwick, Frank Burton, twin brother of the Marquis Cunningham [Conyngham], 2 Bridgemans [Lord Bradford], Dick Trench, Lord Clancarty (in the same room in which I slept), and Sir Thomas Cave; several of the principal Kentish families, Brockmans, Austens, Polhills. Sir John Fagg[e]; Bragge Bathurst, Sir Gilbert Heathcote & his 2 brothers, & John Heathcote, Lord Western [Charles Callis] and his brother, the Shirleys. Creevey was a Newcomite and married Charles Brandling's widowed sister. Skeffington was barely my contemporary. 3 Yorkes, sons of Bishop of Ely, Joseph, James, and Phillip, my crony, Lord Hardwicke's nephews. . . .'

Few of the boys passed on from Newcome's to (Eton at any rate among) public schools. Some did; Canning and Western, and doubtless several more. But Newcome's appears to have been a cross between a public and private school, taking boys of six and seven and keeping those who could survive its rigours until sixteen.

I have seen the account rendered for tuition and boarding fees for a young Master Grey (a relative of Mrs. Creevey's) for the period midsummer to Christmas 1792. It amounted to £27 *2s. 9d.*

So much for Creevey's 'private-public' school.

J. G.

Index

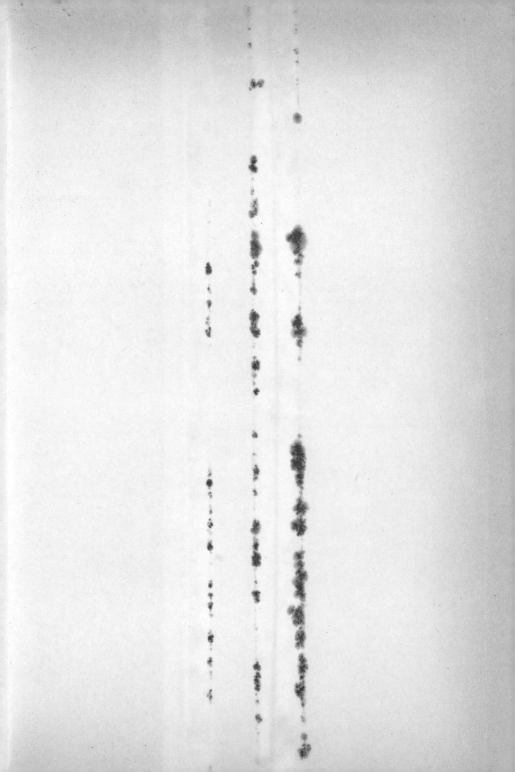

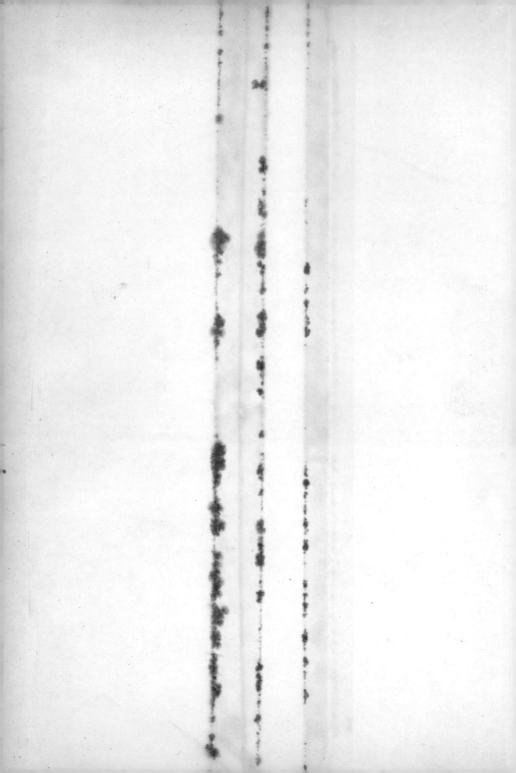